ENERGY
SUPPLIES, SUSTAINABILITY, AND COSTS

ISSN 1534-1585

ENERGY
SUPPLIES, SUSTAINABILITY, AND COSTS

Sandra M. Alters

INFORMATION PLUS® REFERENCE SERIES
Formerly Published by Information Plus, Wylie, Texas

GALE
CENGAGE Learning™

Detroit • New York • San Francisco • New Haven, Conn • Waterville, Maine • London

Energy: Supplies, Sustainability, and Costs

Sandra M. Alters

Paula Kepos, Series Editor

Project Editors: Elizabeth Manar, Kathleen J. Edgar

Rights Acquisition and Management: Jennifer Altschul, Kelly Quin

Composition: Evi Abou-El-Seoud, Mary Beth Trimper

Manufacturing: Cynde Bishop

Product Management: Carol Nagel

Cover photograph: Image copyright Greg Randles, 2008. Used under license from Shutterstock.com.

While every effort has been made to ensure the reliability of the information presented in this publication, Gale, a part of Cengage Learning, does not guarantee the accuracy of the data contained herein. Gale accepts no payment for listing; and inclusion in the publication of any organization, agency, institution, publication, service, or individual does not imply endorsement of the editors or publisher. Errors brought to the attention of the publisher and verified to the satisfaction of the publisher will be corrected in future editions.

Gale
27500 Drake Rd.
Farmington Hills, MI 48331-3535

ISBN-13: 978-0-7876-5103-9 (set)
ISBN-13: 978-1-4144-3373-8

ISBN-10: 0-7876-5103-6 (set)
ISBN-10: 1-4144-3373-5

ISSN 1534-1585

This title is also available as an e-book.
ISBN-13: 978-1-4144-5756-7 (set)
ISBN-10: 1-4144-5756-1 (set)
Contact your Gale sales representative for ordering information.

Printed in the United States of America
1 2 3 4 5 6 7 13 12 11 10 09

TABLE OF CONTENTS

PREFACE

Energy: Supplies, Sustainability, and Costs is part of the *Information Plus Reference Series*. The purpose of each volume of the series is to present the latest facts on a topic of pressing concern in modern American life. These topics include today's most controversial and studied social issues: abortion, capital punishment, care for the elderly, child abuse, crime, energy, the environment, health care, immigration, minorities, national security, social welfare, women, youth, and many more. Even though this series is written especially for high school and undergraduate students, it is an excellent resource for anyone in need of factual information on current affairs.

By presenting the facts, it is the intention of Gale, a part of Cengage Learning, to provide its readers with everything they need to reach an informed opinion on current issues. To that end, there is a particular emphasis in this series on the presentation of scientific studies, surveys, and statistics. These data are generally presented in the form of tables, charts, and other graphics placed within the text of each book. Every graphic is directly referred to and carefully explained in the text. The source of each graphic is presented within the graphic itself. The data used in these graphics are drawn from the most reputable and reliable sources, in particular from the various branches of the U.S. government and from major independent polling organizations. Every effort was made to secure the most recent information available. Readers should bear in mind that many major studies take years to conduct, and that additional years often pass before the data from these studies are made available to the public. Therefore, in many cases the most recent information available in 2009 dated from 2006 or 2007. Older statistics are sometimes presented as well, if they are of particular interest and no more-recent information exists.

Even though statistics are a major focus of the *Information Plus Reference Series*, they are by no means its

only content. Each book also presents the widely held positions and important ideas that shape how the book's subject is discussed in the United States. These positions are explained in detail and, where possible, in the words of those who support them. Some of the other material to be found in these books includes historical background, descriptions of major events related to the subject, relevant laws and court cases, and examples of how these issues play out in American life. Some books also feature primary documents, or have pro and con debate sections giving the words and opinions of prominent Americans on both sides of a controversial topic. All material is presented in an even-handed and unbiased manner; readers will never be encouraged to accept one view of an issue over another.

HOW TO USE THIS BOOK

The United States is the world's largest consumer of energy in all its forms. Gasoline and other fossil fuels power its cars, trucks, trains, and aircraft. Electricity generated by burning oil, coal, and natural gas—or from nuclear or hydroelectric plants—runs Americans' lights, telephones, televisions, computers, and appliances. Without a steady, affordable, and massive amount of energy, modern America could not exist. This book presents the latest information on U.S. energy consumption and production and compares it to years past. Controversial issues such as the U.S. dependence on foreign oil, the possibility of exhausting fossil fuel supplies, and the harm done to the environment by mining, drilling, and pollution are explored.

Energy: Supplies, Sustainability, and Costs consists of nine chapters and three appendixes. Each of the major elements of the U.S. energy system—such as coal, nuclear energy, renewable energy sources, and electricity generation—has a chapter devoted to it. For a summary of the information covered in each chapter, please see the synopses provided in the Table of Contents at the front of the book. Chapters generally begin with an overview of the basic facts and background information on the chapter's topic, then proceed to examine subtopics of particular interest. For example, Chapter 4: Coal begins with a perspective of how coal has been used throughout history as a source for energy. The chapter then examines what coal is and its four classifications: anthracite (hard coal), bituminous (soft coal), subbituminous coal (black lignite), and lignite. Then the locations of coal deposits and how these deposits are mined are examined. Coal mining is a dangerous industry, so the chapter discusses the fatalities and the long-term health risks that miners face. The chapter then shifts to look at the domestic coal market, specifically the production, consumption, and price of coal. Next, the environmental problems of burning coal are detailed, such as the greenhouse effect and acid rain, as are some solutions that help decrease its impact, such as clean coal technology, clean air laws, and carbon dioxide capture. The chapter concludes by examining U.S. exports of coal, international coal production and consumption, and the future trends in the coal industry. Readers can find their way through a chapter by looking for the section and subsection headings, which are clearly set off from the text. Or, they can refer to the book's extensive index, if they already know what they are looking for.

Statistical Information

The tables and figures featured throughout *Energy: Supplies, Sustainability, and Costs* will be of particular use to readers in learning about this topic. These tables and figures represent an extensive collection of the most recent and valuable statistics on energy production and consumption—for example, the amount of coal mined in the United States in a year, the rate at which energy consumption is increasing in the United States, and the percentage of U.S. energy that comes from renewable sources. Gale, a part of Cengage Learning, believes that making this information available to readers is the most important way to fulfill the goal of this book: to help readers understand the topic of energy and reach their own conclusions about controversial issues related to energy use and conservation in the United States.

Each table or figure has a unique identifier appearing above it, for ease of identification and reference. Titles for the tables and figures explain their purpose. At the end of each table or figure, the original source of the data is provided.

To help readers understand these often complicated statistics, all tables and figures are explained in the text. References in the text direct readers to the relevant statistics. Furthermore, the contents of all tables and figures

are fully indexed. Please see the opening section of the index at the back of this volume for a description of how to find tables and figures within it.

Appendixes

Besides the main body text and images, *Energy: Supplies, Sustainability, and Costs* has three appendixes. The first is the Important Names and Addresses directory. Here, readers will find contact information for a number of organizations that study energy. The second appendix is the Resources section, which is provided to assist readers in conducting their own research. In this section, the author and editors of *Energy: Supplies, Sustainability, and Costs* describe some of the sources that were most useful during the compilation of this book. The final appendix is the detailed index.

ADVISORY BOARD CONTRIBUTIONS

The staff of Information Plus would like to extend its heartfelt appreciation to the Information Plus Advisory Board. This dedicated group of media professionals provides feedback on the series on an ongoing basis. Their comments allow the editorial staff who work on the project to make the series better and more user-friendly. Our top priorities are to produce the highest-quality and most useful books possible, and the Advisory Board's contributions to this process are invaluable.

The members of the Information Plus Advisory Board are:

- Kathleen R. Bonn, Librarian, Newbury Park High School, Newbury Park, California
- Madelyn Garner, Librarian, San Jacinto College–North Campus, Houston, Texas
- Anne Oxenrider, Media Specialist, Dundee High School, Dundee, Michigan
- Charles R. Rodgers, Director of Libraries, Pasco-Hernando Community College, Dade City, Florida
- James N. Zitzelsberger, Library Media Department Chairman, Oshkosh West High School, Oshkosh, Wisconsin

COMMENTS AND SUGGESTIONS

The editors of the *Information Plus Reference Series* welcome your feedback on *Energy: Supplies, Sustainability, and Costs*. Please direct all correspondence to:

Editors
Information Plus Reference Series
27500 Drake Rd.
Farmington Hills, MI 48331-3535

CHAPTER 1

AN ENERGY OVERVIEW

Energy is essential to life. Living creatures draw on energy flowing through the environment and convert it to forms they can use. The most fundamental energy flow for living creatures is the energy of sunlight, and the most important conversion is the act of biological primary production, in which plants and sea-dwelling phytoplankton convert sunlight into biomass by photosynthesis. The Earth's web of life, including human beings, rests on this foundation.

—Energy Information Administration, *Energy in the United States: 1635–2000* (2001)

A HISTORICAL PERSPECTIVE

Before the Twentieth Century

People have always found ways to harness energy, such as using animals to do work or inventing machines to tap the power of wind or water. The industrialization of the modern world was accompanied by the widespread use of fossil fuels such as coal, oil, and natural gas.

Significant use and management of energy resulted in one of the most profound social changes in history within a few generations. In the early 1800s most Americans lived in rural areas and worked in agriculture. The country ran mainly on wood fuel. One hundred years later, most Americans were city dwellers and worked in industry. The United States had become the world's largest producer and consumer of fossil fuels, had roughly tripled its use of energy per capita, and had become a global superpower.

The United States has always been a resource-abundant nation, but it was not until the Industrial Revolution in the mid-1800s that the total work output of engines surpassed that of work animals. As the country industrialized, coal began to replace wood as a primary fuel. Then petroleum and natural gas began to replace coal for many applications. The United States has since relied heavily on three fossil fuels: coal, petroleum, and natural gas.

The Twentieth and Early Twenty-First Centuries

For much of its history the United States has been nearly energy self-sufficient, although small amounts of coal were imported from Britain in colonial times. Through the 1950s domestic energy production and consumption were nearly equal. (See Figure 1.1.) During the 1960s consumption slightly outpaced production. In the 1970s the gap widened considerably, narrowed somewhat in the early 1980s, and thereafter widened year after year. By 2007 the gap between domestic energy production and consumption was quite significant. Since the 1970s energy imports have been used to try to close the gap between energy production and consumption. However, the United States' dependence on other countries for energy has created significant problems.

OIL CRISIS IN THE 1970s. In 1973 the United States supported Israel in the Yom Kippur War, which was fought between Israel and neighboring Arab countries. In response, several Arab nations cut off oil exports to the United States and decreased exports to the rest of the world. This embargo was lifted six months later, but the price of oil had tripled from the 1973 average to about $12 per barrel. (See Figure 1.2.) Not only did Americans (and others around the world) face sudden price hikes for products produced from oil, such as gasoline and home heating oil, but they also faced temporary shortages. The energy problem quickly became an energy crisis, which led to occasional blackouts in cities and industries, temporary shutdowns of factories and schools, and frequent lines at gasoline service stations. In 1973 the price of gas at the pump was about $0.39 per gallon ($1.81 in 2007 dollars) but it jumped to $0.52 per gallon ($2.20 in 2007 dollars) by 1974. (See Figure 1.3.) The sudden increase in energy prices in the early 1970s is widely considered to have been a major cause of the economic recession of 1974 and 1975.

Oil prices increased even more in the late 1970s. A revolution in Iran resulted in a significant drop in Iranian

FIGURE 1.1

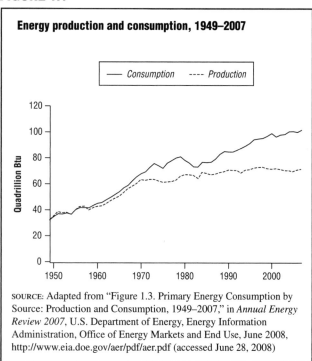

Energy production and consumption, 1949–2007

SOURCE: Adapted from "Figure 1.3. Primary Energy Consumption by Source: Production and Consumption, 1949–2007," in *Annual Energy Review 2007*, U.S. Department of Energy, Energy Information Administration, Office of Energy Markets and End Use, June 2008, http://www.eia.doe.gov/aer/pdf/aer.pdf (accessed June 28, 2008)

oil production from 1978 to 1981. During this same period the Iran-Iraq War (1980–1988) began, and many other Persian Gulf countries decreased their oil output as well. Companies and governments began to stockpile oil. As a result, prices continued to rise.

In early 1981 the U.S. government responded to the oil crisis by removing price and allocation controls on the oil industry. By no longer controlling domestic crude oil prices or restricting exports of petroleum products, it allowed the marketplace and competition to determine the price of crude oil. Domestic oil prices rose to the level of foreign oil prices and peaked in 1981. Oil approached $40 a barrel, and gasoline at the pump rose to $1.38 per gallon ($3.14 in 2007 dollars). (See Figure 1.2 and Figure 1.3.)

OIL PRICES FALL IN THE 1980s. As a result of these increasingly high prices, individuals and industry used less oil, stepped up their conservation efforts, or switched to alternative fuels. The demand for crude oil declined. However, the Organization of Petroleum Exporting Countries (OPEC), and particularly Saudi Arabia, cut its output during the first half of the 1980s to keep the price from

FIGURE 1.2

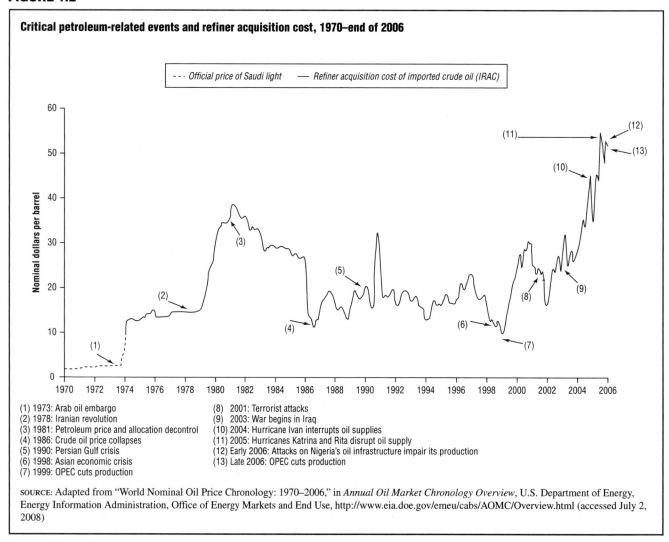

Critical petroleum-related events and refiner acquisition cost, 1970–end of 2006

(1) 1973: Arab oil embargo
(2) 1978: Iranian revolution
(3) 1981: Petroleum price and allocation decontrol
(4) 1986: Crude oil price collapses
(5) 1990: Persian Gulf crisis
(6) 1998: Asian economic crisis
(7) 1999: OPEC cuts production
(8) 2001: Terrorist attacks
(9) 2003: War begins in Iraq
(10) 2004: Hurricane Ivan interrupts oil supplies
(11) 2005: Hurricanes Katrina and Rita disrupt oil supply
(12) Early 2006: Attacks on Nigeria's oil infrastructure impair its production
(13) Late 2006: OPEC cuts production

SOURCE: Adapted from "World Nominal Oil Price Chronology: 1970–2006," in *Annual Oil Market Chronology Overview*, U.S. Department of Energy, Energy Information Administration, Office of Energy Markets and End Use, http://www.eia.doe.gov/emeu/cabs/AOMC/Overview.html (accessed July 2, 2008)

FIGURE 1.3

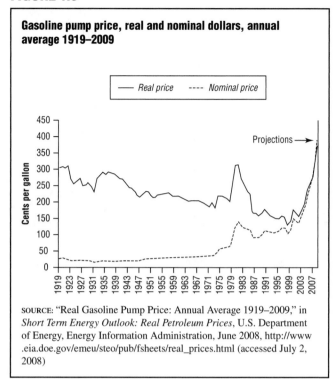

Gasoline pump price, real and nominal dollars, annual average 1919–2009

— Real price   ---- Nominal price

Projections →

Cents per gallon

SOURCE: "Real Gasoline Pump Price: Annual Average 1919–2009," in *Short Term Energy Outlook: Real Petroleum Prices*, U.S. Department of Energy, Energy Information Administration, June 2008, http://www.eia.doe.gov/emeu/steo/pub/fsheets/real_prices.html (accessed July 2, 2008)

declining dramatically. (In the 1980s OPEC member countries were Algeria, Ecuador, Indonesia, Iran, Iraq, Kuwait, Libya, Nigeria, Qatar, Saudi Arabia, the United Arab Emirates, and Venezuela. Angola became a member in 2007.)

In 1985 Saudi Arabia moved to increase its market share of crude oil exports by increasing its production. At the time its production was well below that of Russia and the United States. (See Figure 1.4.) Other OPEC members followed suit, which resulted in a glut of crude oil on the world market. Crude oil prices fell sharply in early 1986, and imports to the United States increased. Eventually, relief was felt by consumers at the gas pump. (See Figure 1.2 and Figure 1.3.)

THE UPS AND DOWNS OF OIL PRICES FROM THE 1990s THROUGH 2002. In August 1990 Iraq invaded Kuwait. The United Nations (UN) responded by placing an embargo on all crude oil and oil products from both countries. Oil prices rose suddenly and sharply, but non-OPEC countries in Central America, western Europe, and Asia, along with the United States, stepped up their production to fill the gap in world supplies. After the UN approved the use of force against Iraq, starting in October 1990, prices fell quickly. (See Figure 1.2.)

The collapse of Asian economies in the mid-1990s led to a further drop in the demand for energy, and petroleum prices dipped sharply in the late 1990s. OPEC reacted by curtailing production, which boosted prices in 2000. (See Figure 1.2.) World crude oil prices then declined through 2001 as global demand dropped because

of weakening economies (especially in the United States) and reduced demand for jet fuel following the September 11, 2001, terrorist attacks in the United States. Fear of an increased worldwide economic downturn also added to the decline in crude oil prices.

In late 2002 attacks and counterattacks between Palestinians and Israelis caused concerns that Iraq might halt its crude oil shipments to countries that supported the Jewish state of Israel over Islamic Palestine. Additionally, concerns existed that the Middle East region might become destabilized should the United States invade Iraq, which had the second-largest oil reserve in the world at that time, according to the Energy Information Administration (EIA), in *Annual Energy Review 2002* (October 2003, http://tonto.eia.doe.gov/FTPROOT/multifuel/038402.pdf). Moreover, Venezuelan oil workers went on strike, which cut off exports from Venezuela. These three factors were the primary causes of the rise in crude oil prices by the end of 2002. (See Figure 1.2.)

VOLATILITY AND RECORD HIGHS IN OIL PRICES FROM 2003 TO 2008. In early 2003 a U.S. war with Iraq seemed imminent. In addition, because of a cold winter and the Venezuelan strike, U.S. crude oil inventories had declined. As a result, the price of crude oil rose to nearly $40 per barrel in February 2003, the highest in twenty-nine months. (See Figure 1.2.) When the war began on March 19, 2003, Iraqi oil fields were shut down. However, other oil-producing countries stepped up production to offset the shortfall. In addition, the Venezuelan strike had ended. The price of oil declined dramatically to about $27 per barrel by the beginning of May 2003.

The lower price did not prevail, however. By June 2003 the price of oil rose above $30 per barrel, largely because supplies of crude oil were low and demand was high—summer, when Americans drive the most, was just starting. (See Figure 1.2.) The price of crude oil continued to climb over the summer and was pushed higher in the fall, when the U.S. dollar sank to a record low against the euro. By December 2003 it had risen to nearly $34 per barrel.

In 2004 crude oil prices continued to rise because of political uncertainty, the weakened U.S. dollar, the weather, and tight supplies. Increases reflected growing demand from the world's three largest oil consumers—the United States, China, and Japan—as well as concern about terrorist attacks in Spain, Iraq, Pakistan, Saudi Arabia, and other areas. Moreover, sabotage of Iraq's northern oil pipelines prevented the country from producing the amount of oil that was expected. By March 2004 the price of oil soared to a thirteen-year high of about $38 per barrel. (See Figure 1.2.) By August the price of crude reached more than $45 per barrel. Then in September Hurricane Ivan hit the Gulf of Mexico, forcing the evacuation of oil workers from offshore platforms and delaying oil tankers from Venezuela. By October 2004 a barrel of crude oil cost more than $50 for the first time.

FIGURE 1.4

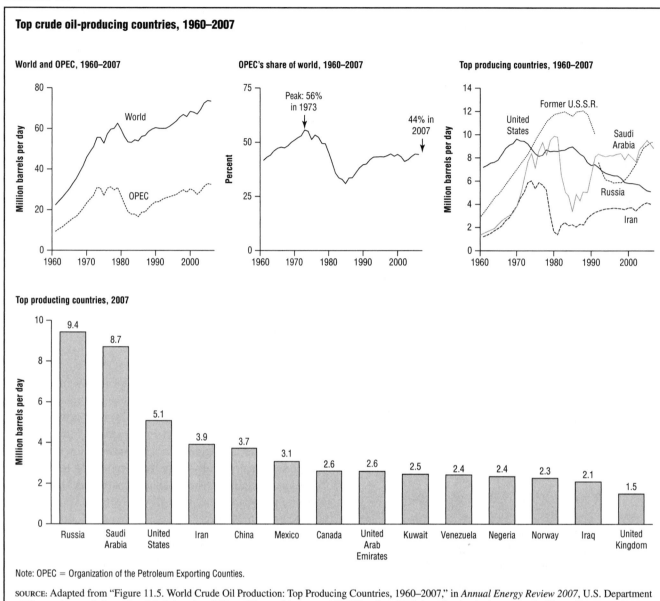

Top crude oil-producing countries, 1960–2007

Note: OPEC = Organization of the Petroleum Exporting Counties.

SOURCE: Adapted from "Figure 11.5. World Crude Oil Production: Top Producing Countries, 1960–2007," in *Annual Energy Review 2007*, U.S. Department of Energy, Energy Information Administration, Office of Energy Markets and End Use, June 2008, http://www.eia.doe.gov/aer/pdf/aer.pdf (accessed June 28, 2008)

In March 2005 sabotage forced Iraq to close the northern pipeline it used to export crude oil. In the following months OPEC agreed to increase its production to allow more oil into the world market to help reduce prices. (See Figure 1.2.) In August 2005, however, Hurricane Katrina hit the Gulf coast of the United States, severely affecting oil and natural gas production and oil refining there. Hurricane Rita struck the Gulf coast a month later. Because of the hurricanes, more than a quarter of U.S. oil refining capacity was shut down. In response, President George W. Bush (1946–) directed the U.S. Department of Energy to release as much as 30 million barrels of crude oil from the Strategic Petroleum Reserve. (See Chapter 2.) To bring the price of oil down on the world market, the International Energy Agency released 66.1

million short tons (60 million tons; approximately 450 million barrels) of crude oil to the United States. The crude oil price began to drop, finally falling below $60 per barrel in October and to $56 per barrel in November. (See Figure 1.2.) However, by December 2005 the price bounced back to slightly more than $60 per barrel.

The effects of the hurricanes on U.S. refining capacity lasted into 2006. The price of oil was pushed higher by other events in the world as well. For example, unrest in Nigeria, the world's twelfth-largest oil producer in 2006, reduced production by more than half a million barrels of crude oil per day. (See Figure 1.4.) By late April 2006 the price of crude oil surpassed $70 per barrel, and by the summer of 2006 the price was higher still at nearly $80 per barrel. (See Figure 1.2.) This rise was attributed to increased gas consumption, the launching of missiles by North Korea, continuing tension between Iran and the United States, and a war between Israel and Lebanon. As tensions eased with Iran during the fall of 2006, oil prices dropped. In October, as oil prices fell below $58 per barrel for the first time since the beginning of that year, OPEC announced that it would cut its crude oil output beginning in November, which halted the price drop.

Oil prices escalated throughout 2007 and into the first half of 2008, surpassing the price spike of the early 1980s for the first time. Figure 1.3 shows this spike in the price of gasoline at the pump in 2007 dollars (real price). One major factor that contributed to the continued price increase of oil in 2007 and 2008 was the falling value of the U.S. dollar. When the value of the U.S. dollar declines against major currencies, the price of oil rises because it is priced in U.S. dollars. Not only did the value of the U.S. dollar decline in 2007 and into 2008 but also the economy was doing poorly, particularly in the housing market sector. Investors were looking for a safe haven for investing, and oil became that safe haven.

In January and February 2008 the price of oil reached $100 per barrel on a few occasions before remaining well above that price into mid-2008. According to the article "Saudis Signal Boost in Production Capacity" (MSNBC, June 21, 2008), Samuel Bodman (1938–), the U.S. secretary of energy, contended that an increasing demand and insufficient supply of oil was the cause of high oil prices, whereas Saudi officials said that investment speculation was the cause. Nevertheless, the Saudi Arabian government pledged to increase output gradually into 2009. The article "Oil Rises to Trading, Closing Records on Falling U.S. Dollar" (*Bloomberg News*, June 28, 2008) notes that the price of crude oil hit an all-time high of $142 per barrel as the stock market fell and investors continued to see oil as a safe haven.

GOVERNMENTAL ENERGY POLICIES
Under President Ronald Reagan

According to the article "Primary Sources: The President's Proposed Energy Policy" (2002, http://www.pbs.org/wgbh/amex/carter/filmmore/ps_energy.html), President Jimmy Carter (1924–), a Democrat, said in a televised speech in April 1977 that the country could have "an effective and comprehensive energy policy only if the government takes responsibility for it and if the people understand the seriousness of the challenge and are willing to make sacrifices." However, when Ronald Reagan (1911–2004), a Republican, took over the presidency in 1981, he downplayed the importance of governmental responsibility. His administration sharply cut federal programs for energy and opposed governmental intervention in energy markets. For example, the administration did not tax energy imports, even though doing so might have stimulated domestic production and conservation. His administration transferred decision making to the states, the private sector, and individuals.

Under President George H. W. Bush

The subsequent Republican administration of President George H. W. Bush (1924–) continued the Reagan policy. In 1991 President Bush unveiled an energy policy that promised to reduce U.S. dependence on foreign oil by expanding domestic oil production into new areas and by simplifying the permit process for construction of nuclear power plants. Both proposals put him in conflict with conservationists, who objected to increased offshore drilling, especially in the coastal plain of the Arctic National Wildlife Refuge in Alaska. They also wanted to see automobile fuel economy improved and conservation methods stressed, rather than the use of nuclear power. President Bush's proposals did not include government-directed conservation efforts, tax incentives conservation, or the use of alternative energy sources.

Under President Bill Clinton

The Democratic administration of President Bill Clinton (1946–) sought a larger role for government in energy and environmental issues, although the major energy bills it proposed were not passed by the Republican-dominated Congress. Nevertheless, the Clinton administration did increase funds for alternative-energy research, mandate new energy-efficiency measures, and enforce emission standards. The administration also opened up several areas for oil exploration, including some Alaskan and offshore areas.

Under President George W. Bush

The major policy goals of the first term of President George W. Bush, a Republican, were to increase and diversify the country's sources of oil and to make energy security a priority. For example, his administration encouraged efforts to import more Russian crude oil into the United States and reopened the U.S. embassy in Equatorial Guinea, an oil-rich nation.

However, in his second term in office, President Bush began to advocate policies that would curb dependence on foreign oil and promote efforts to make the United States less dependent on oil and other fossil fuels. In August 2005 he signed into law the Energy Policy Act of 2005, which set new minimum energy-efficiency standards for appliances; provided tax credits for energy-efficient improvements to homes and for use of energy-efficient heat pumps, water heaters, and air conditioners; and sought to reduce the use of energy by the federal government. President Bush followed that with the Advanced Energy Initiative (http://www.whitehouse.gov/stateoftheunion/2006/energy/print/index.html) in February 2006, the goals of which were "promoting energy conservation, repairing and modernizing our energy infrastructure, and increasing our energy supplies in ways that protect and improve the environment." He also proposed developing new kinds of alternative fuel vehicles and using nuclear, solar, wind, and "clean coal" technologies to help power homes and businesses.

In 2007 and 2008 President Bush moved his agenda forward to improve fuel economy in vehicles and reduce American dependence on foreign oil. In his 2007 State of the Union address, he proposed the "Twenty in Ten" policy (January 2007, http://www.whitehouse.gov/stateoftheunion/2007/initiatives/energy.html) of reducing by 20% the amount of gasoline Americans used within the next ten years by increasing the fuel efficiency of automobiles—increasing the Corporate Average Fuel Economy (CAFE) standards—and using alternative fuels. Congress responded by developing the Energy Independence and Security Act (EISA) of 2007, which mandated that fuel producers make at least 36 billion gallons (136 billion L) of biofuel annually by 2022. EISA also required that the CAFE standard be raised for cars and light trucks to 35 miles per gallon (6.7 L/100 km) by model year 2020. The White House states in the press release "President Bush Discusses Energy" (June 18, 2008, http://www.whitehouse.gov/news/releases/2008/06/20080618.html) that in June 2008 President Bush asked Congress to pass legislation to help increase domestic production of oil by exploring the Outer Continental Shelf for oil resources; allowing the extraction of oil from oil shale located in the Green River Basin of Colorado, Utah, and Wyoming; permitting oil exploration in the Arctic National Wildlife Refuge in Alaska; and expanding and enhancing U.S. oil refinery capacity.

DOMESTIC ENERGY USAGE
Domestic Production

The total domestic energy production of the United States (the amount of fossil fuels and other forms of energy that were mined, pumped, or otherwise originated in the United States) has more than doubled since 1949, rising from 31.7 quadrillion British thermal units (Btu) in 1949 to 71.7 quadrillion Btu in 2007. (See Table 1.1 and Figure 1.5; Figure 1.5 shows how energy production was related to energy consumption in 2007.) One quadrillion Btu equals the energy produced by approximately 170 million barrels of crude oil. Large production and consumption figures are given in these units to make it easier to compare the various types of energy, which come in different forms.

Table 1.1 and Figure 1.6 show that after declining in the 1950s, energy produced from coal increased fairly steadily between 1960 and 2007, with its highest level recorded in 1998 (24 quadrillion Btu). The production of

oil rose from 1949 through 1970, but by 2007 it had declined to about the level produced in 1949. Natural gas production quadrupled between 1949 and 1970, from 5.4 quadrillion Btu to 21.7 quadrillion Btu; after peaking at 22.3 quadrillion Btu in 1971, natural gas production has generally ranged between 17 quadrillion Btu and 20 quadrillion Btu since that time. Energy produced from nuclear power rose dramatically during the 1970s, from 0.2 quadrillion Btu in 1970 to 3 quadrillion Btu in 1978; it continued to rise, doubling to 6.1 quadrillion Btu by 1990 and reaching its highest production level of 8.4 quadrillion Btu in 2007. Hydroelectric power reached its highest level during the mid-1990s but has not shown dramatic changes over the past several decades. The use of biomass (wood, waste, and alcohol) has increased in recent years; the production of energy from biomass reached its highest level ever in 2007 at 3.6 quadrillion Btu. At 23.5 quadrillion Btu, more energy was produced from coal in the United States during 2007 than from any other energy source. Energy produced from natural gas was second (19.8 quadrillion Btu), followed by oil (10.8 quadrillion Btu), and nuclear electric power (8.4 quadrillion Btu).

Domestic Consumption

Even though total domestic energy production more than doubled from 1949 to 2007, total domestic energy consumption (the amount of energy used in the United States) more than tripled during that time. (See Figure 1.1.) This increase did not happen in an even progression over those years. A doubling of domestic energy consumption occurred from 1949 to 1973, increasing from 30 quadrillion Btu to 74 quadrillion Btu. However, after huge oil price increases in 1973, energy consumption fell, then rose, and then fell again, eventually returning to 1973 levels by 1984. The level of domestic energy consumption remained relatively stable through 1986, but following a drop in the price of crude oil that year, imports of oil began to rise and energy consumption increased quite steadily. In 2007 domestic energy consumption reached an all-time high of 101.6 quadrillion Btu.

One of the reasons that energy consumption has increased in the United States is the growing number of people who use it. According to the U.S. Census Bureau, in *Measuring America: The Decennial Censuses from 1790 to 2000* (September 2002, http://www.census.gov/prod/2002pubs/pol02marv.pdf), the U.S. population grew from 151.3 million in 1950 to 281.4 million in 2000, an increase of 86%. Nonetheless, energy consumption has outpaced this increase in population, rising by 181% during the same period. (See Figure 1.1.)

Figure 1.7 shows energy production and consumption flows, including types of energy sources, in 2007. According to the EIA, in *Annual Energy Review 2007*

TABLE 1.1

Energy production by source, selected years 1949–2007

[Quadrillion Btu]

Year	Fossil fuels Coal[b]	Natural gas (dry)	Crude oil[c]	NGPL[d]	Total	Nuclear electric power	Renewable energy[a] Hydro electric power[e]	Geothermal	Solar/PV	Wind	Biomass	Total	Total
1949	11.974	5.377	10.683	0.714	28.748	0.000	1.425	NA	NA	NA	1.549	2.974	31.722
1950	14.060	6.233	11.447	.823	32.563	.000	1.415	NA	NA	NA	1.562	2.978	35.540
1955	12.370	9.345	14.410	1.240	37.364	.000	1.360	NA	NA	NA	1.424	2.784	40.148
1960	10.817	12.656	14.935	1.461	39.869	.006	1.608	.001	NA	NA	1.320	2.929	42.804
1965	13.055	15.775	16.521	1.883	47.235	.043	2.059	.004	NA	NA	1.335	3.398	50.676
1970	14.607	21.666	20.401	2.512	59.186	.239	2.634	.011	NA	NA	1.431	4.076	63.501
1971	13.186	22.280	20.033	2.544	58.042	.413	2.824	.012	NA	NA	1.432	4.268	62.723
1972	14.092	22.208	20.041	2.598	58.938	.584	2.864	.031	NA	NA	1.503	4.398	63.920
1974	14.074	21.210	18.575	2.471	56.331	1.272	3.177	.053	NA	NA	1.540	4.769	62.372
1976	15.654	19.480	17.262	2.327	54.723	2.111	2.976	.078	NA	NA	1.713	4.768	61.602
1978	14.910	19.485	18.434	2.245	55.074	3.024	2.937	.064	NA	NA	2.038	5.039	63.137
1980	18.598	19.908	18.249	2.254	59.008	2.739	2.900	.110	NA	NA	2.476	5.485	67.232
1982	18.639	18.319	18.309	2.191	57.458	3.131	3.266	.105	NA	NA	2.664	6.034	66.623
1984	19.719	18.008	18.848	2.274	58.849	3.553	3.386	.165	(s)	(s)	2.971	6.522	68.924
1986	19.509	16.541	18.376	2.149	56.575	4.380	3.071	.219	(s)	(s)	2.932	6.223	67.178
1988	20.738	17.599	17.279	2.260	57.875	5.587	2.334	.217	(s)	(s)	3.016	5.568	69.030
1990	22.488	18.326	15.571	2.175	58.560	6.104	3.046	.336	.060	.029	2.735	6.206	70.870
1992	21.694	18.375	15.223	2.363	57.655	6.479	2.617	.349	.064	.030	2.933	5.993	70.127
1994	22.202	19.348	14.103	2.391	58.044	6.694	2.683	.338	.069	.036	3.030	6.155	70.893
1996	22.790	19.344	13.723	2.530	58.387	7.087	3.590	.316	.071	.033	3.157	7.167	72.641
1998	24.045	19.613	13.235	2.420	59.314	7.068	3.297	.328	.070	.031	2.933	6.659	73.041
2000	22.735	19.662	12.358	2.611	57.366	7.862	2.811	.317	.066	.057	3.010	6.262	71.490
2002	22.732	19.439	12.163	2.559	56.894	8.143	2.689	.328	.064	.105	2.712	5.899	R70.936
2003	R22.094	19.691	12.026	2.346	R56.157	7.959	2.825	.331	.064	.115	R2.815	6.149	R70.264
2004	R22.852	19.093	11.503	2.466	R55.914	8.222	2.690	.341	.064	.142	3.011	6.248	R70.384
2005	R23.185	R18.574	10.963	2.334	R55.056	8.160	2.703	.343	.066	.178	R3.141	R6.431	R69.647
2006	R23.790	R18.993	R10.801	R2.356	R55.940	R8.214	R2.869	R.343	R.072	R.264	R3.324	R6.872	R71.025
2007P	23.480	19.817	10.802	2.400	56.499	8.415	2.463	.353	.080	.319	3.584	6.800	71.713

[a]Most data are estimates.
[b]Beginning in 1989, includes waste coal supplied. Beginning in 2001, also includes a small amount of refuse recovery.
[c]Includes lease condensate.
[d]Natural gas plant liquids.
[e]Conventional hydroelectric power.
R = Revised.
P = Preliminary.
NA = Not available.
(s) = Less than 0.0005 quadrillion Btu.
Notes: Totals may not equal sum of components due to independent rounding.

SOURCE: Adapted from "Table 1.2. Primary Energy Production by Source, Selected Years, 1949–2007 (Quadrillion Btu)," in *Annual Energy Review 2007*, U.S. Department of Energy, Energy Information Administration, Office of Energy Markets and End Use, June 2008, http://www.eia.doe.gov/aer/pdf/aer.pdf (accessed June 28, 2008)

(June 2008, http://www.eia.doe.gov/aer/pdf/aer.pdf), coal, which accounted for nearly 13 quadrillion Btu (17% of all energy consumed) in 1973, accounted for 22.8 quadrillion Btu (22.4%) in 2007. Nuclear electric power, which contributed 0.9 quadrillion Btu (less than 1%) in 1973, made up 8.4 quadrillion Btu (8.3%) in 2007.

ENERGY IMPORTS AND EXPORTS

As indicated in Figure 1.1, since the late 1950s energy consumption in the United States has outpaced energy production. The difference has been made up by importing energy sources. Imports (mainly oil) grew rapidly from 1953 through 1973 as the U.S. economy expanded using inexpensive oil. The EIA indicates in *Annual Energy Review 2007* that in 1973 net imports of petroleum reached almost 13.5 quadrillion Btu.

Even though the Arab oil embargo of 1973–74—coupled with increased oil prices—momentarily slowed growth in petroleum imports, the general increase continued, with total energy imports exceeding 19 quadrillion Btu in 1977 through 1979. (See Table 1.2.) During those years U.S. dependence on petroleum imports rose to more than 45% of the nation's oil consumption. (See Figure 1.8.) Despite the lesson of 1973, it took a second round of price increases from 1979 to 1980, accompanied by long and frustrating lines at gas stations, to persuade Americans to become less dependent on imported oil, conserve resources, or both. By 1985 U.S. dependence on foreign oil had decreased sharply, to 27.3% of oil consumption.

After 1985 U.S. dependence on foreign sources of oil increased gradually, as a drop in the price of crude oil drove up demand. When Iraq invaded Kuwait in 1990,

FIGURE 1.5

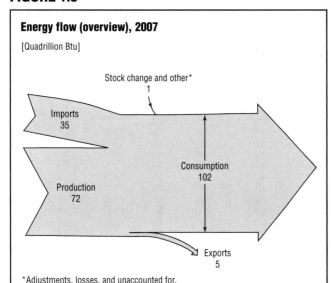

Energy flow (overview), 2007

[Quadrillion Btu]

*Adjustments, losses, and unaccounted for.

SOURCE: Adapted from "Figure 1.1. Primary Energy Overview: Energy Flow, 2007 (Quadrillion Btu)," in *Annual Energy Review 2007*, U.S. Department of Energy, Energy Information Administration, Office of Energy Markets and End Use, June 2008, http://www.eia.doe.gov/aer/pdf/aer.pdf (accessed June 28, 2008)

FIGURE 1.6

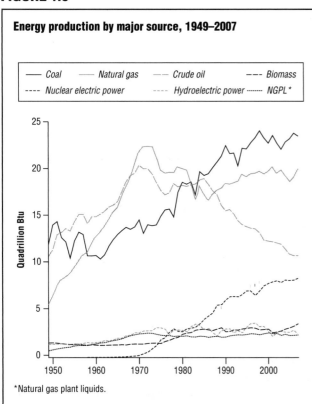

Energy production by major source, 1949–2007

*Natural gas plant liquids.

SOURCE: "Figure 11. Primary Energy Production by Major Source," in *Annual Energy Review 2007*, U.S. Department of Energy, Energy Information Administration, Office of Energy Markets and End Use, June 2008, http://www.eia.doe.gov/aer/pdf/aer.pdf (accessed June 28, 2008)

the potential threat to the flow of oil to the United States and other industrialized nations was one of the reasons the United States challenged Saddam Hussein (1937–2006) in Operation Desert Storm. However, after the terrorist attacks of September 11, 2001, and the Bush administration's subsequent war on terror, the concept of energy independence, or at least reduced energy dependence, became increasingly important. In 2003 the United States was again at war with Iraq, and by 2007 imported oil accounted for a record 58.2% of U.S. oil consumption. (See Figure 1.8.) That year net imports of petroleum (total imports minus total exports) reached 25.8 quadrillion Btu. (See Table 1.2.)

Even though the United States imports energy, primarily in the form of oil, it exports small amounts of energy in the form of coal and oil. In 2007 coal exports totaled 1.5 quadrillion Btu, about 28% of U.S. energy exports. (See Figure 1.9 and Table 1.2.) The United States also exports some oil. The reasons for exporting oil are complicated but have to do with the cost of transporting Alaskan oil; the sale of certain types of petroleum used to make steel; and exchanges with Canada and Mexico of crude products for refined products.

FOSSIL FUEL PRODUCTION PRICES

Production prices are the value of fuel produced. The combined production prices of fossil fuels (crude oil, natural gas, and coal) slowly declined from 1949 through 1972. (See Figure 1.10.) These prices then increased dramatically from 1973 through 1981 and fell almost as dramatically through 1998: the composite value of all fossil fuel prices (in real dollars, which account for inflation and reflect the buying power of the dollar in 2000) dropped from $4.64 per million Btu in 1981 to $1.46 per million Btu in 1998, a decrease of more than two-thirds. (See Table 1.3.) This drop created economic problems in fuel-producing American states, such as Texas, Louisiana, Oklahoma, Montana, West Virginia, and Ohio, and in energy-exporting countries, such as many Middle Eastern nations, Nigeria, Indonesia, Venezuela, and Trinidad. However, it was a windfall for industries that used a lot of energy, such as airlines, electric utilities, steel mills, and trucking companies. Since 1998 the combined production prices of fossil fuels have been generally rising, reaching $4.17 (in real dollars) per million Btu in 2007. These same industries suffered with this rise.

The production prices of both crude oil (the most expensive of the fossil fuels) and natural gas followed a pattern of rising and falling similar to that of the fossil fuel composite price from 1949 to 2005. Crude oil production prices then shot up, whereas natural gas and fossil fuel composite prices declined then leveled off from 2005 to 2007. (See Figure 1.10.)

FIGURE 1.7

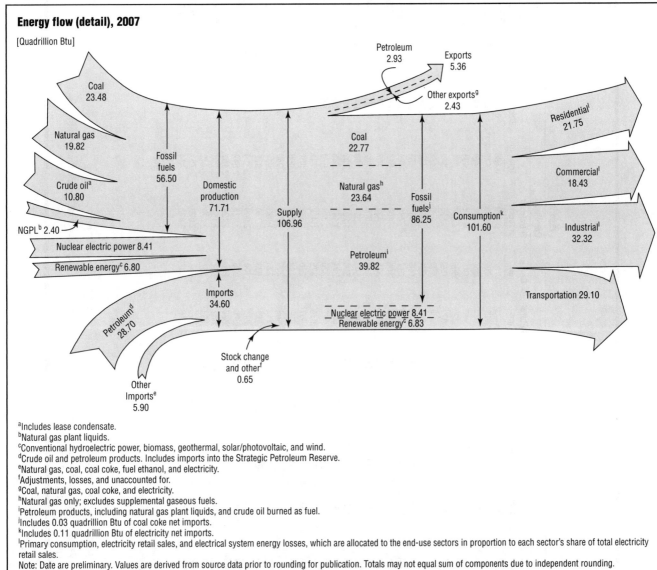

Energy flow (detail), 2007

[Quadrillion Btu]

a Includes lease condensate.
b Natural gas plant liquids.
c Conventional hydroelectric power, biomass, geothermal, solar/photovoltaic, and wind.
d Crude oil and petroleum products. Includes imports into the Strategic Petroleum Reserve.
e Natural gas, coal, coal coke, fuel ethanol, and electricity.
f Adjustments, losses, and unaccounted for.
g Coal, natural gas, coal coke, and electricity.
h Natural gas only; excludes supplemental gaseous fuels.
i Petroleum products, including natural gas plant liquids, and crude oil burned as fuel.
j Includes 0.03 quadrillion Btu of coal coke net imports.
k Includes 0.11 quadrillion Btu of electricity net imports.
l Primary consumption, electricity retail sales, and electrical system energy losses, which are allocated to the end-use sectors in proportion to each sector's share of total electricity retail sales.
Note: Date are preliminary. Values are derived from source data prior to rounding for publication. Totals may not equal sum of components due to independent rounding.

SOURCE: "Diagram 1. Energy Flow, 2007 (Quadrillion Btu)," in *Annual Energy Review 2007*, U.S. Department of Energy, Energy Information Administration, Office of Energy Markets and End Use, June 2008, http://www.eia.doe.gov/aer/pdf/aer.pdf (accessed June 28, 2008)

Even though crude oil production prices have generally followed the fossil fuel composite, its price shifts have been the most dramatic of all the fossil fuel production prices over the decades. After slowly declining from 1949, the crude oil production price rose most dramatically from 1972, when it was $1.94 per million Btu, to 1981, when it topped at $9.27 per million Btu. The price then tumbled to $1.94 in 1998. (See Figure 1.10 and Table 1.3.) However, it rose sharply during the next two years, reaching $4.61 in 2000. After a slight decline in 2001 and 2002, the crude oil production price rose to $4.47 in 2003, $7.67 in 2005, and $9.58 in 2007. For natural gas, the price sank from $3.55 per million Btu in 1984 to $1.83 in 1998. It rose to an all-time high of $5.87 per million Btu by 2005. In 2007 the production price of natural gas had dropped about a dollar to $4.84 per million Btu.

The story of coal prices is a bit different from that of the other fossil fuels. Coal production prices rose from 1970 ($0.97 per million Btu) to 1975 ($2.22), but then—unlike the production prices for natural gas and crude oil—declined quite steadily through 2000 ($0.80). (See Figure 1.10 and Table 1.3.) Coal prices rose to $1.04 per million Btu by 2007.

ENERGY USE BY SECTOR

Energy use can be classified into four main end-use sectors: commercial, industrial, residential, and transportation. Historically, industry has been the largest energy-consuming sector of the economy. In 2007 industry used about 32 quadrillion Btu, compared to approximately 29 quadrillion Btu in the transportation sector, 22 quadrillion

TABLE 1.2

Energy imports, exports, and net imports, selected years 1949–2007

[Quadrillion Btu]

Year	Imports									Exports								Net imports[a]
					Petroleum									Petroleum				
	Coal	Coal coke	Natural gas	Crude oil[b]	Petroleum products[c]	Total	Fuel ethanol	Electricity	Total	Coal	Coal coke	Natural gas	Crude oil	Petroleum products[c]	Total	Electricity	Total	Total
1949	0.008	0.007	0.000	0.915	0.513	1.427	NA	0.006	1.448	0.877	0.014	0.021	0.192	0.488	0.680	0.001	1.592	−0.144
1950	.009	.011	.000	1.056	.830	1.886	NA	.007	1.913	.786	.010	.027	.202	.440	.642	.001	1.465	.448
1955	.008	.003	.011	1.691	1.061	2.752	NA	.016	2.790	1.465	.013	.032	.067	.707	.774	.002	2.286	.504
1960	.007	.003	.161	2.196	1.802	3.999	NA	.018	4.188	1.023	.009	.012	.018	.413	.431	.003	1.477	2.710
1965	.005	.002	.471	2.654	2.748	5.402	NA	.012	5.892	1.376	.021	.027	.006	.386	.392	.013	1.829	4.063
1970	.001	.004	.846	2.814	4.656	7.470	NA	.021	8.342	1.936	.061	.072	.029	.520	.549	.014	2.632	5.709
1971	.003	.004	.964	3.573	4.968	8.540	NA	.024	9.535	1.546	.037	.083	.003	.470	.473	.012	2.151	7.384
1972	.001	.005	1.047	4.712	5.587	10.299	NA	.036	11.387	1.531	.031	.080	.001	.466	.467	.010	2.118	9.269
1974	.052	.088	.985	7.395	5.731	13.127	NA	.053	14.304	1.620	.032	.078	.006	.458	.465	.009	2.203	12.101
1976	.030	.033	.988	11.239	4.434	15.672	NA	.037	16.760	1.597	.033	.066	.017	.452	.469	.008	2.172	14.588
1977	.041	.045	1.037	14.027	4.728	18.756	NA	.069	19.948	1.442	.031	.056	.106	.408	.514	.009	2.052	17.896
1978	.074	.142	.995	13.460	4.364	17.824	NA	.072	19.106	1.078	.017	.053	.335	.432	.767	.005	1.920	17.186
1979	.051	.099	1.300	13.825	4.108	17.933	NA	.077	19.460	1.753	.036	.056	.497	.505	1.002	.007	2.855	16.605
1980	.030	.016	1.006	11.195	3.463	14.658	NA	.085	15.796	2.421	.051	.049	.609	.551	1.160	.014	3.695	12.101
1982	.019	.003	.950	7.418	3.360	10.777	NA	.112	11.861	2.787	.025	.052	.500	1.231	1.732	.012	4.608	7.253
1984	.032	.014	.847	7.302	4.131	11.433	NA	.144	12.471	2.151	.026	.055	.384	1.161	1.545	.009	3.786	8.685
1986	.055	.008	.748	9.002	4.199	13.201	NA	.139	14.151	2.248	.025	.062	.326	1.344	1.670	.016	4.021	10.130
1988	.053	.067	1.296	11.027	4.720	15.747	NA	.133	17.296	2.499	.027	.075	.329	1.412	1.741	.024	4.366	12.929
1990	.067	.019	1.551	12.766	4.351	17.117	NA	.063	18.817	2.772	.014	.087	.230	1.594	1.824	.055	4.752	14.065
1992	.095	.052	2.161	13.253	3.714	16.968	NA	.096	19.372	2.682	.017	.220	.188	1.819	2.008	.010	4.937	14.435
1994	.222	.083	2.682	15.340	R3.904	R19.243	.001	.160	R22.390	1.879	.024	.164	.209	1.779	1.988	.007	4.061	R18.329
1996	.203	.063	3.002	16.341	R3.943	R20.284	.001	.148	R23.702	2.368	.040	.155	.233	1.825	2.059	.011	4.633	R19.069
1998	.218	.095	3.225	18.916	3.992	22.908	(s)	.135	26.581	2.092	.028	.161	.233	1.740	1.972	.047	4.299	22.281
2000	.313	.094	3.869	19.783	R4.749	R24.531	(s)	.166	28.973	1.528	.028	.245	.106	2.048	2.154	.051	4.006	24.967
2002	.422	.080	4.104	19.920	R4.754	R24.674	.001	.125	R29.407	1.032	.020	.520	.019	2.023	2.042	.054	3.668	R25.739
2003	.626	.068	4.042	21.060	R5.159	R26.219	.001	.104	R31.061	1.117	.018	.686	.026	2.124	2.151	.082	4.054	R27.007
2004	.682	.170	4.365	22.082	6.114	R28.196	.013	.117	R33.543	1.253	.033	.862	.057	2.151	2.208	.078	4.433	R29.110
2005	.762	.088	4.450	22.091	R7.157	R29.248	.011	.152	R34.710	1.273	.043	.735	.067	2.374	2.442	.068	4.561	R30.149
2006	.906	.101	R4.291	R22.085	R7.083	R29.168	R.062	R.146	R34.673	1.264	.040	R.730	.052	R2.699	R2.751	R.083	R4.868	R29.805
2007P	.909	.061	4.717	21.868	6.833	28.701	.037	.175	34.599	1.507	.036	.816	.058	2.876	2.934	.069	5.361	29.238

[a]Net imports equal imports minus exports. Minus sign indicates exports are greater than imports.
[b]Crude oil and lease condensate. Includes imports into the Strategic Petroleum Reserve, which began in 1977.
[c]Petroleum products, unfinished oils, pentanes plus, and gasoline blending components. Does not include fuel ethanol.
R = Revised.
P = Preliminary.
NA = Not available.
(s) = Less than 0.0005 quadrillion Btu.
Notes: Includes trade between the United States (50 states and the District of Columbia) and its territories and possessions. Totals may not equal sum of components due to independent rounding.

SOURCE: Adapted from "Table 1.4. Primary Energy Trade by Source, Selected Years, 1949–2007 (Quadrillion Btu)," in *Annual Energy Review 2007*, U.S. Department of Energy, Energy Information Administration, Office of Energy Markets and End Use, June 2008, http://www.eia.doe.gov/aer/pdf/aer.pdf (accessed June 28, 2008)

FIGURE 1.8

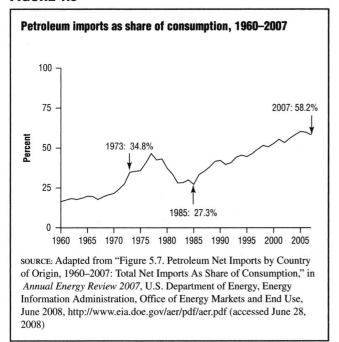

Petroleum imports as share of consumption, 1960–2007

SOURCE: Adapted from "Figure 5.7. Petroleum Net Imports by Country of Origin, 1960–2007: Total Net Imports As Share of Consumption," in *Annual Energy Review 2007*, U.S. Department of Energy, Energy Information Administration, Office of Energy Markets and End Use, June 2008, http://www.eia.doe.gov/aer/pdf/aer.pdf (accessed June 28, 2008)

FIGURE 1.9

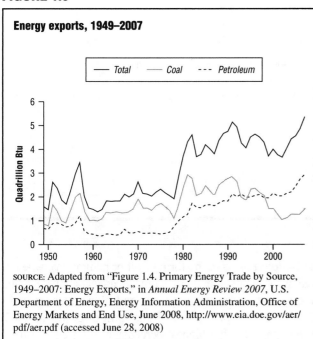

Energy exports, 1949–2007

SOURCE: Adapted from "Figure 1.4. Primary Energy Trade by Source, 1949–2007: Energy Exports," in *Annual Energy Review 2007*, U.S. Department of Energy, Energy Information Administration, Office of Energy Markets and End Use, June 2008, http://www.eia.doe.gov/aer/pdf/aer.pdf (accessed June 28, 2008)

FIGURE 1.10

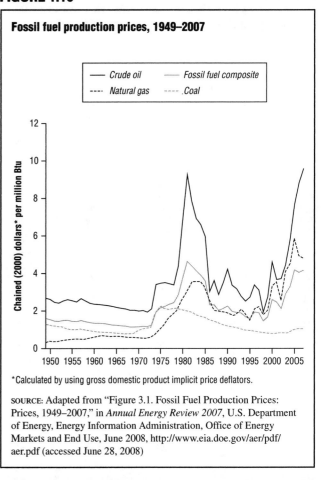

Fossil fuel production prices, 1949–2007

*Calculated by using gross domestic product implicit price deflators.

SOURCE: Adapted from "Figure 3.1. Fossil Fuel Production Prices: Prices, 1949–2007," in *Annual Energy Review 2007*, U.S. Department of Energy, Energy Information Administration, Office of Energy Markets and End Use, June 2008, http://www.eia.doe.gov/aer/pdf/aer.pdf (accessed June 28, 2008)

Btu in the residential sector, and 18 quadrillion Btu in the commercial sector. (See Figure 1.11.)

Within sectors, energy sources have changed over time. For example, in the commercial sector, coal was the leading energy source through 1953 but declined dramatically in favor of petroleum (through 1962) and then natural gas. (See Figure 1.12.) In 1990 energy in the form of electricity pulled ahead as the leading energy source. Similarly, coal was the leading energy source in the residential sector in 1949. (See Figure 1.13.) Natural gas quickly took over, with petroleum in second place. In 1979 electricity took over second place from petroleum. Industry used more coal than natural gas or petroleum through 1957, but after that natural gas and petroleum took over as nearly equally preferred energy sources. (See Figure 1.14.) In transportation, reliance on petroleum has been increasing since 1949. (See Figure 1.15.)

Not included in the four main sectors of energy consumption is the electric power sector. This sector includes electric utilities that generate, transmit, distribute, and sell electricity for use by the other four sectors—in homes, businesses, and industry. Figure 1.16 shows that most of the electricity for the United States is generated by burning coal. The electric power sector consumed nearly 21 quadrillion Btu of coal in 2007, almost all the coal used in the United States. Electricity is also generated by nuclear power, natural gas, renewable energy sources (hydroelectric, wood, waste, geothermal, solar, and wind), and petroleum. As Figure 1.16 shows, renewable sources generate very little of the nation's electricity.

TABLE 1.3

Fossil fuel production prices, selected years 1949–2007

[Dollars per million Btu]

Year	Coal[a] Nominal	Coal[a] Real[e]	Natural gas[b] Nominal	Natural gas[b] Real[e]	Crude oil[c] Nominal	Crude oil[c] Real[e]	Fossil fuel composite[d] Nominal	Fossil fuel composite[d] Real[e]	Fossil fuel composite[d] Percent change[f]
1949	0.21	1.29	0.05	0.33	0.44	2.68	0.26	1.60	—
1950	.21	1.25	.06	.38	.43	2.62	.26	1.54	−3.6
1955	.19	.99	.09	.48	.48	2.55	.27	1.45	−3.7
1960	.19	.92	.13	.60	.50	2.36	.28	1.35	−2.3
1965	.18	.82	.15	.65	.49	2.19	.28	1.23	−1.5
1970	.27	.97	.15	.56	.55	1.99	.32	1.15	.8
1971	.30	1.05	.16	.56	.58	2.02	.34	1.18	2.1
1972	.33	1.09	.17	.57	.58	1.94	.35	1.16	−1.4
1974	.69	1.98	.27	.79	1.18	3.41	.68	1.95	55.8
1975	.85	2.22	.40	1.06	1.32	3.48	.82	2.16	10.9
1976	.86	2.13	.53	1.32	1.41	3.51	.90	2.24	3.8
1978	.98	2.15	.84	1.83	1.55	3.39	1.12	2.44	3.4
1980	1.10	2.04	1.45	2.68	3.72	6.89	2.04	3.78	32.1
1981	1.18	2.00	1.80	3.04	5.48	9.27	2.75	4.64	22.9
1982	1.23	1.95	2.22	3.54	4.92	7.84	2.76	4.40	−5.3
1984	1.16	1.72	2.40	3.55	4.46	6.60	2.65	3.91	−5.6
1986	1.09	1.52	1.75	2.45	2.16	3.03	1.65	2.32	−35.6
1988	1.01	1.34	1.52	2.01	2.17	2.87	1.53	2.03	−12.8
1990	1.00	1.22	1.55	1.90	3.45	4.23	1.84	2.26	6.2
1992	.97	1.12	1.57	1.82	2.76	3.19	1.66	1.92	−3.0
1994	.91	1.01	1.67	1.86	2.27	2.52	1.53	1.69	−10.4
1996	.87	.92	1.96	2.09	3.18	3.39	1.82	1.94	21.3
1998	.83	.86	1.77	1.83	1.87	1.94	1.41	1.46	−22.8
2000	.80	.80	3.32	3.32	4.61	4.61	2.60	2.60	54.2
2002	.87	.84	2.67	2.56	3.88	3.73	2.21	2.12	−14.2
2003	.87	.82	4.41	4.15	4.75	4.47	3.09	2.91	37.1
2004	.98	.89	4.94	R4.51	6.34	5.79	3.61	3.30	13.4
2005	1.16	1.03	R6.63	R5.87	8.67	R7.67	R4.73	R4.19	R27.1
2006	R1.24	R1.06	R5.80	R4.98	10.29	R8.83	R4.73	4.06	R−3.2
2007[P]	1.25	1.04	5.79	4.84	11.47	9.58	4.99	4.17	2.8

[a]Free-on-board (f.o.b.) rail/barge prices, which are the f.o.b. prices of coal at the point of first sale, excluding freight or shipping and insurance costs.
[b]Wellhead prices (converted to dollars per million Btu using marketed production heat contents).
[c]Domestic first purchase prices.
[d]Derived by multiplying the price per Btu of each fossil fuel by the total Btu content of the production of each fossil fuel and dividing this accumulated value of total fossil fuel production by the accumulated Btu content of total fossil fuel production.
[e]In chained (2000) dollars, calculated by using gross domestic product implicit price deflators.
[f]Based on real values.
R = Revised.
P = Preliminary.
— = Not applicable.

SOURCE: Adapted from "Table 3.1. Fossil Fuel Production Prices, Selected Years, 1949–2007 (Dollars per Million Btu)," in *Annual Energy Review 2007*, U.S. Department of Energy, Energy Information Administration, Office of Energy Markets and End Use, June 2008, http://www.eia.doe.gov/aer/pdf/aer.pdf (accessed June 28, 2008)

INTERNATIONAL ENERGY PRODUCTION AND CONSUMPTION

World Production

World production of energy rose from 215.4 quadrillion Btu in 1970 to 460.1 quadrillion Btu in 2005. (See Table 1.4.) The EIA states in *Annual Energy Review 2007* that the world's total output of primary energy increased by 114% from 1970 to 2005. In 2005 fossil fuels accounted for 86% of all energy produced worldwide, whereas renewable energy accounted for 8% and nuclear electric power for 6%.

In 2005 the United States, China, and Russia, respectively, were by far the leading producers of energy, followed by Saudi Arabia, Canada, and Iran. (See Figure 1.17.) According to the EIA, almost all the energy produced in the Middle East is in the form of oil or natural gas, whereas coal is a major source in China. Canada is the leading producer of hydroelectric power and alone accounted for 12.4% of world production of this form of power in 2005. France produces the highest percentage of its energy from nuclear power—about 79% in 2005.

World Consumption

Table 1.5 shows the world consumption of energy by region from 1980 to 2005. The five countries singled out in the table—the United States, China, Russia, Japan, and Germany—together consumed about 51% of the world's total energy supply in 2005. The United States, by far the world's largest consumer of energy, used about 100.7 quadrillion Btu in 2005, or 22% of the energy consumed worldwide. This amount was about 50% more than the 67

FIGURE 1.11

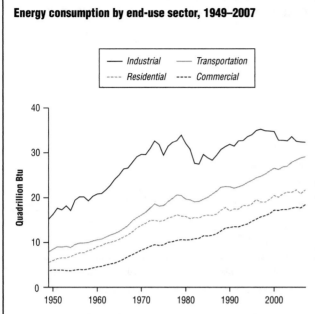

Energy consumption by end-use sector, 1949–2007

SOURCE: Adapted from "Figure 2.1a. Energy Consumption by Sector Overview: Total Consumption by End-Use Sector, 1949–2007," in *Annual Energy Review 2007*, U.S. Department of Energy, Energy Information Administration, Office of Energy Markets and End Use, June 2008, http://www.eia.doe.gov/aer/pdf/aer.pdf (accessed June 28, 2008)

FIGURE 1.12

Commercial sector energy consumption by major source, 1949–2007

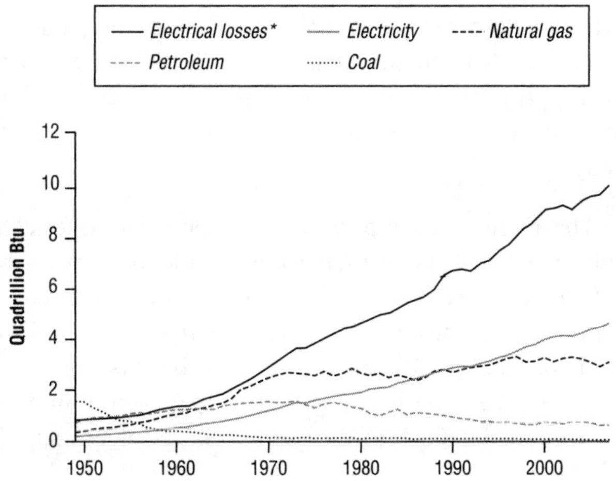

*Electrical system energy losses associated with the generation, transmission, and distribution of energy in the form of electricity.

SOURCE: Adapted from "Figure 2.1b. Energy Consumption by End-Use Sector, 1949–2007: Commercial, by Major Source," in *Annual Energy Review 2007*, U.S. Department of Energy, Energy Information Administration, Office of Energy Markets and End Use, June 2008, http://www.eia.doe.gov/aer/pdf/aer.pdf (accessed June 28, 2008)

FIGURE 1.13

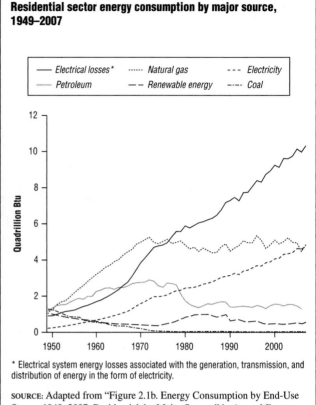

Residential sector energy consumption by major source, 1949–2007

* Electrical system energy losses associated with the generation, transmission, and distribution of energy in the form of electricity.

SOURCE: Adapted from "Figure 2.1b. Energy Consumption by End-Use Sector, 1949–2007: Residential, by Major Source," in *Annual Energy Review 2007*, U.S. Department of Energy, Energy Information Administration, Office of Energy Markets and End Use, June 2008, http://www.eia.doe.gov/aer/pdf/aer.pdf (accessed June 28, 2008)

quadrillion Btu consumed in China. Russia consumed 30.3 quadrillion Btu in 2005.

FUTURE TRENDS IN U.S. ENERGY CONSUMPTION, IMPORTS, AND PRICES

In *Annual Energy Outlook 2008* (June 2008, http://www.eia.doe.gov/oiaf/aeo/pdf/0383(2008).pdf), the EIA forecasts energy supply, demand, and prices, which are used by decision makers in the public and private sectors. The EIA's projections, through 2030, are based on current U.S. laws, regulations, and economic conditions.

Table 1.6 shows total energy supply and disposition, including energy consumption, in the United States in 2006 with projections to 2010, 2020, and 2030. There are two projections for each year: the projection from the *Annual Energy Outlook 2007* (February 2006, http://tonto.eia.doe.gov/ftproot/forecasting/0383(2007).pdf) and the *Annual Energy Outlook 2008*. In 2006 the total energy consumption for the United States was 99.5 quadrillion Btu. By 2030 consumption is projected to increase to between 118 and 131.2 quadrillion Btu. This projection may be greatly affected by factors such as economic growth and world oil prices.

FIGURE 1.14

Industrial sector energy consumption by major source, 1949–2007

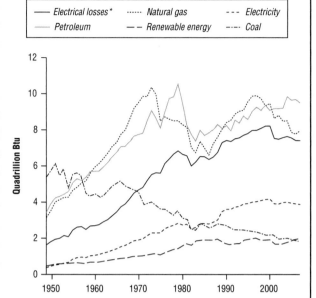

*Electrical system energy losses associated with the generation, transmission, and distribution of energy in the form of electricity.

SOURCE: Adapted from "Figure 2.1b. Energy Consumption by End-Use Sector, 1949–2007: Industrial, by Major Source," in *Annual Energy Review 2007*, U.S. Department of Energy, Energy Information Administration, Office of Energy Markets and End Use, June 2008, http://www.eia.doe.gov/aer/pdf/aer.pdf (accessed June 28, 2008)

FIGURE 1.15

Transportation sector energy consumption by major source, 1949–2007

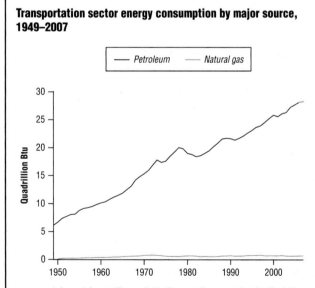

SOURCE: Adapted from "Figure 2.1b. Energy Consumption by End-Use Sector, 1949–2007: Transportation, by Major Source," in *Annual Energy Review 2007*, U.S. Department of Energy, Energy Information Administration, Office of Energy Markets and End Use, June 2008, http://www.eia.doe.gov/aer/pdf/aer.pdf (accessed June 28, 2008)

FIGURE 1.16

Electric power sector energy consumption, 1949–2007

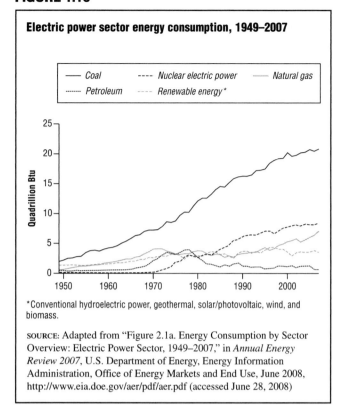

*Conventional hydroelectric power, geothermal, solar/photovoltaic, wind, and biomass.

SOURCE: Adapted from "Figure 2.1a. Energy Consumption by Sector Overview: Electric Power Sector, 1949–2007," in *Annual Energy Review 2007*, U.S. Department of Energy, Energy Information Administration, Office of Energy Markets and End Use, June 2008, http://www.eia.doe.gov/aer/pdf/aer.pdf (accessed June 28, 2008)

The consumption of liquid fuels (from petroleum-based sources and nonpetroleum-based sources, such as biomass, coal, and natural gas), coal, and nonhydroelectric renewables (such as solar and wind) is expected to rise significantly from 2006 to 2030. (See Figure 1.18.) Natural gas consumption is expected to increase until 2016 and then decline until 2030. Conversely, nuclear power use will remain steady from 2006 to 2016, and is then projected to increase slightly until 2030. Consumption of hydroelectric power is expected to remain steady.

The rising consumption of petroleum by Americans is projected to lead to increasing petroleum imports by the United States through 2030. (See Figure 1.19.) Gross oil imports are projected to increase from 13.7 million barrels per day in 2005 to 17.7 million barrels per day in 2030. The EIA projects that gross petroleum imports will account for 66% of the total U.S. petroleum supply in 2030.

After an initial jump, electricity prices in the United States are projected to decline slightly through 2015 because of falling natural gas prices, but will then increase slowly as natural gas prices go up. (See Figure 1.20.) From 2006 to 2030 coal prices will remain relatively stable, but petroleum prices will mirror quite closely the rise, then fall, then slow rise of natural gas prices.

TABLE 1.4

World primary energy production by source, selected years 1970–2005

[Quadrillion Btu]

Year	Coal	Natural gas[a]	Crude oil[b]	Nuclear gas plant liquids	Nuclear electric power[c]	Hydroelectric power[c]	Geothermal[c] and other[d]	Total
1970	62.96	37.09	97.09	3.61	0.90	12.15	1.59	215.39
1971	61.72	39.80	102.70	3.85	1.23	12.74	1.61	223.64
1972	63.65	42.08	108.52	4.09	1.66	13.31	1.68	234.99
1974	63.79	45.35	117.82	4.22	2.86	14.84	1.76	250.64
1976	67.32	47.62	122.92	4.24	4.52	15.08	1.97	263.67
1978	69.56	50.26	128.51	4.55	6.42	16.80	2.32	278.41
1980	R71.31	54.73	128.04	5.10	7.58	17.90	2.94	R287.59
1982	R74.37	55.49	114.45	5.35	9.51	18.71	R3.29	R281.18
1984	R78.48	61.78	116.88	5.73	12.99	20.19	R3.73	R299.79
1986	R84.36	65.32	120.18	6.15	16.25	20.89	R3.83	R316.98
1988	R88.02	71.80	125.84	6.65	19.23	21.48	R4.02	R337.04
1990	R91.02	R75.90	129.35	6.87	20.36	22.35	R3.98	R349.83
1992	R86.21	R76.92	128.93	R7.17	21.28	22.71	R4.35	R347.58
1994	R86.46	R79.19	R130.69	R8.10	22.41	24.15	R4.57	R355.58
1996	R89.14	R84.01	R136.73	R8.59	24.11	25.79	R4.87	R373.24
1998	R91.46	R85.97	R143.24	R9.02	24.32	R26.05	R4.98	R385.03
2000	R90.41	R91.32	R146.83	R9.63	25.66	R26.99	R5.43	R396.26
2001	R95.90	R93.66	R145.57	R10.10	26.39	R26.36	R5.21	R403.19
2002	R97.81	R96.67	R143.54	R10.28	26.68	R26.42	R5.54	R406.94
2003	R105.49	R98.87	R148.44	R10.74	26.45	R26.79	R5.92	R422.69
2004	R114.39	R102.03	R155.42	R11.10	R27.43	R27.65	R6.43	R444.45
2005[p]	122.25	105.33	157.80	11.47	27.47	29.00	6.81	460.14

[a]Dry production.
[b]Includes lease condensate.
[c]Net generation, i.e., gross generation less plant use.
[d]Includes net electricity generation from wood, waste, solar, and wind. Data for the United States also include other renewable energy.
R = Revised.
P = Preliminary.
Notes: Data in this table do not include recent updates for the United States. Totals may not equal sum of components due to independent rounding.

SOURCE: Adapted from "Table 11.1. World Primary Energy Production by Source, 1970–2005 (Quadrillion Btu)," in *Annual Energy Review 2007*, U.S. Department of Energy, Energy Information Administration, Office of Energy Markets and End Use, June 2008, http://www.eia.doe.gov/aer/pdf/aer.pdf (accessed June 28, 2008)

FIGURE 1.17

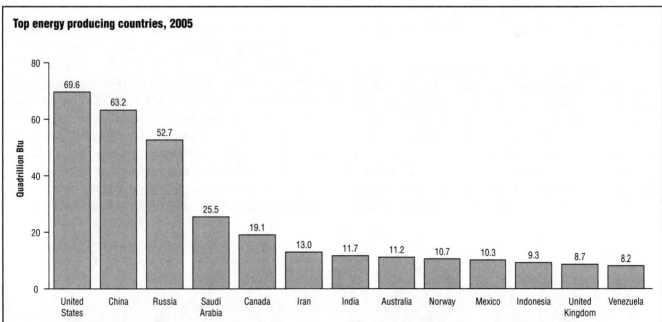

Top energy producing countries, 2005

SOURCE: Adapted from "Figure 11.2. World Primary Energy Production by Region and Country: Top Producing Countries, 2005," in *Annual Energy Review 2007*, U.S. Department of Energy, Energy Information Administration, Office of Energy Markets and End Use, June 2008, http://www.eia.doe .gov/aer/pdf/aer.pdf (accessed June 28, 2008)

TABLE 1.5

World primary energy consumption by region, selected years 1980–2005

[Quadrillion (10^{15}) Btu]

Region/country	1980	1985	1990	1995	2000	2001	2003	2005
United States	78.121	76.491	84.652	91.173	98.975	96.326	98.210	100.691
North America	**91.554**	**91.072**	**100.711**	**108.813**	**118.246**	**115.568**	**118.444**	**121.895**
Europe	**71.883**	**73.170**	**76.385**	**76.709**	**81.419**	**82.683**	**84.226**	**86.294**
Germany	—	—	—	14.326	14.261	14.620	14.599	14.506
Russia	—	—	—	28.299	27.709	27.965	29.051	30.293
Eurasia	**46.735**	**55.689**	**60.976**	**42.581**	**40.789**	**41.201**	**43.604**	**45.817**
Middle East	**5.837**	**8.557**	**11.218**	**13.807**	**17.322**	**17.948**	**19.763**	**22.854**
Africa	**6.795**	**8.508**	**9.466**	**10.649**	**12.023**	**12.592**	**13.308**	**14.433**
China	17.503	22.006	26.999	34.850	37.488	39.378	50.720	67.093
Japan	15.210	15.698	18.488	20.643	22.278	22.096	22.043	22.572
Asia & Oceania	**49.143**	**59.164**	**74.156**	**94.904**	**107.476**	**111.120**	**125.645**	**148.097**
World Total	**283.481**	**308.494**	**347.424**	**365.046**	**398.134**	**402.292**	**426.639**	**462.798**

SOURCE: Adapted from "Table E.1. World Primary Energy Consumption (Quadrillion Btu), 1980–2005," in *International Energy Annual 2005*, U.S. Department of Energy, Energy Information Administration, September 21, 2007, http://www.eia.doe.gov/iea/wecbtu.html (accessed July 7, 2008)

HOW MUCH OIL, NATURAL GAS, AND COAL REMAINS?

As mentioned previously, Figure 1.16 shows that renewable energy sources generate very little of the nation's electricity. Most of the energy sources Americans use are nonrenewable—that is, resources that are consumed faster than they can be generated. By contrast, renewable resources are generated as fast as, or faster than, they are consumed. Examples of renewable resources are solar energy and wind energy; these natural resources are not depleted as they are used. Examples of nonrenewable resources are oil, natural gas, and coal; these natural resources are depleted as they are used. Over hundreds of years of use by billions of human users, the reserves of nonrenewable resources continue to shrink. So how much of these nonrenewable resources remain?

Reserves are estimated volumes of nonrenewable resources in known deposits that are believed to be recoverable in the future. Proved reserves are those volumes that geological and engineering data show with reasonable certainty to be recoverable. According to the EIA, in *Annual Energy Review 2007*, there were 21 billion barrels of proved reserves of crude oil in the United States in 2006. This amount was down from 31.8 billion barrels in 1977. The EIA also reports that on January 1, 2007,

there were between 1.1 trillion barrels and 1.3 trillion barrels of crude oil reserves worldwide.

The volume of natural gas proved reserves can be expressed in crude oil equivalents (COE), which makes comparisons easier. The EIA reports that there were 37.4 billion barrels COE of dry natural gas and 5.8 billion barrels COE of natural gas liquids in proved reserves in 2006, down from 36.5 billion barrels COE in 1977 and up from 5 billion barrels COE in 1978, respectively (see Chapter 3 for a description of these two types of natural gas). Worldwide, there were between 6.2 quadrillion and 6.4 quadrillion cubic feet (175.6 trillion and 181.2 trillion cubic m) of natural gas on January 1, 2007.

The World Energy Council (http://www.worldenergy.org/) has compiled data on the proved reserves of coal throughout the world at the end of 2007. Using these data, Energy.eu (2008, http://www.energy.eu/stats/energy-coal-proved-reserves-total.html) reports that the United States had the largest proved reserves of coal at the end of 2007: 242.7 billion metric tons (267.6 billion short tons). The Russian Federation had approximately two-thirds of the coal reserves of the United States and China about half as much. The total proved coal reserves worldwide at the end of 2007 was 823.6 billion metric tons (907.9 billion short tons).

TABLE 1.6

Summary of projected total energy supply and disposition, selected years 2006–30

Energy and economic factors	2006	2010 AEO2008	2010 AEO2007	2020 AEO2008	2020 AEO2007	2030 AEO2008	2030 AEO2007
Primary energy production (quadrillion Btu)							
Petroleum	13.16	15.03	14.42	15.71	14.85	14.15	13.71
Dry natural gas	19.04	19.85	19.93	20.24	21.41	20.00	21.15
Coal	23.79	23.97	24.47	25.2	26.61	28.63	33.52
Nuclear electricity	8.21	8.31	8.23	9.05	9.23	9.57	9.33
Hydroelectricity	2.89	2.92	3.02	3.00	3.08	3.00	3.09
Biomass	2.94	4.05	4.22	6.42	4.69	8.12	5.26
Other renewable energy	0.88	1.51	1.18	2.00	1.33	2.45	1.44
Other	0.50	0.54	0.67	0.58	0.89	0.64	1.12
Total	**71.41**	**76.17**	**76.13**	**82.21**	**82.09**	**86.56**	**88.63**
Net imports (quadrillion Btu)							
Petroleum	26.69	23.93	25.19	24.03	28.92	26.52	34.74
Natural gas	3.56	3.96	4.67	3.66	5.48	3.28	5.59
Coal/other (−indicates export)	−0.28	−0.84	−0.19	1.06	0.93	1.86	1.57
Total	**29.98**	**27.04**	**29.66**	**28.75**	**35.33**	**31.66**	**41.90**
Consumption (quadrillion Btu)							
Liquid fuels	40.06	40.46	41.76	42.24	46.52	43.99	52.17
Natural gas	22.30	23.93	24.73	24.01	27.04	23.39	26.89
Coal	22.50	23.03	24.24	25.87	27.29	29.90	34.14
Nuclear electricity	8.21	8.31	8.23	9.05	9.23	9.57	9.33
Hydroelectricity	2.89	2.92	3.02	3.00	3.08	3.00	3.09
Biomass	2.50	3.01	3.30	4.50	3.64	5.51	4.06
Other renewable energy	0.88	1.51	1.18	2.00	1.33	2.45	1.44
Net electricity imports	0.19	0.18	0.04	0.17	0.04	0.20	0.04
Total	**99.50**	**103.30**	**106.50**	**110.80**	**118.16**	**118.00**	**131.16**
Liquid fuels (million barrels per day)							
Domestic crude oil production	5.10	5.93	5.67	6.23	5.89	5.59	5.39
Other domestic production	3.19	3.69	4.03	4.46	4.49	4.85	5.08
Net imports	12.45	11.39	11.79	11.36	13.56	12.41	16.37
Consumption	20.65	20.99	21.59	21.96	24.03	22.80	26.95
Natural gas (trillion cubic feet)							
Production	18.57	19.35	19.42	19.73	20.86	19.49	20.61
Net imports	3.46	3.85	4.55	3.55	5.35	3.18	5.45
Consumption	21.66	23.25	24.02	23.33	26.26	22.72	26.12
Coal (million short tons)							
Production	1,177	1,179	1,202	1,281	1,336	1,467	1,704
Net imports	−15	−34	−7	46	41	78	68
Consumption	1,114	1,145	1,195	1,327	1,377	1,545	1,772
Prices (2006 dollars)							
Imported low-sulfur, light crude oil (dollars per barrel)	66.02	74.03	59.23	59.70	53.64	70.45	60.93
Imported crude oil (dollars per barrel)	59.05	65.18	52.76	51.55	47.89	58.66	53.21
Domestic natural gas at wellhead (dollars per thousand cubic feet)	6.42	6.33	5.93	5.44	5.39	6.63	6.16
Domestic coal at mine mouth (dollars per short ton)	24.63	26.16	24.94	22.51	22.24	23.32	23.29
Average electricity price (cents per kilowatthour)	8.9	9.2	8.3	8.6	8.1	8.8	8.3
Economic indicators							
Real gross domestic product (billion 2000 dollars)	11,319	12,453	12,790	15,984	17,077	20,219	22,494
GDP chain-type price index (index, 2000=1.000)	1.166	1.26	1.253	1.52	1.495	1.871	1.815
Real disposable personal income (billion 2000 dollars) . . .	8,397	9,472	9,568	12,654	13,000	16,246	17,535
Value of manufacturing shipments (billion 2000 dollars) . .	5,821	5,997	6,298	7,113	7,779	7,997	9,502
Primary energy intensity (thousand Btu per 2000 dollar of GDP)	**8.79**	**8.30**	**8.33**	**6.93**	**6.92**	**5.84**	**5.83**
Carbon dioxide emissions (million metric tons)	**5,890**	**6,011**	**6,214**	**6,384**	**6,944**	**6,851**	**7,950**

TABLE 1.6

Summary of projected total energy supply and disposition, selected years 2006–30 [CONTINUED]

Notes: Quantities are derived from historical volumes and assumed thermal conversion factors. Other production includes liquid hydrogen, methanol, and some inputs to refineries. Net imports of petroleum include crude oil, petroleum products, unfinished oils, alcohols, ethers, and blending components. Other net imports include coal coke and electricity. For nuclear electricity, both production and consumption numbers are based on its fossil-fuel-equivalent energy content.

SOURCE: "Table 1. Total Energy Supply and Disposition in the *AEO2008* and *AEO2007* Reference Cases, 2006–2030," in *Annual Energy Outlook 2008*, U.S. Department of Energy, Energy Information Administration, Office of Integrated Analysis and Forecasting, June 2008, http://www.eia.doe.gov/oiaf/aeo/pdf/0383 (2008).pdf (accessed July 2, 2008)

FIGURE 1.18

Energy consumption by fuel, 1980–2030

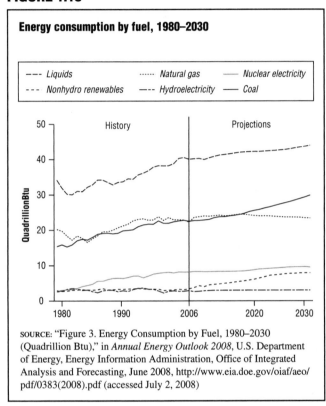

SOURCE: "Figure 3. Energy Consumption by Fuel, 1980–2030 (Quadrillion Btu)," in *Annual Energy Outlook 2008*, U.S. Department of Energy, Energy Information Administration, Office of Integrated Analysis and Forecasting, June 2008, http://www.eia.doe.gov/oiaf/aeo/pdf/0383(2008).pdf (accessed July 2, 2008)

FIGURE 1.19

Gross petroleum imports by source, 2005–30

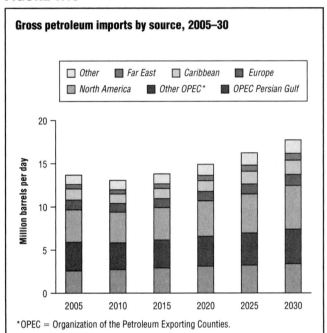

*OPEC = Organization of the Petroleum Exporting Counties.

SOURCE: "Figure 30. U.S. Gross Petroleum Imports by Source, 2005–2030 (Million Barrels per Day)," in *Annual Energy Outlook 2007*, U.S. Department of Energy, Energy Information Administration, Office of Integrated Analysis and Forecasting, February 2007, http://tonto.eia .doe.gov/ftproot/forecasting/0383(2007).pdf (accessed July 2, 2008)

FIGURE 1.20

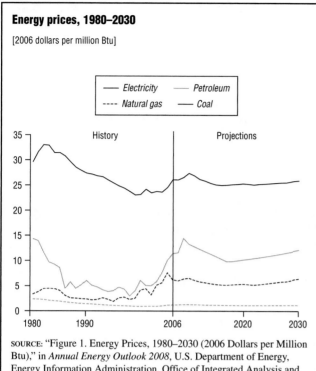

Energy prices, 1980–2030

[2006 dollars per million Btu]

SOURCE: "Figure 1. Energy Prices, 1980–2030 (2006 Dollars per Million Btu)," in *Annual Energy Outlook 2008*, U.S. Department of Energy, Energy Information Administration, Office of Integrated Analysis and Forecasting, June 2008, http://www.eia.doe.gov/oiaf/aeo/pdf/0383 (2008).pdf (accessed July 2, 2008)

CHAPTER 2
OIL

THE QUEST FOR OIL

On August 27, 1859, Edwin Drake (1819–1880) struck oil 69 feet (21 m) below the surface of the earth near Titusville, Pennsylvania. This was the first successful modern oil well, which ushered in the age of petroleum. Not only did petroleum help meet the growing demand for new and better fuels for heating and lighting but also it proved to be an excellent fuel for the internal combustion engine, which was developed in the late 1800s.

Sources of Oil

Almost all oil comes from underground reservoirs. The most widely accepted explanation of how oil and gas are formed within the earth is that these fuels are the products of intense heat and pressure applied over millions of years to organic (formerly alive) sediments buried in geological formations. For this reason they are called fossil fuels. They are limited (nonrenewable) resources, which means that they are formed much more slowly than they are used, so they are finite in supply.

At one time it was believed that crude oil flowed in underground streams and accumulated in lakes or caverns in the earth. In the twenty-first century, scientists know that a petroleum reservoir is usually a solid sandstone or limestone formation overlaid with a layer of impermeable rock or shale, which creates a shield. The petroleum accumulates within the pores and fractures of the rock and is trapped beneath the shield. Anticlines (archlike folds in a bed of rock), faults, and salt domes are common trapping formations. (See Figure 2.1.) Oil deposits can be found at varying depths. Wells are drilled to reach the reservoirs and extract the oil.

How Oil Is Drilled and Recovered

Most oil wells are drilled with a rotary drilling system, or rotary rig, as illustrated in Figure 2.2. The rotating bit at the end of a pipe drills a hole into the ground.

Drilling mud is pushed down through the pipe and the drill bit, forcing small pieces of drilled rock to the surface, as shown by the arrows in the diagram. As the well gets deeper, more pipe is added. The oil derrick above the ground supports equipment that can lift the pipe and drill bit from the well when drill bits need to be changed or replaced.

After oil reservoirs have been tapped for several years or decades, their supply of oil becomes depleted. Several techniques can be used to recover additional petroleum, including the injection of water, chemicals, or steam to force more oil from the rock. These recovery techniques can be expensive and add to the cost of producing each barrel of crude oil.

Oil can also be recovered from oil sands, which are deposits of a thick, tarlike form of crude oil called bitumen that is mixed with sand and water and buried in the earth. Oil sands that are near the surface of the earth are recovered by open-pit mining, a process in which huge shovels and trucks dig it up after removing the soil, clay, and gravel that lie on top. Oil sands that are deep within the earth are recovered by drilling to the deposit and then injecting steam to bring bitumen to the surface. Other processes are sometimes used as well. It takes about 2 short tons (1.8 t) of oil sands to produce one barrel of oil and is an extremely expensive and specialized process. (A short ton is 2,000 pounds [907 k].) As oil prices escalated in the middle of the first decade of the 2000s and new oil sands technologies became available, extracting this crude product from oil sands and processing it became profitable.

In "Alberta Oil Sands" (August 25, 2008, http://www.ags.gov.ab.ca/energy/oilsands/alberta_oil_sands.html), the Alberta Geological Survey states that even though oil sands are found in about seventy countries worldwide, the largest deposit is the Athabasca oil sands of Alberta, Canada. According to the article "Oil Sands Facts" (June 20, 2007, http://www.energy.gov.ab.ca/OilSands/790.asp), oil derived

FIGURE 2.1

Petroleum traps

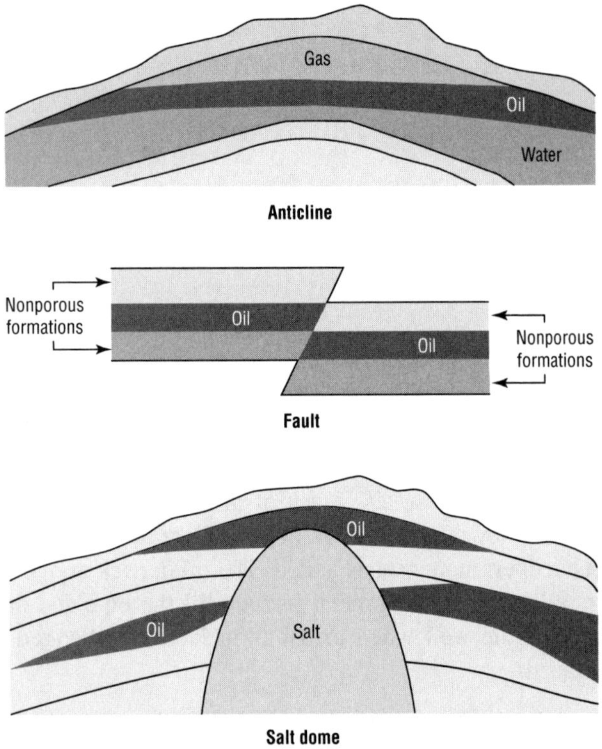

Anticline

Gas

Oil

Water

Anticline

Nonporous formations

Oil

Oil

Nonporous formations

Fault

Oil

Oil

Salt

Salt dome

FIGURE 2.2

A rotary drilling system

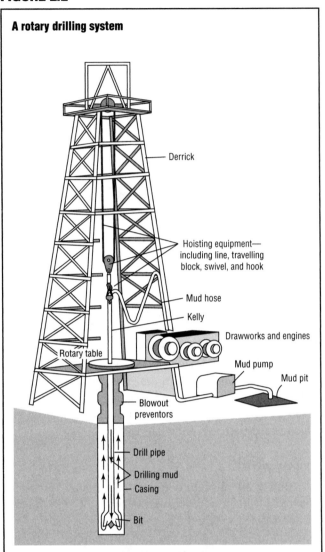

Derrick

Hoisting equipment— including line, travelling block, swivel, and hook

Mud hose

Kelly

Drawworks and engines

Rotary table

Mud pump

Mud pit

Blowout preventors

Drill pipe

Drilling mud

Casing

Bit

from oil sands made up 42% of Canada's crude output in 2006. Large quantities of oil sands are also found in Venezuela. Eastern Utah is the primary location of the tar sands in the United Sates, but these reserves are small in comparison to the reserves of Canada and Venezuela. The Oil Shale and Tar Sands Programmatic Environmental Impact Statement Information Center estimates in "About Tar Sands" (2008, http://ostseis.anl.gov/guide/ tarsands/index.cfm) that the oil sands reserves of Utah hold approximately 12 billion barrels to 19 billion barrels of oil.

TYPES OF OIL

While crude oil is usually dark when it comes from the ground, it may also be green, red, yellow, or colorless, depending on its chemical composition and the amount of sulfur, oxygen, nitrogen, and trace minerals present. Its viscosity (thickness, or resistance to flow) can range from as thin as water to as thick as tar. Crude oil is refined, or chemically processed, into finished petroleum products; it has limited uses in its natural form.

Crude oils vary in quality. "Sweet" crudes have little sulfur, refine easily, and are worth more than "sour" crudes, which contain more impurities. "Light" crudes, which have more short molecules, yield more gasoline and are more profitable than "heavy" crudes, which have more long molecules and bring a lower price in the market.

Besides crude oil, there are two other sources of petroleum: lease condensate and natural gas plant liquids. Lease condensate is a liquid recovered from natural gas at the well. It consists primarily of chemical compounds called pentanes and heavier hydrocarbons and is generally blended with crude oil for refining. Natural gas plant liquids, such as butane and propane, are recovered during the refinement of natural gas in processing plants.

USES FOR OIL

Many of the uses for petroleum are well known: gasoline, diesel fuel, jet fuel, and lubricants for transportation; heating oil, residual oil, and kerosene for heat; and heavy residuals for paving and roofing. Petroleum by-products are also vital to the chemical industry, ending up in many different foams, plastics, synthetic fabrics, paints, dyes, inks, and even pharmaceutical drugs. Many chemical plants, because of their dependence on petroleum, are directly connected by pipelines to nearby refineries.

HOW OIL IS REFINED

Before they can be used by consumers, crude oil, lease condensate, and natural gas plant liquids must be processed into finished products. The first step in refining is distillation, in which crude oil molecules are separated according to size and weight.

During distillation, crude oil is heated until it turns to vapor. (See Figure 2.3.) The vaporized crude oil enters the bottom of a distillation column, where it rises and condenses on trays. The lightest vapors, such as those of gasoline, rise to the top. The middleweight vapors, such as those of kerosene, rise about halfway up the column. The heaviest vapors, such as those of heavy gas oil, stay at the bottom. The vapors at each level condense into liquids as they are cooled. These liquids are drawn off, and processes called cracking and reforming further refine each portion. Cracking converts the heaviest fractions of separated petroleum into lighter fractions to produce jet fuel, motor gasoline, home heating oil, and less-residual fuel oils, which are heavier and used for naval ships, commercial and industrial heating, and some power generation. Reforming is used to increase the octane rating of gasoline.

Refining is a continuous process, with crude oil entering the refinery at the same time that finished products leave by pipeline, truck, and train. At most refineries storage capacity is limited, so if there is a malfunction and products cannot be refined, the oil may be burned off (flared) rather than stored. Whereas a small flare is normal at a refinery or a chemical plant, large flares or many flares likely indicate a processing problem.

REFINERY NUMBERS AND CAPACITY

One hundred forty-nine refineries were operating in the United States in 2007, a drop from 336 in 1949 and 324 in 1981. (See Table 2.1.) Refinery capacity in 2007 was about 17.4 million barrels per day (mbpd), below the 1981 peak of 18.6 mbpd. As of 2007 U.S. refineries were operating near full capacity. Utilization rates generally increased from a low of 68.6% in 1981 (a period of low demand because of economic recession) to a high of 95.6% in 1998. Even though capacity has fallen since 1998, in 2007 it was still high at 88.5%.

As Table 2.1 shows, fewer refineries were operating in the United States in the early twenty-first century than in the past. The number dropped partly because the petroleum industry shut down older, inefficient refineries and concentrated production in more efficient plants, which tended to be newer and larger. The industry also consolidated. For example, the merging of Gulf Oil Corporation into Chevron Corporation in 1984 led to the closing of two large refineries. Many other large mergers and closings followed. According to the U.S. Government Accountability Office (GAO), in *Energy Markets: Effects of Mergers and Market Concentration in the U.S. Petroleum Industry* (May 2004; http://www.gao.gov/highlights/d0496high.pdf), more than twenty-six hundred mergers have occurred in the U.S. petroleum industry since the 1990s, "most frequently among firms involved in exploration and production." Industry officials told the GAO that mergers increase efficiency, reduce costs, and improve a company's ability to control prices.

An equally important reason for the drop in the number of U.S. refineries is that some members of the Organization of Petroleum Exporting Countries (OPEC) started refining their own oil products to obtain higher prices in the world market. This strategy, employed particularly by Saudi Arabia, was intended to maximize profits.

The last large refinery built in the United States was completed in 1976, and the last new refinery of any size began operation in Valdez, Alaska, in 1993. However, the demand for U.S.-refined petroleum continues to grow. The Energy Information Administration (EIA) states in *Annual Energy Outlook 2006* (February 2006, http://www.eia.doe.gov/oiaf/archive/aeo06/pdf/0383(2006).pdf) that refinery expansion is expected from 2010 to 2030. A startup company has announced plans to open a major new refinery in Arizona in 2010.

LOSS AND VOLATILITY OF OIL INDUSTRY JOBS

The oil industry has experienced both rapid expansions and contractions in its history as it responds to changes in demand, the development of new technologies, and other economic imperatives. For example, corporate mergers not only restructure companies and reduce the number of refineries but they also affect the number of jobs. In "Oil and Gas Extraction" (August 27, 2008, http://www.bls.gov/iag/tgs/iag211.htm), the U.S. Bureau of Labor Statistics explains that the oil and gas extraction industry has been in an employment decline since reaching a peak of 264,800 employees in April 1982. By April 1992, when employees numbered 187,600, about 29% of petroleum jobs had been lost. As of June 2008 employment in the oil and gas extraction industry segment was up 35%, to 160,500, from the all-time low of 118,400 experienced in December 2003, but 39% below the 1982 figure.

FIGURE 2.3

Crude oil distillation

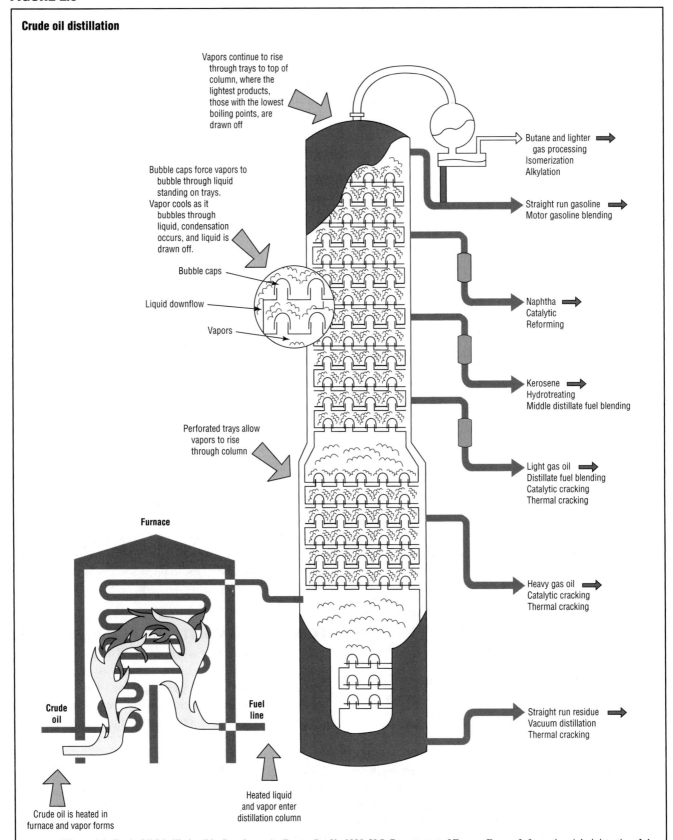

Vapors continue to rise through trays to top of column, where the lightest products, those with the lowest boiling points, are drawn off

Bubble caps force vapors to bubble through liquid standing on trays. Vapor cools as it bubbles through liquid, condensation occurs, and liquid is drawn off.

Bubble caps

Liquid downflow

Vapors

Perforated trays allow vapors to rise through column

Furnace

Crude oil

Fuel line

Crude oil is heated in furnace and vapor forms

Heated liquid and vapor enter distillation column

Butane and lighter gas processing
Isomerization
Alkylation

Straight run gasoline
Motor gasoline blending

Naphtha
Catalytic Reforming

Kerosene
Hydrotreating
Middle distillate fuel blending

Light gas oil
Distillate fuel blending
Catalytic cracking
Thermal cracking

Heavy gas oil
Catalytic cracking
Thermal cracking

Straight run residue
Vacuum distillation
Thermal cracking

SOURCE: "Figure 5.1. Crude Oil Distillation," in *Petroleum: An Energy Profile 1999*, U.S. Department of Energy, Energy Information Administration, July 1999, http://www.eia.doe.gov/pub/oil_gas/petroleum/analysis_publications/petroleum_profile_1999/profile99v8.pdf (accessed July 2, 2008)

TABLE 2.1

Refinery capacity and utilization, selected years 1949–2007

Year	Operable refineries[a] Number	Operable refineries capacity — On January 1 Thousand barrels per day	Operable refineries capacity — Annual average[b] Thousand barrels per day	Gross input to distillation units Thousand barrels per day	Utilization[c] Percent
1949	336	6,231	NA	5,556	89.2
1950	320	6,223	NA	5,980	92.5
1955	296	8,386	NA	7,820	92.2
1960	309	9,843	NA	8,439	85.1
1965	293	10,420	NA	9,557	91.8
1970	276	12,021	NA	11,517	92.6
1971	272	12,860	NA	11,881	90.9
1972	274	13,292	NA	12,431	92.3
1974	273	14,362	NA	12,689	86.6
1976	276	15,237	NA	13,884	87.8
1978	296	17,048	NA	15,071	87.4
1980	319	17,988	NA	13,796	75.4
1981	324	18,621	18,603	12,752	68.6
1982	301	17,890	17,432	12,172	69.9
1984	247	16,137	16,035	12,216	76.2
1986	216	15,459	15,459	12,826	82.9
1988	213	15,915	15,927	13,447	84.7
1990	205	15,572	15,623	13,610	87.1
1992	199	15,696	15,460	13,600	87.9
1994	179	15,034	15,150	14,032	92.6
1996	170	15,333	15,239	14,337	94.1
1998	163	15,711	15,802	15,113	95.6
2000	158	16,512	16,525	15,299	92.6
2002	153	16,785	16,744	15,180	90.7
2003	149	16,757	16,748	15,508	92.6
2004	149	16,894	16,974	15,783	93.0
2005	148	17,125	17,196	15,578	90.6
2006	149	17,339	R17,385	R15,602	89.7
2007P	149	17,443	17,447	15,449	88.5

[a]Through 1956, includes only those refineries in operation on January 1; beginning in 1957, includes all "operable" refineries on January 1.
[b]Weighted average of monthly capacity data.
[c]Through 1980, utilization is calculated by dividing gross input to distillation units by one-half of the sum of the current year's January 1 capacity and the following year's January1 capacity. Beginning in 1981, utilization is calculated by dividing gross input to distillation units by the annual average capacity.
R = Revised.
P = Preliminary.
NA = Not available.

SOURCE: Adapted from "Table 5.9. Refinery Capacity and Utilization, Selected Years, 1949–2007," in *Annual Energy Review 2007*, U.S. Department of Energy, Energy Information Administration, Office of Energy Markets and End Use, June 2008, http://www.eia.doe.gov/aer/pdf/aer.pdf (accessed June 28, 2008)

Oil prices have created some of the volatility experienced in oil employment. In 1996, after a decade of low oil prices (except for one short-term spike in 1991; see Figure 1.2 in Chapter 1), drilling slowed and the demand for rigs collapsed. New rig construction stopped altogether. Thousands of rigs were left idle, sold for scrap metal, or shipped overseas, and their crews were put out of work. Idle rigs became a source of spare parts for those still operating. In 1997, following a rise in oil prices, the demand for rigs soared, but by 1998 the market for rigs had once again dwindled as oil prices sank. Rising oil prices in 1999 eventually boosted the demand for drilling equipment. Even though crude oil prices declined in 2001, they rose again in 2003 and continued to rise, again spurring demand

for oil rigs. In "Baker Hughes Rigs Running by Week in the U.S. 1990–2008" (2008, http://files.shareholder.com/downloads/BHI/354184748x0x210176/A4F015D6-B26E-49F3-88EC-7CF675D9DA62/US_Rig_Report_070208.xls), Baker Hughes Inc., a company that has tallied weekly U.S. drilling activity since 1940, states that domestic oil drilling has rebounded sharply since late April 1999. In 1999 an average of 629 rigs ran weekly, compared to 1,768 in 2007.

DOMESTIC PRODUCTION

U.S. production of petroleum (including crude oil and natural gas plant liquids) reached its highest level in 1970 at 11.3 mbpd. (See Table 2.2.) Of that amount, 9.6 mbpd were crude oil. After 1970 domestic production of petroleum first declined, then rose from 1977 through 1985, and finally declined fairly steadily. (See Figure 2.4.) By 2007 U.S. domestic production averaged about 6.9 mbpd, a decrease of 39% from the 1970 production level. Of the 6.9 mbpd, 5.1 mbpd were crude oil.

The decline in the U.S. production of petroleum is due to a decline in both the number of producing wells and the number of barrels produced per day per well. In *Annual Energy Review 2007* (June 2008, http://www.eia.doe.gov/aer/pdf/aer.pdf), the EIA indicates that the 500,000 producing wells in the United States in 2007 yielded 10.2 barrels per day per well, compared to the 531,000 producing wells in 1970, each yielding 18.1 barrels per day.

Figure 2.5 shows the overall flow of petroleum in the United States for 2007. Most of the domestic crude oil production shown (5.1 mbpd) occurs in only a few states. According to the EIA, in "Crude Oil Production" (January 2008, http://www.eia.doe.gov/neic/infosheets/crudeproduction.html), in 2006 these states were Texas (21%), Alaska (15%), California (12%), Louisiana (4%), Oklahoma (3%), and New Mexico (3%). Most domestic oil (3.4 mbpd, or about 66% in 2007) came from onshore drilling, whereas the remaining 1.7 mbpd came from offshore sources. (See Figure 2.6.)

Supplies from Alaska, which increased with the construction of a pipeline in the late 1970s, have begun to decline. Notice the gap between "Total" and "48 states" in Figure 2.7; the difference is Alaska's share of U.S. oil production. The EIA explains in "Alaska" (August 21, 2008, http://tonto.eia.doe.gov/state/state_energy_profiles.cfm?sid=AK) that Alaska oil production peaked in 1988 at 2 mbpd and has since been in decline. Unless protected wildlife refuges in Alaska are opened for drilling, U.S. oil production there will likely continue to decline. The Alaskan government and the administration of President George W. Bush (1946–) strongly support drilling for oil in Alaska's Arctic National Wildlife Refuge (ANWR). In June 2008 President Bush once again asked Congress to consider legislation that would allow drilling in the ANWR as one measure to increase domestic oil production. However, this

TABLE 2.2

Petroleum production, selected years 1949–2007

[Thousand barrels per day]

Year	Field production[a] Crude oil[b] 48 states[c]	Field production[a] Crude oil[b] Alaska	Field production[a] Crude oil[b] Total	Field production[a] Natural gas plant liquids	Field production[a] Total	Processing gain[d]	Trade Imports[e]	Trade Exports	Trade Net imports[f]	Stock change[g]	Adjustments[h]	Petroleum products supplied
1949	5,046	0	5,046	430	5,477	−2	645	327	318	−8	−38	5,763
1950	5,407	0	5,407	499	5,906	2	850	305	545	−56	−51	6,458
1955	6,807	0	6,807	771	7,578	34	1,248	368	880	(s)	−37	8,455
1960	7,034	2	7,035	929	7,965	146	1,815	202	1,613	−83	−8	9,797
1965	7,774	30	7,804	1,210	9,014	220	2,468	187	2,281	−8	−10	11,512
1970	9,408	229	9,637	1,660	11,297	359	3,419	259	3,161	103	−16	14,697
1971	9,245	218	9,463	1,693	11,155	382	3,926	224	3,701	71	45	15,212
1972	9,242	199	9,441	1,744	11,185	388	4,741	222	4,519	−232	43	16,367
1974	8,581	193	8,774	1,688	10,462	480	6,112	221	5,892	179	−2	16,653
1976	7,958	173	8,132	1,604	9,736	477	7,313	223	7,090	−58	101	17,461
1977	7,781	464	8,245	1,618	9,862	524	8,807	243	8,565	548	28	18,431
1978	7,478	1,229	8,707	1,567	10,275	496	8,363	362	8,002	−94	−20	18,847
1980	6,980	1,617	8,597	1,573	10,170	597	6,909	544	6,365	140	64	17,056
1982	6,953	1,696	8,649	1,550	10,199	531	5,113	815	4,298	−147	121	15,296
1984	7,157	1,722	8,879	1,630	10,509	553	5,437	722	4,715	280	228	15,726
1985	7,146	1,825	8,971	1,609	10,581	557	5,067	781	4,286	−103	200	15,726
1986	6,814	1,867	8,680	1,551	10,231	616	6,224	785	5,439	202	197	16,281
1988	6,123	2,017	8,140	1,625	9,765	655	7,402	815	6,587	−28	249	17,283
1990	5,582	1,773	7,355	1,559	8,914	683	8,018	857	7,161	107	338	16,988
1992	5,457	1,714	7,171	1,697	8,868	772	7,888	950	6,938	−68	386	17,033
1994	5,103	1,559	6,662	1,727	8,388	768	8,996	942	8,054	15	523	17,718
1996	5,071	1,393	6,465	1,830	8,295	837	9,478	981	8,498	−151	528	18,309
1998	5,077	1,175	6,252	1,759	8,011	886	10,708	945	9,764	239	495	18,917
2000	4,851	970	5,822	1,911	7,733	948	11,459	1,040	10,419	−69	532	19,701
2002	4,761	984	5,746	1,880	7,626	957	11,530	984	10,546	−105	527	19,761
2003	4,706	974	5,681	1,719	7,400	974	12,264	1,027	11,238	56	478	20,034
2004	4,510	908	5,419	1,809	7,228	1,051	13,145	1,048	12,097	209	564	20,731
2005	4,314	864	5,178	1,717	6,895	989	13,714	1,165	12,549	145	513	20,802
2006	R4,361	741	R5,102	R1,739	R6,841	R994	R13,707	R1,317	R12,390	R60	R522	R20,687
2007[p]	4,384	719	5,103	1,776	6,879	1,005	13,439	1,399	12,040	−162	611	20,698

[a]Crude oil production on leases, and natural gas liquids (liquefied petroleum gases, pentanes plus, and a small amount of finished petroleum products) production at natural gas processing plants. Excludes what was previously classified as "field production" of finished motor gasoline, motor gasoline blending components, and other hydrocarbons and oxygenates; these are now included in "adjustments."
[b]Includes lease condensate.
[c]United States excluding Alaska and Hawaii.
[d]Refinery and blender net production minus refinery and blender net inputs.
[e]Includes crude oil imports for the Strategic Petroleum Reserve, which began in 1977.
[f]Net imports equal imports minus exports.
[g]A negative value indicates a decrease in stocks and a positive value indicates an increase. Includes crude oil stocks in the Strategic Petroleum Reserve, but excludes distillate fuel oil stocks in the Northeast Heating Oil Reserve.
[h]An adjustment for crude oil, finished motor gasoline, motor gasoline blending components, fuel ethanol, and distillate fuel oil.
R = Revised.
P = Preliminary.
(s) = Less than 500 barrels per day.
Notes: Totals may not equal sum of components due to independent rounding.

SOURCE: Adapted from "Table 5.1. Petroleum Overview, Selected Years, 1949–2007 (Thousand Barrels per Day)," in *Annual Energy Review 2007*, U.S. Department of Energy, Energy Information Administration, Office of Energy Markets and End Use, June 2008, http://www.eia.doe.gov/aer/pdf/aer.pdf (accessed June 28, 2008)

proposal is highly controversial for environmental reasons. Legislation to allow the drilling has been stalled in Congress several times.

Not only is domestic oil production affected by the availability of this resource and the legislative and legal approval to drill for it, but also production is affected by the expense of drilling and extraction. For example, U.S. producers spend more money than Middle Eastern producers to drill and extract crude oil, because oil is available in enormous, easily accessible reservoirs in the Middle East. U.S. oil is not as easily recovered. When

the cost of oil recovery severely reduces the profit margin on a barrel of oil, U.S. producers may shut down their most expensive wells, especially in times when oil prices are low. When oil prices are high, even the most expensive extraction methods, such as those used to recover oil from the oil sands of Canada and Venezuela, are still cost effective.

DOMESTIC CONSUMPTION

In 2007 most petroleum was used for transportation (14.3 mbpd, or 69%), followed by industrial use (5.1 mbpd;

FIGURE 2.4

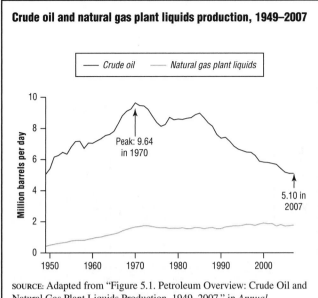

Crude oil and natural gas plant liquids production, 1949–2007

SOURCE: Adapted from "Figure 5.1. Petroleum Overview: Crude Oil and Natural Gas Plant Liquids Production, 1949–2007," in *Annual Energy Review 2007*, U.S. Department of Energy, Energy Information Administration, Office of Energy Markets and End Use, June 2008, http://www.eia.doe.gov/aer/pdf/aer.pdf (accessed June 28, 2008)

25%), residential use (0.8 mbpd; 4%), electric utilities (0.3 mbpd; 1%), and commercial use (0.3 mbpd; 1%). (See Figure 2.8.)

Most petroleum used in the transportation sector is for motor gasoline. In the residential and commercial sectors, distillate fuel oil (light fuel oils; refined fuels used for space heaters, diesel engines, and electric power generation) accounts for most petroleum use. Liquid petroleum gas is the primary oil used in the industrial sector. In electric utilities residual fuel oils (heavy fuel oils) are used the most.

In *Annual Energy Review 2007*, the EIA shows that from 1979 through 1982 there was a decline in the amount of motor gasoline used in the transportation sector, which was attributed to the federal Corporate Average Fuel Economy (CAFE) regulations. The CAFE regulations required increased miles-per-gallon efficiency in new automobiles. However, motor gasoline use has increased relatively steadily since then, partly because the number of users has increased and partly because vehicle efficiency has leveled off—consumers once again preferred

FIGURE 2.5

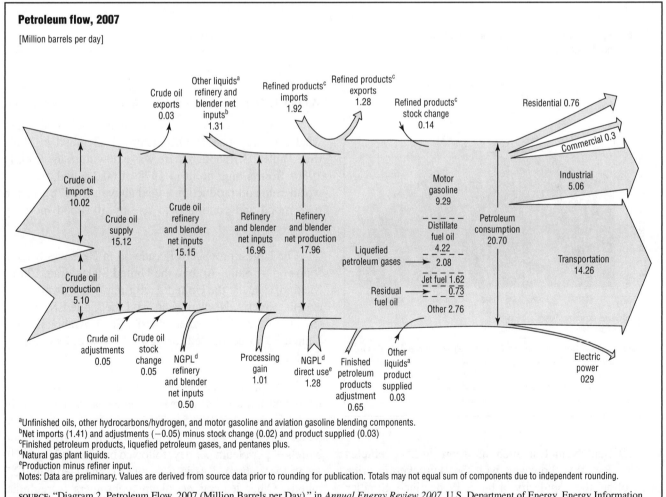

Petroleum flow, 2007

[Million barrels per day]

[a]Unfinished oils, other hydrocarbons/hydrogen, and motor gasoline and aviation gasoline blending components.
[b]Net imports (1.41) and adjustments (−0.05) minus stock change (0.02) and product supplied (0.03)
[c]Finished petroleum products, liquefied petroleum gases, and pentanes plus.
[d]Natural gas plant liquids.
[e]Production minus refiner input.
Notes: Data are preliminary. Values are derived from source data prior to rounding for publication. Totals may not equal sum of components due to independent rounding.

SOURCE: "Diagram 2. Petroleum Flow, 2007 (Million Barrels per Day)," in *Annual Energy Review 2007*, U.S. Department of Energy, Energy Information Administratin, Office of Energy Markets and End Use, June 2008, http://www.eia.doe.gov/aer/pdf/aer.pdf (accessed June 28, 2008)

FIGURE 2.6

Crude oil production and crude oil well productivity, by site, 1954–2007

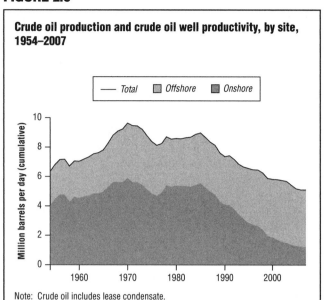

Note: Crude oil includes lease condensate.

SOURCE: Adapted from "Figure 5.2. Crude Oil Production and Crude Oil Well Productivity, 1954–2007: By Site," in *Annual Energy Review 2007*, U.S. Department of Energy, Energy Information Administration, Office of Energy Markets and End Use, June 2008, http://www.eia.doe .gov/aer/pdf/aer.pdf (accessed June 28, 2008)

FIGURE 2.7

Crude oil production and crude oil well productivity, by geographic location, 1954–2007

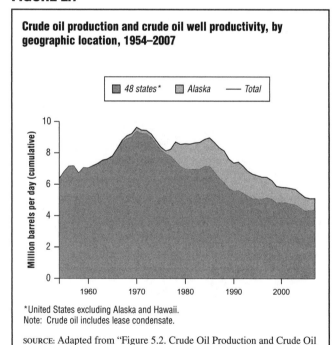

*United States excluding Alaska and Hawaii.
Note: Crude oil includes lease condensate.

SOURCE: Adapted from "Figure 5.2. Crude Oil Production and Crude Oil Well Productivity, 1954–2007: By Geographic Location," in *Annual Energy Review 2007*, U.S. Department of Energy, Energy Information Administration, Office of Energy Markets and End Use, June 2008, http://www.eia.doe.gov/aer/pdf/aer.pdf (accessed June 28, 2008)

less efficient vehicles, such as sport utility vehicles (SUVs). By 2008, however, with the skyrocketing price of gasoline, the popularity of the SUV declined. Smaller "crossover" SUVs and economy models came into favor with much of the American public.

FIGURE 2.8

Estimated petroleum consumption by sector, 2007

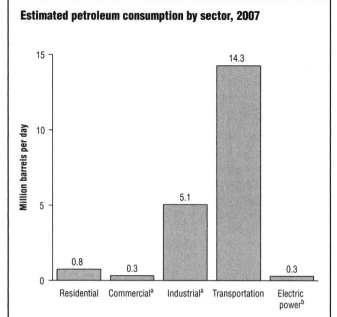

[a]Includes combined-heat-and-power plants and a small number of electricity-only plants.
[b]Electricity-only and combined-heat-and-power plants whose primary business is to sell electricity, or electricity and heat, to the public.

SOURCE: Adapted from "Figure 5.13a. Estimated Petroleum Consumption by Sector: By Sector, 2007," in *Annual Energy Review 2007*, U.S. Department of Energy, Energy Information Administration, Office of Energy Markets and End Use, June 2008, http://www.eia.doe .gov/aer/pdf/aer.pdf (accessed June 28, 2008)

WORLD OIL PRODUCTION AND CONSUMPTION

Total world crude oil production has increased somewhat steadily since 1960, reaching 73.3 mbpd in 2007. (See Table 2.3.) Though there was a downturn in the early 1980s from a high point in 1978 of 60.2 mbpd, by 1996 world crude oil production edged above the 1978 value to 63.8 mbpd and continued to rise by 10 mbpd more by 2007.

The largest producer of crude oil in 2007 was Russia, followed by Saudi Arabia, the United States, Iran, China, Mexico, Canada, the United Arab Emirates, Kuwait, Venezuela, Nigeria, Norway, Iraq, and the United Kingdom. (See Figure 2.9.) Together, Russia, Saudi Arabia, and the United States accounted for 32% of the world's crude oil production.

Like total world crude oil production, total world petroleum consumption has increased somewhat steadily, reaching 84.6 mbpd in 2006. (See Table 2.4.) In 2006 the United States was by far the leading consumer, using 20.7 million barrels of petroleum per day, followed by China (7.2 mbpd), Japan (5.2 mbpd), Russia (2.8 mbpd), and Germany (2.7 mbpd). Other leading petroleum consumers were India, Canada, Brazil, South Korea, Mexico, France, the United Kingdom, Italy, and Spain. (See Figure 2.10.)

TABLE 2.3

World crude oil production, selected years 1960–2007

[Million barrels per day]

Year	Selected OPEC producers									Selected non-OPEC producers									World
	Persian Gulf nations[a]	Iran	Iraq	Kuwait[b]	Nigeria	Saudi Arabia[b]	United Arab Emirates	Venezuela	Total OPEC[c]	Canada	China	Mexico	Norway	Former U.S.S.R.	Russia	United Kingdom	United States	Total non-OPEC[c]	
1960	5.27	1.07	0.97	1.69	0.02	1.31	0.00	2.85	R8.68	0.52	0.10	0.27	0.00	2.91	—	(s)	7.04	R12.31	20.99
1962	6.19	1.33	1.01	1.96	.07	1.64	.01	3.20	R10.50	.67	.12	.31	.00	3.67	—	(s)	7.33	R13.85	24.35
1964	7.61	1.71	1.26	2.30	.12	1.90	.19	3.39	12.98	.75	.18	.32	.00	4.60	—	(s)	7.61	15.20	28.18
1966	9.32	2.13	1.39	2.48	.42	2.60	.36	3.37	R15.75	.88	.29	.33	.00	5.23	—	(s)	8.30	R17.20	32.96
1968	10.91	2.84	1.50	2.61	.14	3.04	.50	3.60	18.71	1.19	.30	.39	.00	6.08	—	(s)	9.10	R19.93	38.63
1970	13.39	3.83	1.55	2.99	1.08	3.80	.78	3.71	23.42	1.26	.60	.49	.00	6.99	—	(s)	9.64	R22.47	45.89
1972	17.54	5.02	1.47	3.28	1.82	6.02	1.20	3.22	27.11	1.53	.90	.51	.03	7.89	—	(s)	9.44	R24.03	51.14
1974	21.28	6.02	1.97	2.55	2.26	8.48	1.68	2.98	30.70	1.55	1.32	.57	.04	8.91	—	(s)	8.77	R25.02	55.72
1976	21.51	5.88	2.42	2.15	2.07	8.58	1.94	2.29	R30.62	1.31	1.67	.83	.28	10.06	—	.25	8.13	R26.72	57.34
1978	20.61	5.24	2.56	2.13	1.90	8.30	1.83	2.17	29.80	1.32	2.08	1.21	.36	11.11	—	1.08	8.71	R30.36	60.16
1980	17.96	1.66	2.51	1.66	2.06	9.90	1.71	2.17	26.96	1.44	2.11	1.94	.49	11.71	—	1.62	8.60	R32.60	59.56
1982	12.16	2.21	1.01	.82	1.30	6.48	1.25	1.90	R19.11	1.27	2.05	2.75	.49	11.91	—	2.07	8.65	R34.34	53.45
1984	10.78	2.17	1.21	1.16	1.39	4.66	1.15	1.80	17.91	1.44	2.30	2.78	.71	11.86	—	2.48	8.88	R36.59	54.50
1986	11.70	2.04	1.69	1.42	1.47	4.87	1.33	1.79	R18.85	1.47	2.62	2.44	.84	11.90	—	2.54	8.68	R37.35	56.20
1988	13.46	2.24	2.69	1.49	1.45	5.09	1.57	1.90	21.08	1.62	2.73	2.51	1.11	12.05	—	2.23	8.14	R37.61	58.69
1990	15.28	3.09	2.04	1.18	1.81	6.41	2.12	2.14	23.96	1.55	2.77	2.55	1.63	10.98	—	1.82	7.36	R36.54	60.49
1992	15.97	3.43	.43	1.06	1.94	8.33	2.27	2.37	R25.25	1.61	2.85	2.67	2.13	—	7.63	1.83	7.17	R34.87	60.12
1994	16.96	3.62	.55	2.03	1.93	8.12	2.19	2.59	R26.41	1.75	2.94	2.69	2.57	—	6.14	2.37	6.66	R34.69	R61.10
1996	17.37	3.69	.58	2.06	2.00	8.22	2.28	2.94	27.57	1.84	3.13	2.86	3.09	—	5.85	2.57	6.46	R36.19	R63.75
1998	19.34	3.63	2.15	2.09	2.15	8.39	2.35	3.17	R29.88	1.98	3.20	3.07	3.01	—	5.85	2.62	6.25	R37.08	R66.97
2000	19.89	3.70	2.57	2.08	2.17	8.40	2.37	3.16	30.41	1.98	3.25	3.01	3.22	—	6.48	2.28	5.82	R38.09	68.49
2001	19.10	3.72	2.39	2.00	2.26	8.03	2.21	3.01	R29.50	2.03	3.30	3.13	3.23	—	6.92	2.28	5.80	R38.60	68.10
2002	17.79	3.44	2.02	1.89	2.12	7.63	2.08	2.60	27.64	2.17	3.39	3.18	3.13	—	7.41	2.29	5.75	R39.53	67.17
2003	19.06	3.74	1.31	2.14	2.28	8.78	2.35	2.34	29.14	2.31	3.41	3.37	3.04	—	8.13	2.09	5.68	40.31	69.45
2004	20.79	4.00	2.01	2.38	2.33	9.10	2.48	2.56	R31.50	2.40	3.49	3.38	2.95	—	8.80	1.85	5.42	41.01	R72.51
2005	21.50	4.14	1.88	2.53	2.63	9.55	2.54	2.56	R32.94	2.37	3.61	3.33	2.70	—	9.04	1.65	5.18	40.87	R73.81
2006	21.23	4.03	2.00	2.54	2.44	9.15	2.64	2.51	R32.61	2.53	R3.67	3.26	2.49	—	9.25	1.49	R5.10	R40.93	R73.54
2007P	20.68	3.92	2.09	2.46	2.35	8.72	2.60	2.43	32.18	2.61	3.73	3.08	2.27	—	9.44	1.50	5.10	41.09	73.27

[a]Bahrain, Iran, Iraq, Kuwait, Qatar, Saudi Arabia, United Arab Emirates, and the neutral zone (between Kuwait and Saudi Arabia).

[b]Includes about one-half of the production in the neutral zone between Kuwait and Saudi Arabia.

[c]On this table, "total OPEC" for all years includes Algeria, Angola, Ecuador, Indonesia, Iran, Iraq, Kuwait, Libya, Nigeria, Qatar, Saudi Arabia, United Arab Emirates, Venezuela, and the neutral zone (between Kuwait and Saudi Arabia). Data for all countries not included in "total OPEC" are included in "total Non-OPEC."

R = Revised

P = Preliminary.

— = Not applicable.

(s) = Less than 0.005 million barrels per day.

U.S.S.R. = Union of Soviet Socialist Republics.

OPEC = Organization of the Petroleum Exporting Countries.

Notes: Data are for crude oil, including extra heavy crude oil, lease condensate, and liquids processed from Canadian oil sands; they exclude natural gas plant liquids. Totals may not equal sum of components due to independent rounding.

SOURCE: Adapted from "Table 11.5. World Crude Oil Production, 1960–2007 (Million Barrels per Day)," in *Annual Energy Review 2007*, U.S. Department of Energy, Energy Information Administration, Office of Energy Markets and End Use, June 2008, http://www.eia.doe.gov/aer/pdf/aer.pdf (accessed June 28, 2008). Non-U.S. governmental data from the U.S.S.R. Central Statistical Office, *Narodnoye Khozyaystvo SSSR* (National Economy USSR) for the years 1960–1969; and OPEC, *Annual Statistical Bulletin 1979* for the years 1960–1972.

FIGURE 2.9

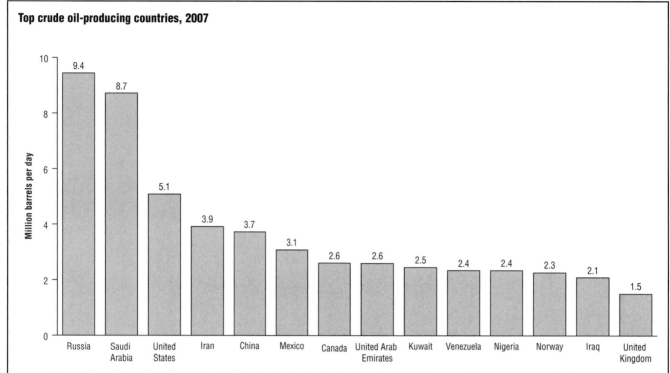

Top crude oil-producing countries, 2007

SOURCE: Adapted from "Figure 11.5. World Crude Oil Production: Top Producing Countries, 2007," in *Annual Energy Review 2007*, U.S. Department of Energy, Energy Information Administration, Office of Energy Markets and End Use, June 2008, http://www.eia.doe.gov/aer/pdf/aer.pdf (accessed June 28, 2008)

OIL IMPORTS AND EXPORTS

Countries that have surplus oil (e.g., Saudi Arabia) sell their excess to countries that need more than they can produce, such as the United States, China, Japan, and west European countries. They sell petroleum as both crude oil and refined products, although the trend has been moving toward refined products because they bring higher profits. According to the EIA, in *Annual Energy Review 2007*, the leading supplier of petroleum to the United States in 2007 was Canada, followed by Mexico, Saudi Arabia, Venezuela, Nigeria, Iraq, Russia, the United Kingdom, and Brazil.

Even though the United States produces a significant amount of petroleum, it has been importing oil since World War II (1939–1945). Initially, the imported oil was cheap and available, suiting the demands of a growing American population and economy. Furthermore, relatively low world crude oil prices often resulted in reduced domestic oil production: when the world price was lower than the cost of producing oil from some U.S. wells, domestic oil became unprofitable and was not produced. So more oil was imported.

The amount of oil imported to the United States has fluctuated over the years. Total net imports (imports minus exports) rose from 4.3 mbpd in 1982 to 12 mbpd by 2007, down from 12.5 in 2005. (See Table 2.2.) In 1985 imported oil supplied only 27.3% of American oil consumption. (See Figure 1.8 in Chapter 1.) Just five years later, in 1990, the proportion had risen to 42% and by 2007 to 58.2%.

CONCERN ABOUT OIL DEPENDENCY

In the 1970s U.S. leaders were concerned that so much of the country's economic structure, based heavily on imported oil, was dependent on decisions in OPEC countries. Oil resources became an issue of national security, and OPEC countries, especially the Arab members, were often portrayed as potentially strangling the U.S. economy. Efforts were made to reduce imports by raising public awareness and by encouraging industry to create more energy-efficient products, such as automobiles that got better gas mileage. Nonetheless, the EIA notes in *Annual Energy Review 2007* that total petroleum imports rose from 3.4 mbpd in 1970 to 8.5 mbpd in 1979, but dropped to 6.9 mbpd in 1980.

The Ronald Reagan (1911–2004) and George H. W. Bush (1924–) administrations, which ran from 1981 to 1989 and from 1989 to 1993, respectively, took a different view. They saw oil supply as an economic, rather than as a political, issue and allowed energy issues to be handled by the marketplace. According to the EIA, during those years total petroleum imports dropped dramatically, from 6 mbpd in 1980 to a low of about 5.1 mbpd from 1981 to 1985, but then increased to 8.6 mbpd by 1993.

TABLE 2.4

World petroleum consumption, selected years 1960–2006

[Million barrels per day]

Year	Selected OECD consumers											Selected non-OECD consumers						World
	Canada	France	Germany[a]	Italy	Japan	Mexico[b]	South Korea[b]	Spain	United Kingdom	United States	Total OECD[c]	Brazil	China	India	Former U.S.S.R.	Russia	Total non-OECD	World
1960	0.84	0.56	0.63	0.44	0.66	0.30	0.01	0.10	0.94	9.80	15.78	0.27	0.17	0.16	2.38	—	5.56	21.34
1962	.92	.73	1.00	.67	.93	.30	.02	.12	1.12	10.40	18.06	.31	.14	.18	2.87	—	6.83	24.89
1964	1.05	.98	1.36	.90	1.48	.33	.02	.20	1.36	11.02	21.05	.35	.20	.22	3.58	—	8.03	29.08
1966	1.21	1.19	1.80	1.08	1.98	.36	.04	.31	1.58	12.08	24.60	.38	.30	.28	3.87	—	8.96	33.56
1968	1.34	1.46	1.99	1.40	2.66	.41	.10	.46	1.82	13.39	28.56	.46	.31	.31	4.48	—	10.40	38.96
1970	1.52	1.94	2.83	1.71	3.82	.50	.20	.58	2.10	14.70	34.69	.53	.62	.40	5.31	—	12.12	46.81
1972	1.66	2.32	3.10	1.95	4.36	.59	.24	.68	2.28	16.37	38.95	.66	.91	.46	6.12	—	14.15	53.09
1974	1.78	2.45	3.03	2.00	4.86	.71	.29	.86	2.21	16.65	40.38	.86	1.19	.47	7.28	—	16.30	56.68
1976	1.82	2.42	3.21	1.97	4.84	.83	.36	.97	1.89	17.46	41.72	1.00	1.53	.51	7.78	—	17.96	59.67
1978	1.90	2.41	3.29	1.95	4.95	.99	.48	.98	1.94	18.85	43.98	1.11	1.79	.62	8.48	—	20.18	64.16
1980	1.87	2.26	3.08	1.93	4.96	1.27	.54	.99	1.73	17.06	41.76	1.15	1.77	.64	9.00	—	21.35	63.11
1982	1.58	1.88	2.74	1.78	4.58	1.48	.53	1.00	1.59	15.30	37.77	1.06	1.66	.74	9.08	—	21.78	59.54
1984	1.52	1.77	2.56	1.72	4.67	R1.40	.55	.85	1.83	15.73	37.69	1.03	1.74	.82	8.91	—	22.12	59.82
1986	1.53	1.76	2.79	1.73	4.50	1.52	.59	.87	1.64	16.28	38.60	1.24	2.00	.95	8.98	—	23.21	61.81
1988	1.68	1.80	2.72	1.83	4.85	1.60	.75	.98	1.69	17.28	40.65	1.30	2.27	1.08	8.89	—	24.32	64.97
1990	1.73	1.83	2.68	1.87	R5.30	1.75	1.05	1.01	1.78	16.99	R41.61	1.47	2.30	1.17	8.39	—	25.07	R66.68
1992	1.72	1.93	2.84	1.89	R5.47	1.86	1.53	1.10	R1.82	17.03	R42.95	1.52	2.66	1.27	—	4.42	24.51	R67.46
1994	1.77	R1.87	2.88	1.87	R5.65	1.93	1.84	1.12	1.83	17.72	R44.44	1.67	3.16	1.41	—	3.18	24.43	R68.86
1996	1.86	1.95	2.92	1.92	R5.74	1.79	2.10	1.20	1.85	18.31	R45.98	1.90	3.61	1.68	—	2.62	25.65	R71.63
1998	1.94	2.04	2.92	1.94	R5.50	1.95	1.92	1.36	1.79	18.92	R46.89	2.10	4.11	1.84	—	2.49	R27.12	74.00
2000	2.03	2.00	2.77	1.85	R5.50	2.04	2.14	1.43	1.76	19.70	R47.88	2.17	4.80	2.13	—	2.58	R28.79	R76.66
2001	2.06	2.05	2.81	1.84	R5.39	2.01	2.13	1.49	R1.74	19.65	R47.94	2.21	4.92	2.18	—	2.59	R29.46	R77.40
2002	2.08	1.98	2.72	1.87	5.30	1.95	2.15	1.50	R1.73	19.76	R47.89	2.13	5.16	2.26	—	2.64	R30.15	R78.04
2003	2.21	2.00	2.68	1.87	5.42	1.95	2.18	1.54	R1.76	20.03	R48.60	2.06	5.58	2.35	—	2.68	R31.01	79.61
2004	R2.30	2.01	2.67	1.79	5.29	2.00	2.16	1.57	R1.80	20.73	R49.36	R2.12	6.44	2.43	—	2.75	R32.97	R82.33
2005	R2.30	R1.99	R2.65	R1.75	R5.31	R2.05	R2.19	R1.61	R1.83	20.80	R49.66	R2.17	R6.72	2.44	—	R2.76	R33.99	R83.65
2006P	2.26	1.96	2.66	1.73	5.16	2.00	2.17	1.59	1.83	20.69	49.34	2.22	7.20	2.57	—	2.81	35.29	84.62

[a]Through 1969, the data for Germany are for the former West Germany only. For 1970 through 1990, this is East and West Germany. Beginning in 1991, this is unified Germany.

[b]Mexico, which joined the OECD on May 18, 1994, and South Korea, which joined the OECD on December 12, 1996, are included in the OECD for all years shown in this table.

[c]Hungary and Poland, which joined the OECD on May 7, 1996, and November 22, 1996, respectively, are included in total OECD beginning in 1970, the first year that data for these countries were available. Total OECD includes Czechoslovakia from 1970–1992, and Czech Republic and Slovakia from 1993 forward.

R = Revised.

P = Preliminary.

— = Not applicable.

U.S.S.R. = Union of Soviet Socialist Republics

Notes: OECD = Organization for Economic Cooperation and Development.

Totals may not equal sum of components due to independent rounding.

SOURCE: Adapted from "Table 11.10. World Petroleum Consumption, 1960–2006 (Million Barrels per Day)," in *Annual Energy Review 2007*, U.S. Department of Energy, Energy Information Administration, Office of Energy Markets and End Use, June 2008, http://www.eia.doe.gov/aer/pdf/aer.pdf (accessed June 28, 2008)

FIGURE 2.10

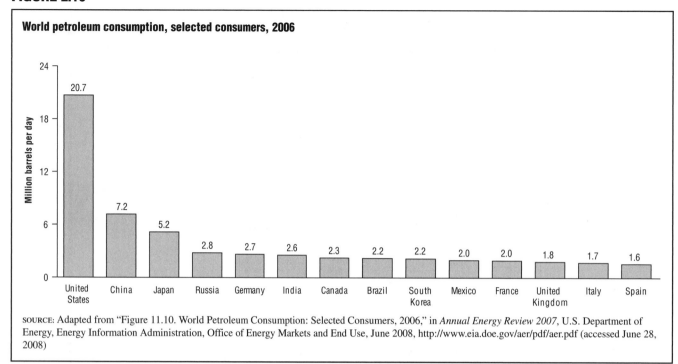

World petroleum consumption, selected consumers, 2006

SOURCE: Adapted from "Figure 11.10. World Petroleum Consumption: Selected Consumers, 2006," in *Annual Energy Review 2007*, U.S. Department of Energy, Energy Information Administration, Office of Energy Markets and End Use, June 2008, http://www.eia.doe.gov/aer/pdf/aer.pdf (accessed June 28, 2008)

During the Bill Clinton (1946–) administration, which ran from 1993 to 2001, U.S. dependence on foreign oil continued largely because low prices throughout most of the 1990s set back energy-conservation efforts. In fact, efficiency gains in automobiles were offset by the public's growing preference for large vehicles, such as SUVs. Total imports of petroleum grew steadily. In 2001 the United States imported 11.9 mbpd, up from 8.6 mbpd in 1993.

Many factors diverted the public's attention from U.S. dependence on foreign oil. For example, a comfort level had been achieved through oil reserves, such as the U.S. Strategic Petroleum Reserve and the U.S. government-required reserves in Europe, and the knowledge that, in emergencies, non-OPEC oil producers such as the United Kingdom and Norway could increase their output. Furthermore, increased use of pipelines across Saudi Arabia and Turkey lessened concern about the disruption of supplies. The pipelines allow tankers to load oil in the Red Sea or the Mediterranean Sea, rather than in the potentially dangerous Persian Gulf. Tankers do not have to navigate through the narrow Strait of Hormuz, where saboteurs might be able to stop the flow of oil.

Heavy dependence on foreign oil continued during the George W. Bush (1946–) administration (from 2001 to 2009), and by 2007 about 65% of the nation's crude oil supply (10 mbpd out of a total 15.1 mbpd) came from outside the country. (See Figure 2.5.) According to the EIA, in *Annual Energy Review 2007*, nearly 45% of that crude oil came from OPEC nations.

Concern that U.S. dependence on foreign oil, especially OPEC oil, represented a threat to national security

or national stability changed somewhat after the terrorist attacks of September 11, 2001. It was heightened by the war on terror, the war with Iraq, and the consequent unrest in Middle Eastern nations. Still, demand for the product persisted. By mid-2008 demand had continued to grow, oil prices had increased dramatically, and oil supplies and reserves were tight.

PROJECTED OIL SUPPLY AND CONSUMPTION

The EIA projects in *Annual Energy Outlook 2006* that domestic crude oil production will increase from 5.4 mbpd in 2004 to a peak of 5.9 mbpd in 2014, with the peak attributed to offshore production, particularly in the deep water of the Gulf of Mexico. After 2014 production is projected to fall to 4.6 mbpd in 2030. However, even though domestic supply is expected to remain relatively constant though 2030, demand is projected to increase significantly. (See Figure 2.11.) Thus, the agency foresees an increasing dependence on petroleum imports.

STRATEGIC PETROLEUM RESERVE

Early in the twentieth century the Naval Petroleum Reserve was established to ensure that the U.S. Navy would have adequate fuel in the event of war. Large tracts of government land with known deposits of oil were set aside. In 1975, in response to the growing concern over U.S. energy dependence, Congress expanded this concept by creating the Strategic Petroleum Reserve. Oil and refined products are stored in forty-one deep salt caverns in Louisiana and Texas. (The caverns are used because oil does not dissolve salt the way water does.) If

FIGURE 2.11

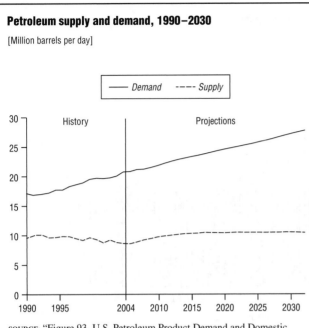

Petroleum supply and demand, 1990–2030

[Million barrels per day]

SOURCE: "Figure 93. U.S. Petroleum Product Demand and Domestic Petroleum Supply, 1990–2030 (Million Barrels per Day)," in *Annual Energy Outlook 2006*, U.S. Department of Energy, Energy Information Administration, Office of Integrated Analysis and Forecasting, February 2006, http://www.eia.doe.gov/oiaf/archive/aeo06/pdf/0383(2006).pdf (accessed July 2, 2008)

FIGURE 2.12

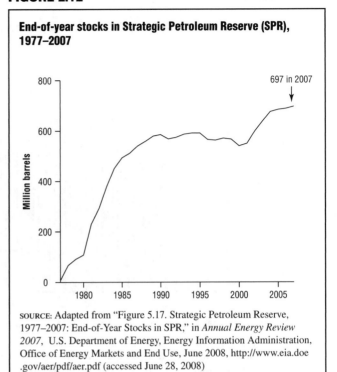

End-of-year stocks in Strategic Petroleum Reserve (SPR), 1977–2007

SOURCE: Adapted from "Figure 5.17. Strategic Petroleum Reserve, 1977–2007: End-of-Year Stocks in SPR," in *Annual Energy Review 2007*, U.S. Department of Energy, Energy Information Administration, Office of Energy Markets and End Use, June 2008, http://www.eia.doe.gov/aer/pdf/aer.pdf (accessed June 28, 2008)

the United States suddenly finds its supplies cut off, the reserves can be connected to existing pipelines and the oil pumped out.

At the end of 2004 the Strategic Petroleum Reserve contained 697 million barrels of oil (see Figure 2.12), equal to fifty-eight days' worth of imported oil. Figure 2.13 shows a decline in the reserves in terms of days' worth of net imports, from a high of 115 days in 1985, to a low of 50 days in 2001, to 58 days in 2007. This decline reflects the country's increasing reliance on imports since 1985. As the nation has imported a greater amount of oil, the days of net import replacement represented by the amount of oil in the reserves have dropped, even though the amount of oil in the reserves has increased.

OIL PRICES

The law of supply (availability) and demand (need) often explains changes in the price of oil. Higher prices lead to increased production—it becomes profitable to operate more expensive wells—and reduced demand—consumers lower usage and increase conservation efforts. The factors also work the other way: Reduced demand or increased supply generally causes the price of oil to drop. The demand for petroleum products varies. Heating oil demand rises during the winter. A cold spell, which leads to a sharp rise in demand, may result in a corresponding price increase. A warm winter may be reflected in lower

prices as suppliers try to clear out their inventory. Gasoline demand rises during the summer—people drive more for recreation—so gas prices rise as a consequence.

Wars and other types of political unrest in oil-producing nations add volatility to petroleum prices, which fluctuate—sometimes dramatically—depending on the situation at the time. Wars, such as the war in Iraq, can also seriously affect the oil extraction and refining capabilities of a country, which, in turn, affects oil prices. Weather disasters, such as Hurricane Katrina along the Gulf coast in the summer of 2005, affect these capabilities and the price of oil as well.

Petroleum demand also reflects the general condition of the economy. During a recession, demand for and production of petroleum products usually drop. On the edge of recession in late 2007 and early 2008, the United States saw its dollar decline in value dramatically and its housing market crumble, so investors looked to oil as a safe haven for their money. Even though oil prices would be expected to drop in such poor economic times, oil market speculation appeared to be a major factor in the rise of oil prices in 2007 and 2008. (See Chapter 1.)

The Organization of Petroleum Exporting Countries

Consumers prefer low prices that allow them to save money or get more for the same price, whereas producers naturally prefer to keep prices high. With this goal in mind, some oil-producing countries formed OPEC in 1960. OPEC is a cartel (a group of businesses that agree to control

FIGURE 2.13

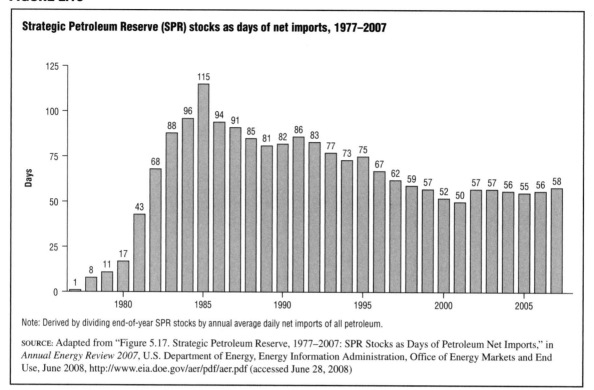

Strategic Petroleum Reserve (SPR) stocks as days of net imports, 1977–2007

Note: Derived by dividing end-of-year SPR stocks by annual average daily net imports of all petroleum.

SOURCE: Adapted from "Figure 5.17. Strategic Petroleum Reserve, 1977–2007: SPR Stocks as Days of Petroleum Net Imports," in *Annual Energy Review 2007*, U.S. Department of Energy, Energy Information Administration, Office of Energy Markets and End Use, June 2008, http://www.eia.doe.gov/aer/pdf/aer.pdf (accessed June 28, 2008)

production and marketing to avoid competing with one another). Since 1973 OPEC has tried to control the oil supply to achieve higher prices.

OPEC has faced long-term problems, however, because high prices in the late 1970s to mid-1980s encouraged conservation, thereby reducing demand for oil and leading to a sharp decline in oil prices. As a result of the decreased demand for oil and lower prices, OPEC lost some of its ability to control its members and, consequently, prices.

Nevertheless, OPEC actions can still effectively influence the petroleum market. For example, in an attempt to halt the downward slide of oil prices in 1999, Saudi Arabia, Mexico, and Venezuela agreed to cut production by 1.6% to 2 mbpd. Many other oil-producing nations also limited their production. The limitations worked: During the summer of 2000 oil prices climbed. The EIA explains in *Annual Energy Review 2000* (August 2001, http://tonto .eia.doe.gov/ftproot/multifuel/038400.pdf) that refiners paid $16.71 in real dollars per barrel of crude oil in 1999. In 2000 the price had risen to $26.40 per barrel. More recently, OPEC agreed to cut its crude oil output by 1.2 mbpd by November 2006, and by an additional 500,000 barrels per day in February 2007. The price of oil then began to rise. (See Figure 1.2 in Chapter 1.)

Gasoline Prices

Many older Americans can remember when gas cost thirty cents per gallon. From 1972 to 1980 the price of a gallon of regular leaded gasoline (in dollars

of that time, [nominal] dollars that do not consider inflation) more than tripled, whereas the price in real dollars, which account for inflation and in Table 2.5 reflect the buying power of the dollar in 2000, rose 83%. In 1981 the price of a gallon of regular unleaded gasoline was $2.33 in real dollars. However, after 1981, as a result of the international oil glut, real prices tumbled. In 1998 the price per gallon was only $1.10, and after price increases in 1999 the price of unleaded gas still averaged only $1.51 in 2000 and less in 2001 through 2003.

By the end of April 2006, prices at the pump had soared in the United States. In many major cities prices hovered around $3 per gallon (in nominal dollars) for regular gasoline. Table 2.5 shows that regular unleaded gasoline in 2006 cost $2.22 per gallon in real (2000) dollars—close to $2.33 per gallon in real dollars in 1981. Oil prices were rising all over the world in response to high demand, especially in the United States, China, Japan, and India. In addition, the U.S. government was changing the additives required in certain fuel blends, which caused shortages in parts of the country, pushing fuel prices up even more.

The White House explains in the press release "President Bush's Four-Part Plan to Confront High Gasoline Prices" (April 25, 2006, http://www.whitehouse.gov/ news/releases/2006/04/20060425-2.html) that to confront the high gasoline prices, President Bush announced a four-part plan in April 2006. The plan included:

TABLE 2.5

Retail motor gasoline and on-highway diesel fuel prices, selected years 1949–2007

[Dollars per gallon]

| | Motor gasoline by grade | | | | | | | | Regular motor gasoline by area type | | | On-highway diesel fuel |
| | Leaded regular | | Unleaded regular | | Unleaded premium | | All grades | | Conventional gasoline areas[a, b] | Reformulated gasoline areas[c, d] | All areas | |
Year	Nominal	Real[e]	Nominal	Real[e]	Nominal	Real[e]	Nominal	Real[e]	Nominal	Nominal	Nominal	Nominal
1949	0.27	1.64	NA	NA	NA	NA	NA	NA	NA	NA	NA	NA
1950	.27	1.62	NA	NA	NA	NA	NA	NA	NA	NA	NA	NA
1955	.29	1.55	NA	NA	NA	NA	NA	NA	NA	NA	NA	NA
1960	.31	1.48	NA	NA	NA	NA	NA	NA	NA	NA	NA	NA
1965	.31	1.39	NA	NA	NA	NA	NA	NA	NA	NA	NA	NA
1970	.36	1.30	NA	NA	NA	NA	NA	NA	NA	NA	NA	NA
1971	.36	1.26	NA	NA	NA	NA	NA	NA	NA	NA	NA	NA
1972	.36	1.20	NA	NA	NA	NA	NA	NA	NA	NA	NA	NA
1974	.53	1.53	NA	NA	NA	NA	NA	NA	NA	NA	NA	NA
1976	.59	1.47	.61	1.53	NA	NA	NA	NA	NA	NA	NA	NA
1978	.63	1.37	.67	1.46	NA	NA	.65	1.43	NA	NA	NA	NA
1980	1.19	2.20	1.25	2.30	NA	NA	1.22	2.26	NA	NA	NA	NA
1981	1.31	2.22	1.38	2.33	1.47	2.49	1.35	2.29	NA	NA	NA	NA
1982	1.22	1.95	1.30	2.07	1.42	2.26	1.28	2.04	NA	NA	NA	NA
1984	1.13	1.67	1.21	1.79	1.37	2.02	1.20	1.77	NA	NA	NA	NA
1986	.86	1.20	.93	1.30	1.09	1.52	.93	1.31	NA	NA	NA	NA
1988	.90	1.19	.95	1.25	1.11	1.46	.96	1.27	NA	NA	NA	NA
1990	1.15	1.41	1.16	1.43	1.35	1.65	1.22	1.49	NA	NA	NA	NA
1992	NA	NA	1.13	1.31	1.32	1.52	1.19	1.38	1.09	NA	1.09	NA
1994	NA	NA	1.11	1.23	1.31	1.45	1.17	1.30	b1.07	NA	1.08	NA
1996	NA	NA	1.23	1.31	1.41	1.51	1.29	1.37	b1.19	d1.28	1.22	1.24
1998	NA	NA	1.06	1.10	1.25	1.30	1.12	1.16	b1.02	d1.08	1.03	1.04
2000	NA	NA	1.51	1.51	1.69	1.69	1.56	1.56	b1.46	d1.54	1.48	1.49
2001	NA	NA	1.46	1.43	1.66	1.62	1.53	1.50	1.38	1.50	1.42	1.40
2002	NA	NA	1.36	1.30	1.56	1.49	1.44	1.38	1.31	1.41	1.35	1.32
2003	NA	NA	1.59	1.50	1.78	1.67	1.64	1.54	1.52	1.66	1.56	1.51
2004	NA	NA	1.88	1.72	2.07	1.89	1.92	1.76	1.81	1.94	1.85	1.81
2005	NA	NA	2.30	R2.03	2.49	R2.20	2.34	2.07	2.24	2.34	2.27	2.40
2006	NA	NA	2.59	R2.22	2.81	R2.41	2.64	R2.26	2.53	2.65	2.57	2.71
2007	NA	NA	2.80	2.34	3.03	2.54	2.85	2.38	2.77	2.86	2.80	2.89

[a]Any area that does not require the sale of reformulated gasoline.
[b]For 1993–2000, data collected for oxygenated areas are included in "conventional gasoline areas."
[c]"Reformulated gasoline areas" are ozone nonattainment areas designated by the Environmental Protection Agency that require the use of reformulated gasoline.
[d]For 1995–2000, data collected for combined oxygenated and reformulated areas are included in "reformulated gasoline areas."
[e]In chained (2000) dollars, calculated by using gross domestic product implicit price deflators.
R = Revised.
NA = Not available.

SOURCE: Adapted from "Table 5.24. Retail Motor Gasoline and On-Highway Diesel Fuel Prices, Selected Years, 1949–2007 (Dollars per Gallon)," in *Annual Energy Review 2007*, U.S. Department of Energy, Energy Information Administration, Office of Energy Markets and End Use, June 2008, http://www.eia.doe.gov/aer/pdf/aer.pdf (accessed June 28, 2008). Non-U.S. governmental data for the years 1949–1973 from *Platt's Oil Price Handbook and Oilmanac, 1974,* 51st ed.

1. Investigating whether the price of gas had been unfairly manipulated since Hurricanes Katrina and Rita hit the Gulf coast in the summer 2005

2. Promoting greater fuel efficiency by providing tax credits for all hybrid and "clean diesel" vehicles sold in 2006

3. Boosting supplies of crude oil and gas by temporarily halting deposits to the Strategic Petroleum Reserve

4. Calling on Congress to support the Advanced Energy Initiative (February 2006, http://www.whitehouse.gov/stateoftheunion/2006/energy/print/index.html), the goals of which were "promoting energy conservation, repairing and modernizing our energy infrastructure, and increasing our energy supplies in ways that protect and improve the environment"

However, by 2007 gasoline prices had risen above the high recorded in 1981, to $2.34 per gallon in real (2000) dollars. Figure 1.3 in Chapter 1 shows the tremendous price spike in both real and nominal gasoline prices during this period. In "Weekly Retail Gasoline and Diesel Prices" (August 25, 2008, http://tonto.eia.doe.gov/dnav/pet/pet_pri_gnd_a_epmr_pte_cpgal_w.htm), the EIA notes that gasoline prices at the pump in nominal dollars the week of July 21, 2008, averaged over $4.06 in the United States.

In 2007 and 2008 President Bush moved his agenda forward to improve fuel economy in vehicles and reduce U.S. dependence on foreign oil. In his 2007 State of the Union address, he proposed a "Twenty in Ten" policy (January 2007, http://www.whitehouse.gov/stateoftheunion/2007/initiatives/energy.html) of reducing by 20% the amount of gasoline Americans used within the next ten years by increasing the fuel efficiency of automobiles—increasing the CAFE standards—and using alternative fuels. Congress responded by developing the Energy Independence and Security Act (EISA) of 2007, which mandated that fuel producers make at least 36 billion gallons (136 billion L) of biofuel annually by 2022. EISA also required that the CAFE standard be raised for cars and light trucks to 35 miles per gallon (6.7 L/100 km) by model year 2020. In the press release "President Bush Discusses Energy" (June 18, 2008, http://www.whitehouse.gov/news/releases/2008/06/20080618.html), the White House explains that in June 2008 President Bush asked Congress to pass legislation to help increase domestic production of oil by exploring the Outer Continental Shelf for oil resources; allowing the extraction of oil from oil shale located in the Green River Basin of Colorado, Utah, and Wyoming; permitting exploration in the Arctic National Wildlife Refuge in Alaska; and expanding and enhancing U.S. oil refinery capacity.

ENVIRONMENTAL CONCERNS ABOUT OIL TRANSPORTATION

Transporting oil carries significant environmental risks. According to the U.S. Department of the Interior, oil tanker accidents are the cause of most transportation spills.

The *Exxon Valdez* Oil Spill

Even though a number of events have influenced American attitudes toward oil production and use, one of the most notable occurred in March 1989, when the oil tanker *Exxon Valdez* hit a reef in Alaska and spilled 11 million gallons (41.6 million L) of crude oil into the waters of Prince William Sound. The cleanup cost Exxon nearly $1.3 billion, a sum that does not include legal costs or any valuation for the wildlife lost. The spill was an environmental disaster for a formerly pristine area. Even measures used to clean up the spill, such as washing the beaches with hot water, caused additional damage.

Adam Liptak reports in "Damages Cut against Exxon in Valdez Case" (*New York Times*, June 26, 2008) that the legal arguments about the extent of Exxon's liability were ended on June 25, 2008, when the U.S. Supreme Court ruled that the $5 billion punitive (punishment) damage award previously set by an appeals court was too high. To the dismay of many of the people affected by the spill, the punitive damages were reduced to about $500 million. The ruling had broad implications for the lowering of punitive damages in general.

The Oil Pollution Act of 1990

The *Exxon Valdez* spill led to debate in the United States about tanker safety and design. Over the years, oil tankers have grown in size. The American Petroleum Institute indicates in *Large Tankers: Our Energy Lifelines* (1976) that in 1945 the largest tanker held 16,500 short tons (15,000 t) of oil; by 1976 supertankers carried more than 550,000 short tons (499,000 t). These ships are difficult to maneuver because of their size and are likely to spill more oil if damaged.

The *Exxon Valdez* oil spill led Congress to pass the Oil Pollution Act of 1990, which increased, but still limited, oil spillers' federal liability (financial responsibility) as long as spills were not the result of "gross negligence." The bill also mandated compensation to those who were economically injured by oil spills. Damages that can be charged to oil companies were limited to $60 million for tanker accidents and $75 million for accidents at offshore facilities. The law specified that the rest of the cleanup costs were to be paid from a $500 million oil-spill fund generated by a $0.013-per-barrel tax on oil. Individual states still have the right to impose unlimited liability on spillers. Oil companies were also required to phase in double-hulled vessels by 2015. Essentially, a double-hulled vessel carries its oil in a container inside another container, providing extra protection in case of an accident.

Oil Spills Still Occur Worldwide

In November 2002 the twenty-six-year-old, single-hulled tanker *Prestige* was damaged off the coast of Spain and spilled approximately 5,000 short tons (4,500 t) of heavy fuel oil, according to Spanish government estimates. The ship continued to leak, so Spanish authorities ordered the leaking vessel towed to the open ocean. Several thousand more short tons of oil were released as it sank, although much of the oil may have solidified inside the ship in the cold water at the bottom of the ocean. Scientists estimate the oil spilled from the *Prestige* caused the deaths of nearly 250,000 seabirds. It also killed unknown numbers of fish and dolphins and was responsible for economic damage to the Spanish fish and shellfish industries.

In December 2007 a Samsung-owned barge collided with the *Heibei Spirit* oil tanker, which was anchored off the west coast of South Korea. About 10,500 short tons (9,500 t) of crude oil were spilled, destroying the ecology of the region and damaging the southwestern coastline. The *Heibei Spirit* was a single-hulled tanker, a key factor in what is considered to be the worst Asian oil spill in a decade.

These examples of oil spills are only that—examples. Oil spills occur relatively frequently around the world. Smaller oil spills occur as well. For example, oil frequently washes ashore on Newfoundland's south coast. The oil often comes from bilge water (waste water contaminated with oil that accumulates in the bottoms of ships). Bilge water should be properly dumped, but it is often pumped into the ocean to save dumping costs.

Not All Oil Spills Are Due to Oil Transportation

According to the Natural Resources Defense Council (NRDC), in "Recovering from Katrina: Greater New Orleans Region, 2005–Present Day" (2008, http://www.nrdc.org/ej/partnerships/katrina.asp), Hurricane Katrina, which hit the coast of Louisiana and Mississippi in 2005, triggered spills of more than 8 million gallons (30.3 million L) of petroleum and hazardous chemicals (generally refinery products). The Gulf coast is home to many oil refineries with scores of oil storage tanks and miles of oil pipeline. Some tanks and pipelines did not withstand the floodwater, releasing oil and refinery products into the soil and buildings of New Orleans. Before people can safely move back into these areas, the oil and other refinery products must be cleaned up because these chemicals can be hazardous: short-term exposure to certain chemicals in the oil causes dizziness and nausea; long-term exposure is linked to leukemia and other serious ailments. The NRDC is working with local groups to identify contaminated soils and sediments and remove them.

CHAPTER 3
NATURAL GAS

Natural gas is an important source of energy in the United States. Like petroleum, natural gas is composed of hydrocarbons, which are chemical compounds containing both hydrogen and carbon. The molecular structure of hydrocarbon compounds varies from the simplest, methane, to very heavy and very complex molecules, such as those found in petroleum.

Methane, ethane, and propane are the primary constituents of natural gas, with methane making up 73% to 95% of the total. Consumer-grade natural gas is "dry gas," which means that it has been processed to remove water vapor, nonhydrocarbon gases (such as helium and nitrogen), and certain compounds that liquefy during the processing (such as lease condensate and natural gas plant liquids). Lease condensate is a liquid mix of heavy hydrocarbons recovered during natural gas processing at a lease, or field separation, facility. Natural gas plant liquids are compounds such as propane and butane that are recovered as liquids at other facilities later in the processing.

The natural gas industry developed out of the petroleum industry. Wells drilled for oil often produced considerable amounts of natural gas, but early oilmen had no idea what to do with it. Originally considered a waste by-product, natural gas had no market. Even if a use for natural gas had been known at the time, there were no transmission lines to deliver it. As a result, the gas was flared, or burned off. Pictures of southeastern Texas in the early twentieth century show thousands of wooden drilling rigs, each topped with a plume of flaming gas. Even today, flaring sites are sometimes the brightest spots in nighttime satellite images, outshining even the largest urban areas.

Eventually, researchers found ways to use natural gas for lighting, cooking, and heat. In 1925 the first natural gas pipeline, more than 200 miles (322 km) long, was built from Louisiana to Texas. U.S. demand grew rapidly, especially after World War II (1939–1945). By the 1950s

natural gas was providing a quarter of the nation's energy needs. At the beginning of the twenty-first century natural gas was second only to coal in the share of U.S. energy produced. (See Table 1.1 in Chapter 1.) Crude oil was third. A vast pipeline transmission system now connects production facilities in the United States, Canada, and Mexico with natural gas distributors.

Figure 3.1 shows the overview of production and consumption of natural gas for 2007. Notice how imports make up only a small share of the natural gas that is consumed in the United States. The industrial sector consumed the largest amount of natural gas resources in 2007, and the transportation sector consumed the least amount.

Figure 3.2 shows the pattern of natural gas supply and distribution in the United States in 2006. Not all the gas withdrawn from gas and oil wells ends up as dry gas that can be immediately used; about 20% is lost during extraction and processing. Some natural gas is imported, primarily from Canada, a small amount is exported, and some is stored. Natural gas that is produced in this country, imported, and withdrawn from storage is then used immediately as fuel primarily in the residential, commercial, industrial, and electric power sectors. A small amount is used by the gas industry itself and in transportation.

THE PRODUCTION OF NATURAL GAS

As mentioned previously, natural gas is produced from gas and oil wells; there is little delay between production and consumption, except for gas that is placed in storage. Therefore, changes in demand are almost immediately reflected by changes in wellhead flows, or supply.

The Energy Information Administration (EIA) reports in *Annual Energy Review 2007* (June 2008, http://www.eia.doe.gov/aer/pdf/aer.pdf) that from 1970 through 1973 the total U.S. natural gas production peaked at around 21 trillion cubic feet (Tcf; 594.6 billion cubic m

FIGURE 3.1

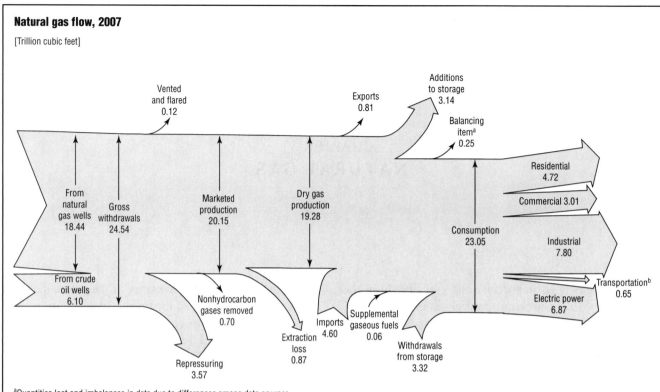

Natural gas flow, 2007

[Trillion cubic feet]

Vented and flared 0.12

Exports 0.81

Additions to storage 3.14

Balancing item[a] 0.25

From natural gas wells 18.44

Gross withdrawals 24.54

Marketed production 20.15

Dry gas production 19.28

Consumption 23.05

Residential 4.72

Commercial 3.01

Industrial 7.80

Transportation[b] 0.65

Electric power 6.87

From crude oil wells 6.10

Nonhydrocarbon gases removed 0.70

Repressuring 3.57

Extraction loss 0.87

Imports 4.60

Supplemental gaseous fuels 0.06

Withdrawals from storage 3.32

[a]Quantities lost and imbalances in data due to differences among data sources.
[b]Natural gas consumed in the operation of pipelines (primarily in compressors), and as fuel in the delivery of natural gas to consumers; plus a small quantity used as vehicle fuel.
Nores: Data are preliminary. Values are derived from source data prior to rounding for publication. Totals may not equal sum of components due to independent rounding.

SOURCE: "Diagram 3. Natural Gas Flow, 2007 (Trillion Cubic Feet)." in *Annual Energy Review 2007*, U.S. Department of Energy, Energy Information Administration, Office of Energy Markets and End Use, June 2008, http://www.eia.doe.gov/aer/pdf/aer.pdf (accessed June 28, 2008)

[bcm]). By 2007 it had dropped to 19.3 Tcf (538 bcm). (See Figure 3.3.). The EIA notes that Texas, Louisiana, and Oklahoma accounted for 38% of the natural gas produced in the United States in 2007. Even though production is increasing because of demand and rising prices, it continues to be outpaced by consumption. Imported gas makes up the difference between supply and demand.

Natural Gas Wells

In 2007 there were 427,000 gas wells in operation in the United States. (See Figure 3.4.) Even though the number of producing wells increased steadily after 1960 and more sharply after the mid-1970s, the number of gas wells in operation fluctuates from year to year because new wells are opened and old wells are closed. Weather and economic conditions also affect well operations.

The average productivity of natural gas wells peaked in 1971, then dropped throughout most of the 1970s and the mid-1980s. It has remained at a relatively steady low level since then. At the peak of productivity in 1971, U.S. natural gas wells averaged 435,000 cubic feet of natural gas per day per well. (See Figure 3.5.) In 2007 they averaged 118,000 cubic feet per day per well.

Offshore Production

Most offshore natural gas wells are located in the Gulf of Mexico and off the coast of California. Offshore wells accounted for about 3.5 Tcf (99.1 bcm) of the estimated 24.5 Tcf (693.8 bcm) of gross withdrawals of natural gas in 2007, or about 14% of the total U.S. production. (See Figure 3.6.) This percentage does not include wells off the shores of states, but includes only federal (Outer Continental Shelf) offshore wells.

Most offshore drilling occurs on the Outer Continental Shelf, in waters up to 600 feet (183 m) deep. Figure 3.7 is a diagram of a continental margin. The continental shelf varies from one coastal area to another: the shelf is relatively narrow along the Pacific coast, wide along much of the Atlantic coast and the Gulf of Alaska, and widest in the Gulf of Mexico.

The development of offshore oil and gas resources began with the drilling of the Summerland oil field along the coast of California in 1896, where about four hundred wells were drilled. Since then the industry has continually improved drilling technology. In the twenty-first century, deepwater petroleum and natural gas exploration occurs from platforms and drill ships, and shallow-water exploration occurs from gravel islands and mobile units.

FIGURE 3.2

Natural gas supply and disposition in the United States, 2006

[Trillion cubic feet]

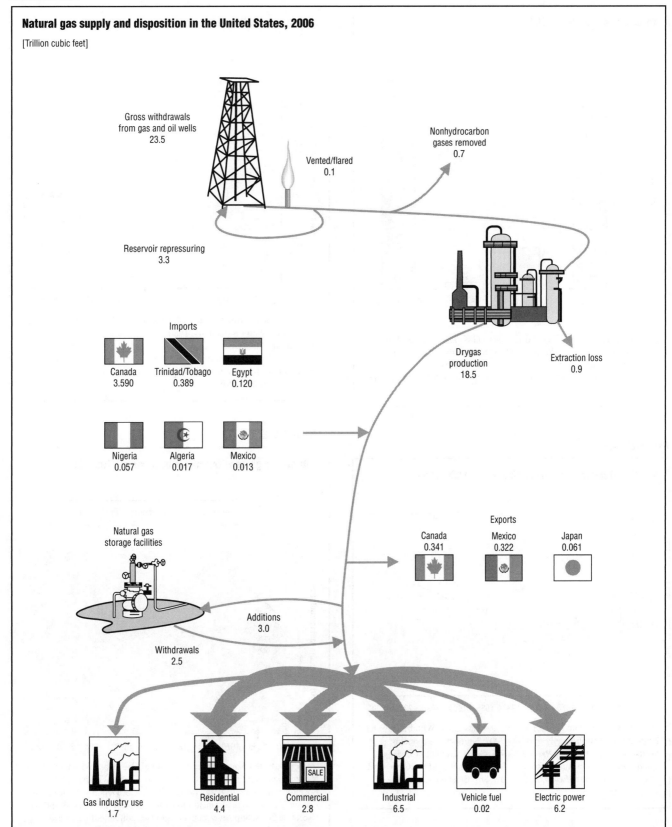

SOURCE: "Figure 2. Natural Gas Supply and Disposition in the United States, 2006," in *Natural Gas Annual 2006*, U.S. Department of Energy, Energy Information Administration, Office of Oil and Gas, October 2007, http://www.eia.doe.gov/pub/oil_gas/natural_gas/data_publications/natural_gas_annual/current/pdf/nga06.pdf (accessed July 2, 2008)

FIGURE 3.3

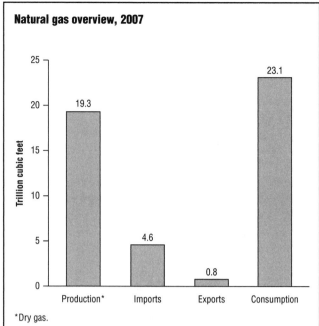

Natural gas overview, 2007

SOURCE: Adapted from "Figure 6.1. Natural Gas Overview: Overview, 2007," in *Annual Energy Review 2007*, U.S. Department of Energy, Energy Information Administration, Office of Energy Markets and End Use, June 2008, http://www.eia.doe.gov/aer/pdf/aer.pdf (accessed June 28, 2008)

FIGURE 3.4

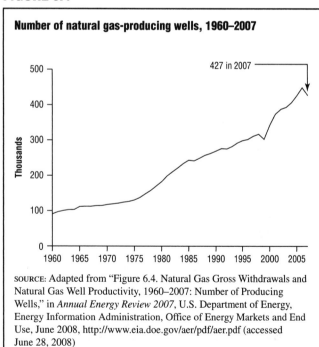

Number of natural gas-producing wells, 1960–2007

SOURCE: Adapted from "Figure 6.4. Natural Gas Gross Withdrawals and Natural Gas Well Productivity, 1960–2007: Number of Producing Wells," in *Annual Energy Review 2007*, U.S. Department of Energy, Energy Information Administration, Office of Energy Markets and End Use, June 2008, http://www.eia.doe.gov/aer/pdf/aer.pdf (accessed June 28, 2008)

FIGURE 3.5

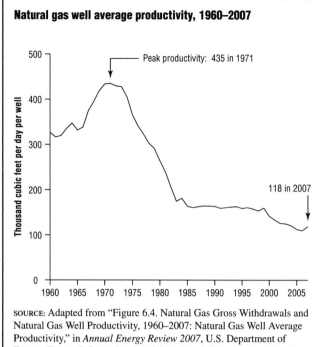

Natural gas well average productivity, 1960–2007

SOURCE: Adapted from "Figure 6.4. Natural Gas Gross Withdrawals and Natural Gas Well Productivity, 1960–2007: Natural Gas Well Average Productivity," in *Annual Energy Review 2007*, U.S. Department of Energy, Energy Information Administration, Office of Energy Markets and End Use, June 2008, http://www.eia.doe.gov/aer/pdf/aer.pdf (accessed June 28, 2008)

FIGURE 3.6

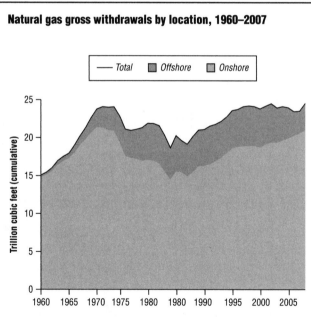

Natural gas gross withdrawals by location, 1960–2007

SOURCE: Adapted from "Figure 6.4. Natural Gas Gross Withdrawals and Natural Gas Well Productivity, 1960–2007: Gross Withdrawals by Location," in *Annual Energy Review 2007*, U.S. Department of Energy, Energy Information Administration, Office of Energy Markets and End Use, June 2008, http://www.eia.doe.gov/aer/pdf/aer.pdf (accessed June 28, 2008)

Even though most natural gas is transported by pipelines, rather than by tanker ships, accidents such as the 1989 *Exxon Valdez* oil spill in Alaska and the 2002 *Prestige* oil spill off the coast of Spain have focused attention on all types of offshore drilling and tanker transport. Even before the *Exxon Valdez* oil spill, environmentalists were calling for the curtailment of offshore drilling for both oil and gas. The spills from refining and storage facilities triggered by Hurricane Katrina in 2005 raised additional concerns. (See Chapter 2.)

Natural Gas Reserves

Reserves are estimated volumes of gas in known deposits that are believed to be recoverable in the future. Proved reserves are those gas volumes that geological and engineering data show with reasonable certainty to be recoverable. Proved reserves of natural gas amounted to 211.1 Tcf (5.9 trillion cubic m [Tcm]) in 2006. (See Table 3.1.)

Natural gas reserves in North America are generally more abundant than crude oil reserves. In *U.S. Crude Oil, Natural Gas, and Natural Gas Liquids Reserves: 2006 Annual Report* (November 2007, http://www.eia.doe.gov/pub/oil_gas/natural_gas/data_publications/crude_oil_natural_gas_reserves/current/pdf/arr.pdf), the EIA indicates that in 2006 Texas had the largest percentage of the U.S. dry natural gas proved reserves at 61.8 Tcf (1.7 Tcm), which represented 29% of the U.S. natural gas reserves. Wyoming had 23.5 Tcf (11%; 665.4 bcm) and New Mexico, Oklahoma, and Colorado each had over 17 Tcf (481.4 bcm), representing 8% of the proved natural gas reserves for each of these states.

According to the EIA, the North Slope fields of Alaska were estimated to contain reserves amounting to 10.2 Tcf in 2006, or 5% of the U.S. natural gas reserves. As of September 2008, there was still no easy way to transport those reserves to the lower forty-eight states, but progress was being made. The Federal Energy Regulatory Commission explains in *Fifth Report to Congress on Progress Made in Licensing and Constructing the Alaska Natural Gas Pipeline* (February 2008, http://www.ferc.gov/legal/staff-reports/angta-fifth.pdf) that in May 2007 the Alaska legislature passed the Alaska Gasline Inducement Act (AGIA), which allowed the state to choose an

FIGURE 3.7

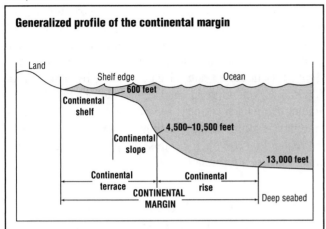

Generalized profile of the continental margin

Note: Depths and gradients are approximate.

SOURCE: George Dellagiarino and Keith Meekins, "Figure 1. Profile of the Continental Margin," in *The Resource Evaluation Program: Structure and Mission on the Outer Continental Shelf*, U.S. Department of the Interior, Minerals Management Service, Resource Evaluation Division, 1998, http://www.mms.gov/itd/pubs/1998/98-0028.pdf (accessed July 2, 2008)

TABLE 3.1

Crude oil and natural gas cumulative production, proved reserves, and proved ultimate recovery, selected years 1977–2006

Year	Crude oil and lease condensate*			Natural gas (dry)		
	Cumulative production	Proved reserves	Proved ultimate recovery	Cumulative production	Proved reserves	Proved ultimate recovery
	Billion barrels			Trillion cubic feet		
1977	118.1	31.8	149.9	514.4	207.4	721.9
1978	121.3	31.4	152.6	533.6	208.0	741.6
1980	127.5	31.3	158.9	572.6	199.0	771.6
1982	133.8	29.5	163.3	609.6	201.5	811.1
1984	140.2	30.0	170.2	643.2	197.5	840.7
1986	146.7	28.3	175.0	675.7	191.6	867.3
1988	152.7	28.2	180.9	709.4	168.0	877.4
1990	158.2	27.6	185.7	744.5	169.3	913.9
1992	163.5	25.0	188.5	780.1	165.0	945.1
1994	168.4	23.6	192.0	817.0	163.8	980.8
1996	173.2	23.3	196.5	854.5	166.5	1,020.9
1998	177.8	22.4	200.2	892.4	164.0	1,056.4
2000	182.1	23.5	205.6	930.4	177.4	1,107.8
2002	186.3	24.0	210.4	968.9	186.9	1,155.9
2003	188.4	23.1	211.5	988.0	189.0	1,177.1
2004	190.4	22.6	213.0	1,006.6	192.5	1,199.1
2005	192.3	23.0	215.3	1,024.6	204.4	1,229.0
2006	194.1	22.1	216.3	1,043.1	211.1	1,254.2

*Lease condensate is the portion of natural gas liquids that is separated from the wellhead gas stream at a lease or field separation facility.
Note: Data are at end of year.
Web Pages: See http://www.eia.doe.gov/oil_gas/petroleum/info_glance/petroleum.html and http://www.eia.doe.gov/oil_gas/natural_gas/info_glance/natural_gas.html for related information.

SOURCE: Adapted from "Table 4.2. Crude Oil and Natural Gas Cumulative Production, Proved Reserves, and Proved Ultimate Recovery, 1977–2006," in *Annual Energy Review 2007*, U.S. Department of Energy, Energy Information Administration, Office of Energy Markets and End Use, June 2008, http://www.eia.doe.gov/aer/pdf/aer.pdf (accessed June 28, 2008)

FIGURE 3.8

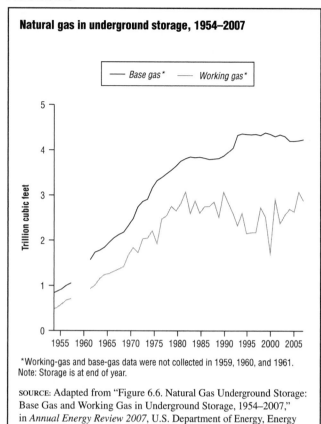

Natural gas in underground storage, 1954–2007

*Working-gas and base-gas data were not collected in 1959, 1960, and 1961.
Note: Storage is at end of year.

SOURCE: Adapted from "Figure 6.6. Natural Gas Underground Storage: Base Gas and Working Gas in Underground Storage, 1954–2007," in *Annual Energy Review 2007*, U.S. Department of Energy, Energy Information Administration, Office of Energy Markets and End Use, June 2008, http://www.eia.doe.gov/aer/pdf/aer.pdf (accessed June 28, 2008)

applicant to proceed with a federal application to construct an Alaskan natural gas pipeline. In July 2008 Alaska had chosen an applicant, and in August 2008 the Alaska legislature authorized the awarding of the AGIA license to TransCanada Alaska.

Underground Storage

Because of seasonal, daily, and even hourly changes in demand, substantial natural gas storage facilities have been created. Many are depleted gas reservoirs located near transmission lines and marketing areas. Gas is injected into storage when market needs are lower than the available gas flow, and gas is withdrawn from storage when supplies from producing fields and the capacity of transmission lines are not adequate to meet peak demands. At the end of 2007 gas in underground storage totaled approximately 7.1 Tcf (198.2 bcm). This natural gas consisted of base gas (permanently stored gas needed to maintain the proper pressure in the storage area) plus working gas (gas that can be released from storage and used). (See Figure 3.8.)

TRANSMISSION OF NATURAL GAS

A vast network of natural gas pipelines crisscrosses the United States. The natural gas in this 250,000-mile (402,000-km) system generally flows northeastward, primarily from Texas and Louisiana, the two major gas-producing states, and from Oklahoma and New Mexico. (See Figure 3.9.) It also flows west to California.

Imports of natural gas enter the United States via pipeline from Canada into Idaho, Maine, Michigan, Montana, New Hampshire, New York, North Dakota, Washington, and Vermont. Natural gas also enters via pipeline into Texas from Mexico. According to the EIA, in *Natural Gas Annual 2006* (October 2007, http://www.eia.doe.gov/pub/oil_gas/natural_gas/data_publications/natural_gas_annual/current/pdf/nga06.pdf), 86% of imported natural gas arrived in the United States by pipeline in 2006. The remainder was shipped as liquefied natural gas, arriving by tanker from Algeria, Egypt, Nigeria, and Trinidad/Tobago. (For the amount from each country, see Figure 3.2.) Liquefied natural gas is produced by cooling natural gas to −260° Fahrenheit (−162° C); at this temperature natural gas changes from a gas to a liquid.

DOMESTIC NATURAL GAS CONSUMPTION

Natural gas fulfills an important part of the country's energy needs. It is an attractive fuel not only because its price is relatively low but also because it burns cleanly and efficiently, which helps the country meet its environmental goals.

Nationally, natural gas consumption rose from 1949 through 1972, then generally declined through 1986. Since 1986 natural gas consumption has been rising, hitting an all-time high of 23.3 Tcf (651.3 bcm) in 2000. (See Table 3.2.) From 2000 through 2007, prices have fluctuated slightly but remained somewhat stable.

In 2007, 7.8 Tcf (34% of the natural gas consumed; 226.5 bcm) was used by industry; 6.9 Tcf (30%; 198.2 bcm) was used by electric utilities; 4.9 Tcf (20%; 141.6 bcm) was used by residences; 3 Tcf (13%; 85 bcm) was used by commercial customers; and 0.7 Tcf (3%; 21.2 bcm) was used to transport the gas through pipelines, deliver gas to consumers, and fuel vehicles. (See Figure 3.1 and Table 3.2.)

Residential energy consumption depends heavily on weather-related heating demands and the number and types of uses of this energy source. According to the U.S. Census Bureau (June 3, 2008, http://www.census.gov/prod/2007pubs/08abstract/construct.pdf), about 52% of all residential energy consumers in the United States used gas to heat their homes in 2005. Residential consumption is also affected by conservation practices and the efficiency of gas appliances such as water heaters, stoves, and gas clothes dryers. In *Natural Gas Annual 2006*, the EIA lists Texas, California, Louisiana, and New York, respectively, as having been the largest residential users of natural gas by volume in 2006. According to the Census Bureau (December 22, 2006, http://www.census.gov/compendia/statab/tables/08s0013.pdf), California, Texas, and New York were the top three most populous states, in that

FIGURE 3.9

Principal interstate natural gas flow summary, 2006

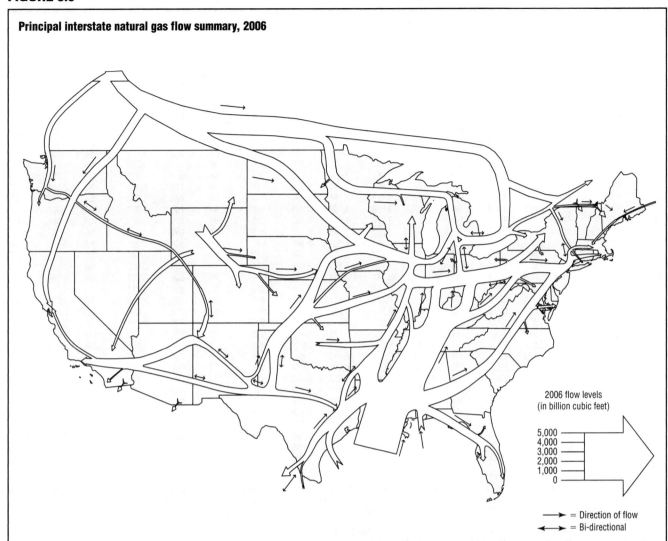

2006 flow levels
(in billion cubic feet)

5,000
4,000
3,000
2,000
1,000
0

→ = Direction of flow
↔ = Bi-directional

SOURCE: "Figure 12. Principal Interstate Natural Gas Flow Summary, 2006," in *Natural Gas Annual 2006*, U.S. Department of Energy, Energy Information Administration, Office of Oil and Gas, October 2007, http://www.eia.doe.gov/pub/oil_gas/natural_gas/data_publications/natural_gas_annual/current/pdf/nga06.pdf (accessed July 2, 2008)

order, as of July 1, 2006, which would help explain their high volume of natural gas consumption. Louisiana was the twenty-fifth most populous state at that time.

In 2007 the commercial sector used 3 Tcf (85 bcm)of natural gas. (See Table 3.2.) Its use, as with residential consumption, depends heavily on seasonal requirements and on the number of users and conservation measures they have taken.

The industrial sector has historically been the largest consumer of natural gas. Consumption in this sector was 7.8 Tcf (226.5 bcm) in 2007, up slightly from 7.6 Tcf (170 bcm) in 2006, but below the high of 10.2 Tcf (283.2 bcm) used in 1973. (See Table 3.2.) After 1973 natural gas consumption in the industrial sector declined quite steadily through 1986, increased through 1997, and then generally declined through 2007. Industrial use grew

from 1986 through 1997 because natural gas was substituted for petroleum for some purposes.

NATURAL GAS PRICES

Natural gas prices can vary across the nation because federal and state rate structures differ. Region also plays a role. For example, prices are lower in major natural gas–producing areas where transmission costs are lower.

From the mid-twentieth century through the early 1970s natural gas prices were relatively stable. (See Figure 3.10.) Then governmental deregulation of the industry and the restructuring of companies brought about a period of sharply rising prices, with wellhead prices (the value of natural gas at the mouth of the well) reaching a high in 1983, generally declining through 1995, and then generally increasing through 2005. Prices fell in 2006 and

TABLE 3.2

Natural gas consumption by sector, selected years 1949–2007

[Billion cubic feet]

Year	Residential sector	Commercial sector			Industrial sector					Transportation sector			Electric power sector[a]			Total
		CHP[b]	Other[c]	Total	Lease and plant fuel	Other industrial			Total	Pipelines and distribution[g]	Vehicle fuel[h]	Total	Electricity only	CHP	Total	
						CHP[d]	Non-CHP[e]	Total								
1949	993	(j)	348	348	835	(i)	2,245	2,245	3,081	NA	NA	NA	550	NA	550	4,971
1950	1,198	(i)	388	388	928	(i)	2,498	2,498	3,426	126	NA	126	629	NA	629	5,767
1955	2,124	(i)	629	629	1,131	(i)	3,411	3,411	4,542	245	NA	245	1,153	NA	1,153	8,694
1960	3,103	(i)	1,020	1,020	1,237	(i)	4,535	4,535	5,771	347	NA	347	1,725	NA	1,725	11,967
1965	3,903	(i)	1,444	1,444	1,156	(i)	5,955	5,955	7,112	501	NA	501	2,321	NA	2,321	15,280
1970	4,837	(i)	2,399	2,399	1,399	(i)	7,851	7,851	9,249	722	NA	722	3,932	NA	3,932	21,139
1971	4,972	(i)	2,509	2,509	1,414	(i)	8,181	8,181	9,594	743	NA	743	3,976	NA	3,976	21,793
1972	5,126	(i)	2,608	2,608	1,456	(i)	8,169	8,169	9,624	766	NA	766	3,977	NA	3,977	22,101
1973	4,879	(i)	2,597	2,597	1,496	(i)	8,689	8,689	10,185	728	NA	728	3,660	NA	3,660	22,049
1974	4,786	(i)	2,556	2,556	1,477	(i)	8,292	8,292	9,769	669	NA	669	3,443	NA	3,443	21,223
1976	5,051	(i)	2,668	2,668	1,634	(i)	6,964	6,964	8,598	548	NA	548	3,081	NA	3,081	19,946
1978	4,903	(i)	2,601	2,601	1,648	(i)	6,757	6,757	8,405	530	NA	530	3,188	NA	3,188	19,627
1980	4,752	(i)	2,611	2,611	1,026	(i)	7,172	7,172	8,198	635	NA	635	3,682	NA	3,682	19,877
1982	4,633	(i)	2,606	2,606	1,109	(i)	5,831	5,831	6,941	596	NA	596	3,226	NA	3,226	18,001
1984	4,555	(i)	2,524	2,524	1,077	(i)	6,154	6,154	7,231	529	NA	529	3,111	NA	3,111	17,951
1986	4,314	(i)	2,318	2,318	923	(i)	5,579	5,579	6,502	485	NA	485	2,602	NA	2,602	16,221
1988	4,630	(i)	2,670	2,670	1,096	(i)	6,383	6,383	7,479	614	NA	614	2,636	NA	2,636	18,030
1990	4,391	46	2,576	2,623	1,236	1,055	k5,963	k7,018	8,255	660	(s)	660	k2,794	k451	k3,245	k19,174
1992	4,690	62	2,740	2,803	1,171	1,107	k6,420	k7,527	8,698	588	2	590	k2,829	k619	k3,448	k20,228
1994	4,848	72	2,823	2,895	1,124	1,176	6,613	7,790	8,913	685	3	689	3,065	838	3,903	21,247
1996	5,241	82	3,076	3,158	1,250	1,289	7,146	8,435	9,685	711	6	718	2,824	983	3,807	22,609
1997	4,984	87	3,128	3,215	1,203	1,282	7,229	8,511	9,714	751	8	760	3,039	1,026	4,065	22,737
1998	4,520	87	2,912	2,999	1,173	1,355	6,965	8,320	9,493	635	9	645	3,544	1,044	4,588	22,246
2000	4,996	85	3,098	3,182	1,151	1,386	6,757	8,142	9,293	642	13	655	4,093	1,114	5,206	23,333
2002	4,889	74	3,070	3,144	1,113	1,240	6,267	7,507	8,620	667	15	682	4,258	1,413	5,672	23,007
2003	5,079	58	3,121	3,179	1,122	1,144	6,007	7,150	8,273	591	18	610	3,780	1,355	5,135	22,277
2004	4,869	72	3,057	3,129	1,098	1,191	6,052	7,243	8,341	566	21	587	4,142	1,322	5,464	22,389
2005	R4,827	75	R2,924	R2,999	1,112	1,084	R5,514	R6,597	R7,709	R584	R23	607	4,592	1,277	5,869	R22,011
2006	R4,368	R82	P2,753	P2,835	R1,124	R1,115	R5,380	R6,495	R7,618	R584	R25	R609	R5,091	R1,131	R6,222	R21,653
2007P	4,724	83	2,924	3,008	1,168	1,202	5,430	6,632	7,800	622	26	649	5,607	1,267	6,874	23,055

[a]Electricity-only and combined-heat-and-power (CHP) plants within the NAICS (North American Industry Classification System) 22 category whose primary business is to sell electricity, or electricity and heat, to the public. Through 1988, data are for electric utilities only; beginning in 1989, data are for electric utilities and independent power producers. Electric utility CHP plants are included in "electricity only."
[b]Commercial combined-heat-and-power (CHP) and a small number of commercial electricity-only plants.
[c]All commercial sector fuel use other than that in "commercial CHP."
[d]Industrial combined-heat-and-power (CHP) and a small number of industrial electricity-only plants.
[e]All industrial sector fuel other than that in "I ease and plant fuel" and "industrial CHP."
[f]Natural gas consumed in the operation of pipelines, primarily in compressors.
[g]Natural gas used as fuel in the delivery of natural gas to consumers.
[h]Vehicle fuel data do not reflect revised data shown.
[i]Included in "commercial other."
[j]Included in "industrial non-CHP."
[k]For 1989–1992, a small amount of consumption at independent power producers may be counted in both "other industrial" and "electric power sector."
R = Revised.
P = Preliminary.
NA = Not available.
(s) = Less than 0.5 billion cubic feet.
Notes: Data are for natural gas, plus a small amount of supplemental gaseous fuels. Beginning with 1965, all volumes are shown on a pressure base of 14.73 p.s.i.a. at 60°F. For prior years, the pressure base was 14.65 p.s.i.a. at 60°F. Totals may not equal sum of components due to independent rounding.

SOURCE: Adapted from "Table 6.5. Natural Gas Consumption by Sector, Selected Years, 1949–2007 (Billion Cubic Feet)," in *Annual Energy Review 2007*, U.S. Department of Energy, Energy Information Administration, Office of Energy Markets and End Use, June 2008, http://www.eia.doe.gov/aer/pdf/aer.pdf (accessed June 28, 2008)

2007. According to the EIA, in *Annual Energy Review 2007*, the average price of natural gas at the wellhead was $5.34 in real dollars (i.e., adjusted for inflation) per 1,000 cubic feet in 2007, sharply up from $2.83 in 2002.

At the retail price level (in real dollars), residential customers paid $10.87 per 1,000 cubic feet of natural gas in 2007, compared to $7.57 in 2002. (See Table 3.3.) Commercial consumers paid $9.45 per 1,000 cubic feet in

2007, and industrial consumers paid $6.36 per 1,000 cubic feet that year.

Much of the variation in natural gas prices through the years can be attributed to changes in the natural gas industry. The passage of the Natural Gas Policy Act of 1978 allowed prices at the wellhead to rise sharply. (See Figure 3.10.) On January 1, 1985, prices for new gas (that which was produced from new formations and fields or

FIGURE 3.10

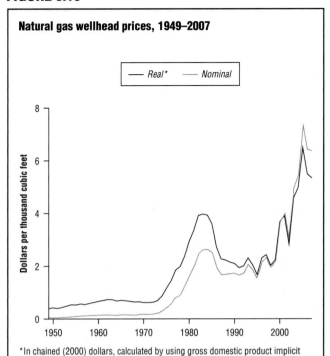

Natural gas wellhead prices, 1949–2007

— Real* — Nominal

*In chained (2000) dollars, calculated by using gross domestic product implicit price deflators.

SOURCE: Adapted from "Figure 6.7. Natural Gas Wellhead, City Gate, and Imports Prices: Wellhead, 1949–2007," in *Annual Energy Review 2007*, U.S. Department of Energy, Energy Information Administration, Office of Energy Markets and End Use, June 2008, http://www.eia.doe.gov/aer/pdf/aer.pdf (accessed June 28, 2008)

drilling after April 1977) were deregulated, and additional volumes of onshore production were deregulated on July 1, 1987. In 1988 President Ronald Reagan (1911–2004) signed legislation removing all remaining wellhead price controls by 1993.

The 1978 law not only allowed prices to go up but it also opened the market to the forces of supply and demand. Now that prices are deregulated and the industry is no longer constrained by federal controls, the natural gas industry has become more sensitive to market signals and responds more quickly to changes in economic conditions.

NATURAL GAS IMPORTS AND EXPORTS

U.S. natural gas trading was limited to the neighboring countries of Mexico and Canada until shipment of natural gas in liquefied form became a feasible alternative to pipelines. In 1969 the first shipments of liquefied natural gas were sent from Alaska to Japan, and U.S. imports of liquefied natural gas from Algeria began the following year.

The EIA states in *Annual Energy Review 2007* that in 2007 U.S. net imports of natural gas (total imports minus total exports) by all routes totaled 3.8 Tcf (113.2 bcm), or 16.5% of domestic consumption. Natural gas imports have been increasing significantly since 1986. Historically, Canada has been by far the major supplier of U.S.

natural gas imports, accounting for 82% of the natural gas imported in 2007. (See Figure 3.11.)

The EIA notes that the United States exported 809 billion cubic feet of natural gas in 2007. (See Figure 3.11.) Canada bought the largest amount (472 billion cubic feet), followed by Mexico (288 billion cubic feet), and Japan (47 billion cubic feet).

INTERNATIONAL NATURAL GAS USAGE
World Production

The world production of dry natural gas totaled 104.7 Tcf (2.9 Tcm) in 2006. (See Table 3.4.) Russia and the United States were the two top producers of this energy source. Russia accounted for 23.2 Tcf (651.3), or 22% of the world production, and the United States produced 18.5 Tcf (538 bcm), or 18% of the world production.

World Consumption

In *Annual Energy Review 2007*, the EIA shows that the world consumption of natural gas has increased steadily over the past several decades, from 52.9 Tcf (1.5 Tcm) in 1980 to 105.4 Tcf (2.9 Tcm) in 2006. The United States consumed the largest amount of natural gas in 2006, followed by Russia. (See Figure 3.12.) Combined, they accounted for 36% of world consumption in 2006.

FUTURE TRENDS IN THE GAS INDUSTRY

The EIA predicts in *Annual Energy Outlook 2008* (June 2008, http://www.eia.doe.gov/oiaf/aeo/pdf/0383(2008).pdf) that from 2006 to 2030 the total U.S. natural gas production will grow modestly. Consumption will increase through 2016 and then decrease through 2030, but its share of total energy consumption during these years will fall from 22% in 2006 to 20% in 2030. The importation of liquid natural gas from overseas will increase from 2006 to 2030, but imports of natural gas from Canada are expected to decline during this period. Natural gas prices for residential customers are projected to increase after 2016.

Domestic Production

According to the EIA, in *Annual Energy Outlook 2008*, total domestic natural gas production is projected to increase somewhat from 2006 (18.5 Tcf; 523.8 bcm) through 2030 (19.4 Tcf; 538 bcm), primarily from two sources: unconventional resources in the lower forty-eight states and Alaska, if a natural gas pipeline becomes operational in 2020. Other sources are expected to decline. Figure 3.13 shows projected figures for these different types of natural gas production. Unconventional sources are those from which it is more difficult and less economically sound to extract natural gas, because the technology to reach it has not been developed fully or is too expensive.

TABLE 3.3

Natural gas prices by sector, selected years 1967–2007

[Dollars per thousand cubic feet]

	Residential sector			Commercial sector[a]			Industrial sector[b]			Transportation sector		Electric power sector[c]		
	Prices		Percentage of sector[f]	Prices		Percentage of sector[f]	Prices		Percentage of sector[f]	Vehicle fuel[d] prices		Prices		Percentage of sector[f]
Year	Nominal	Real[e]		Nominal	Real[e]		Nominal	Real[e]		Nominal	Real[e]	Nominal	Real[e]	
1967	1.04	4.35	NA	0.74	3.10	NA	0.34	1.42	NA	NA	NA	0.28	1.17	NA
1968	1.04	4.17	NA	.73	2.93	NA	.34	1.36	NA	NA	NA	.22	.88	NA
1970	1.09	3.96	NA	.77	2.80	NA	.37	1.34	NA	NA	NA	.29	1.05	NA
1972	1.21	4.01	NA	.88	2.92	NA	.45	1.49	NA	NA	NA	.34	1.13	NA
1974	1.43	4.12	NA	1.07	3.08	NA	.67	1.93	NA	NA	NA	.51	1.47	92.7
1976	1.98	4.93	NA	1.64	4.08	NA	1.24	3.08	NA	NA	NA	1.06	2.64	96.2
1978	2.56	5.59	NA	2.23	4.87	NA	1.70	3.72	NA	NA	NA	1.48	3.23	98.0
1980	3.68	6.81	NA	3.39	6.27	NA	2.56	4.74	NA	NA	NA	2.27	4.20	96.9
1982	5.17	8.24	NA	4.82	7.68	NA	3.87	6.17	85.1	NA	NA	3.48	5.55	92.6
1984	6.12	9.05	NA	5.55	8.20	NA	4.22	6.24	74.7	NA	NA	3.70	5.47	94.4
1986	5.83	8.18	NA	5.08	7.13	NA	3.23	4.53	59.8	NA	NA	2.43	3.41	91.7
1988	5.47	7.23	NA	4.63	6.12	90.7	2.95	3.90	42.6	NA	NA	2.33	3.08	89.6
1990	5.80	7.11	99.2	4.83	5.92	86.6	2.93	3.59	35.2	3.39	4.15	2.38	2.92	76.8
1992	5.89	6.82	99.1	4.88	5.65	83.2	2.84	3.29	30.3	4.05	4.69	2.36	2.73	76.5
1994	6.41	7.10	99.1	5.44	6.03	79.3	3.05	3.38	25.5	4.11	4.55	2.28	2.53	73.4
1996	6.34	6.76	99.0	5.40	5.75	77.6	3.42	3.64	19.4	4.34	4.62	2.69	2.87	68.4
1998	6.82	7.07	97.7	5.48	5.68	67.0	3.14	3.25	16.1	4.59	4.76	2.40	2.49	63.7
2000	7.76	7.76	92.6	6.59	6.59	63.9	4.45	4.45	19.8	5.54	5.54	4.38	4.38	50.5
2001	9.63	9.40	92.4	8.43	8.23	66.0	5.24	5.12	20.8	6.60	6.45	4.61	4.50	40.2
2002	7.89	7.57	97.9	6.63	6.36	77.4	4.02	3.86	22.7	5.10	4.90	c3.68	c3.53	c83.9
2003	9.63	9.05	97.5	8.40	7.89	78.2	5.89	5.54	22.1	6.19	5.82	5.57	5.23	91.2
2004	10.75	9.82	97.7	9.43	R8.61	78.0	6.53	5.97	23.7	7.16	6.54	6.11	5.58	89.8
2005	R12.70	R11.24	98.2	R11.34	R10.04	R82.1	8.56	R7.58	R24.1	R9.14	R8.09	R8.47	R7.50	R91.3
2006	R13.75	R11.80	R98.1	R11.99	R10.29	R80.7	R7.86	R6.74	R23.5	R8.78	R7.53	R7.11	R6.10	R93.4
2007	P13.01	P10.87	E98.0	P11.31	P9.45	P79.1	P7.60	P6.35	P22.2	NA	NA	P7.31	P6.11	P93.2

[a]Commercial sector, including commercial combined-heat-and-power (CHP) and commercial electricity-only plants.
[b]Industrial sector, including industrial combined-heat-and-power (CHP) and industrial electricity-only plants.
[c]Electricity-only and combined-heat-and-power (CHP) plants within the NAICS 22 category whose primary business is to sell electricity, or electricity and heat, to the public. Through 2001, data are for electric utilities only; beginning in 2002, data are for electric utilities and independent power producers.
[d]Much of the natural gas delivered for vehicle fuel represents deliveries to fueling stations that are used primarily or exclusively by fleet vehicles. Thus, the prices are often those associated with the cost of gas in the operation of fleet vehicles.
[e]In chained (2000) dollars, calculated by using gross domestic product implicit price deflators.
[f]The percentage of the sector's consumption for which price data are available.
R = Revised.
P = Preliminary.
E = Estimate.
NA = Not available.
Notes: Prices are for natural gas, plus a small amount of supplemental gaseous fuels. The average for each end-use sector is calculated by dividing the total value of the natural gas consumed by each sector by the total quantity consumed. Prices are intended to include all taxes.
Web Page: See http://www.eia.doe.gov/oil_gas/natural_gas/info_glance/natural_gas.html for related information.

SOURCE: Adapted from "Table 6.8. Natural Gas Prices by Sector, 1967–2007 (Dollars per Thousand Cubic Feet)," in *Annual Energy Review 2007*, U.S. Department of Energy, Energy Information Administration, Office of Energy Markets and End Use, June 2008, http://www.eia.doe.gov/aer/pdf/aer.pdf (accessed June 28, 2008)

Domestic Consumption

In *Annual Energy Outlook 2008*, the EIA projects that consumption of natural gas will increase from 21.7 Tcf (623 bcm) in 2006 to a peak of 23.8 Tcf (679.6 bcm) in 2016. At that time the price of natural gas is projected to rise, and consumption is expected to decline to 22.7 Tcf (651.3 bcm) in 2030. Demand for natural gas by industrial consumers is expected to grow slowly because of high prices from 7.6 Tcf (212.4 bcm) in 2006 to 8.1 Tcf (226.5 bcm) in 2030. High prices will also limit growth in the residential and commercial sectors, where natural gas use will grow from a combined 7.2 Tcf (198.2 bcm) in 2006 to 8.8 Tcf (254.9 bcm) in 2030. (See Figure 3.14.) High prices will result in a projected decrease in the use of natural gas for electricity generation.

Imports and Exports

Net imports of natural gas are projected to increase to meet demand from 2006 to 2030. Most of these imports will come from overseas in the form of liquefied natural gas. (See Figure 3.15.) A decline in Canada's non-Arctic conventional natural gas production will be only partially offset by its Arctic and unconventional production. This estimation is based on projections that the Canada natural gas pipeline will not be built by 2020 due to reportedly high costs for its construction, along with the development costs for three natural gas fields that would supply the gas. Natural gas exports to Mexico peaked in 2004 (shown as a negative import value in Figure 3.15) and then declined for a period as Mexico developed its own natural gas infrastructure. However, exports to Mexico are expected to increase again fairly steadily beginning in about 2012.

FIGURE 3.11

Natural gas trade overview, 1949–2007

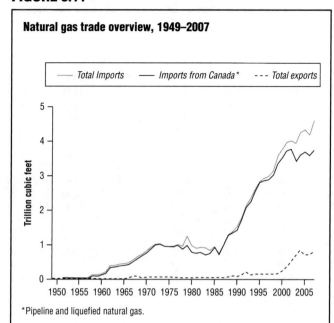

*Pipeline and liquefied natural gas.

SOURCE: Adapted from "Figure 6.3. Natural Gas Imports, Exports, and Net Imports: Trade Overview, 1949–2007," in *Annual Energy Review 2007*, U.S. Department of Energy, Energy Information Administration, Office of Energy Market and End Use, June 2008, http://www.eia.doe.gov/aer.pdf (assessed June 28, 2008)

TABLE 3.4

World dry natural gas production, 1997–2006

[Trillion cubic feet]

Region and country	1997	1998	1999	2000	2001	2002	2003	2004	2005	2006[P]
North, Central, and South America	**28.75**	**29.39**	**29.53**	**30.40**	**31.17**	**30.56**	**31.02**	**[R]31.08**	**31.00**	**31.93**
Argentina	.97	1.04	1.22	1.32	1.31	1.28	1.45	1.58	1.61	1.63
Canada	5.76	5.98	6.27	6.47	6.60	6.63	6.45	6.48	6.56	6.55
Mexico	1.17	1.27	1.29	1.31	1.30	1.33	1.40	1.46	1.52	1.71
United States	18.90	19.02	18.83	19.18	19.62	18.93	19.10	18.59	18.05	18.48
Venezuela	.99	1.11	.95	.96	1.12	1.00	.86	.96	1.01	1.01
Other	.96	.96	.98	1.15	1.22	1.39	1.76	2.00	2.24	2.56
Europe[a]	**10.68**	**10.49**	**10.72**	**10.98**	**11.10**	**11.41**	**11.48**	**11.89**	**11.42**	**11.18**
Germany	.79	.77	.82	.78	.79	.79	.78	.73	.70	.69
Italy	.68	.67	.62	.59	.54	.52	.49	.46	.43	.39
Netherlands	2.99	2.84	2.65	2.56	2.75	2.68	2.57	3.04	2.78	2.73
Norway	1.62	1.63	1.76	1.87	1.95	2.41	2.70	2.95	3.07	3.20
Romania	.61	.52	.50	.48	.51	.47	.43	.42	.41	.42
United Kingdom	3.03	3.14	3.49	3.83	3.69	3.66	3.63	3.39	3.10	2.83
Other	.95	.92	.88	.88	.89	.88	.86	.92	.92	.92
Eurasia[b]	**23.88**	**24.31**	**24.59**	**25.43**	**25.65**	**26.26**	**27.25**	**28.16**	**28.79**	**29.46**
Russia	20.17	20.87	20.83	20.63	20.51	21.03	21.77	22.39	22.62	23.17
Turkmenistan	.90	.47	.79	1.64	1.70	1.89	2.09	2.07	2.22	2.23
Ukraine	.64	.64	.63	.64	.64	.65	.69	.68	.69	.69
Uzbekistan	1.74	1.94	1.96	1.99	2.23	2.04	2.03	2.11	2.11	2.22
Other	.44	.40	.39	.53	.57	.65	.68	.91	1.15	1.16
Middle East and Africa	**9.74**	**10.30**	**10.95**	**12.01**	**12.61**	**13.39**	**[R]14.29**	**15.23**	**17.31**	**18.60**
Algeria	2.43	2.60	2.88	2.94	2.79	2.80	2.85	2.83	3.11	3.07
Egypt	.48	.49	.52	.65	.87	.88	1.06	1.15	1.50	1.86
Iran	1.66	1.77	2.04	2.13	2.33	2.65	2.86	2.96	3.56	3.71
Qatar	.61	.69	.78	1.03	.95	1.04	1.11	1.38	1.62	1.75
Saudi Arabia	1.60	1.65	1.63	1.76	1.90	2.00	2.12	2.32	2.52	2.59
United Arab Emirates	1.28	1.31	1.34	1.36	1.39	1.53	1.58	1.63	1.66	1.67
Other	1.67	1.79	1.76	2.15	2.39	2.48	[R]2.71	2.95	3.35	3.9
Asia and Oceania[a]	**[R]8.64**	**[R]8.70**	**[R]9.29**	**[R]9.60**	**[R]10.02**	**[R]10.72**	**[R]11.47**	**[R]12.17**	**13.00**	**13.50**
Australia	1.06	1.10	1.12	1.16	1.19	1.23	1.27	1.31	1.44	1.51
China	.80	.82	.89	.96	1.07	1.15	1.21	1.44	1.76	2.07
India	.72	.76	.75	.79	.85	.93	.96	1.00	1.06	1.07
Indonesia	2.37	2.27	2.51	2.36	2.34	2.48	2.61	2.66	2.61	2.61
Malaysia	1.36	1.37	1.42	1.50	1.66	1.71	2.01	2.20	2.24	2.22
Pakistan	.70	.71	.78	.86	.77	.81	.89	.97	1.09	1.11
Other	[R]1.64	[R]1.68	[R]1.82	[R]1.97	[R]2.14	[R]2.40	[R]2.52	[R]2.59	2.81	2.91
World	**[R]81.70**	**[R]83.19**	**[R]85.08**	**[R]88.42**	**[R]90.56**	**[R]92.33**	**[R]95.52**	**[R]98.53**	**101.52**	**104.67**

[a]Excludes countries that were part of the former U.S.S.R.
[b]Includes only countries that were part of the former U.S.S.R.
R = Revised.
P = Preliminary.
U.S.S.R. = Union of Soviet Socialist Republics
Note: Totals may not equal sum of components due to independent rounding.

SOURCE: "Table 11.11. World Dry Natural Gas Production, 1997–2006 (Trillion Cubic Feet)," in *Annual Energy Review 2007*, U.S. Department of Energy, Energy Information Administration, Office of Energy Markets and End Use, June 2008, http://www.eia.doe.gov/aer/pdf/aer.pdf (accessed June 28, 2008)

FIGURE 3.12

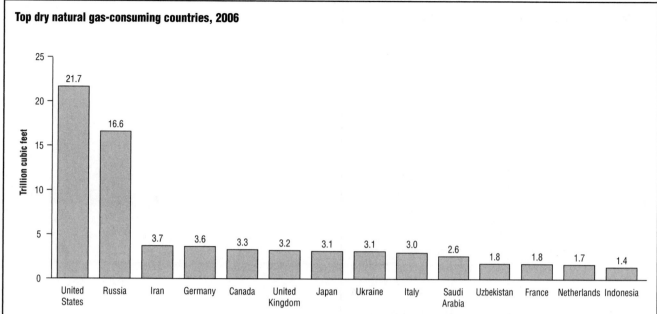

Top dry natural gas-consuming countries, 2006

SOURCE: Adapted from "Figure 11.12. World Dry Natural Gas Consumption: Top Consuming Countries, 2006," in *Annual Energy Rreview 2007*, U.S. Department of Energy, Energy Information Administration, Office of Energy Markets and End Use, June 2008, http://www.eia.doe.gov/aer/pdf/aer.pdf (accessed June 28, 2008)

FIGURE 3.13

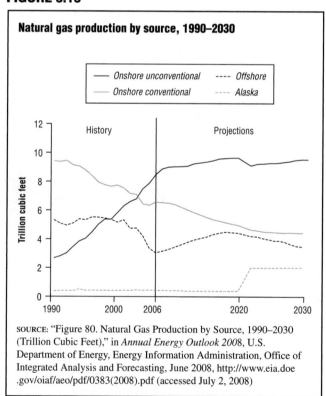

Natural gas production by source, 1990–2030

SOURCE: "Figure 80. Natural Gas Production by Source, 1990–2030 (Trillion Cubic Feet)," in *Annual Energy Outlook 2008*, U.S. Department of Energy, Energy Information Administration, Office of Integrated Analysis and Forecasting, June 2008, http://www.eia.doe .gov/oiaf/aeo/pdf/0383(2008).pdf (accessed July 2, 2008)

FIGURE 3.14

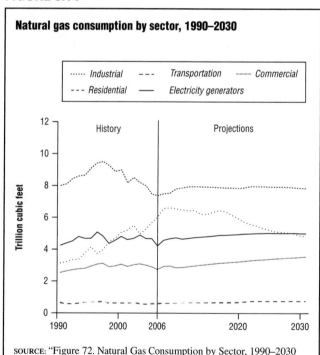

Natural gas consumption by sector, 1990–2030

SOURCE: "Figure 72. Natural Gas Consumption by Sector, 1990–2030 (Trillion Cubic Feet)," in *Annual Energy Outlook 2008*, U.S. Department of Energy, Energy Information Administration, Office of Integrated Analysis and Forecasting, June 2008, http://www.eia.doe .gov/oiaf/aeo/pdf/0383(2008).pdf (accessed July 2, 2008)

FIGURE 3.15

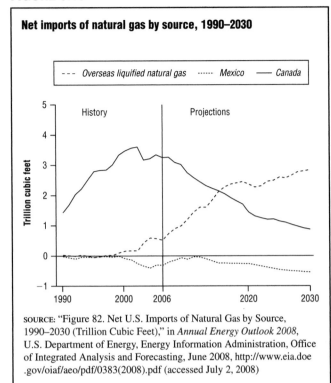

Net imports of natural gas by source, 1990–2030

SOURCE: "Figure 82. Net U.S. Imports of Natural Gas by Source, 1990–2030 (Trillion Cubic Feet)," in *Annual Energy Outlook 2008*, U.S. Department of Energy, Energy Information Administration, Office of Integrated Analysis and Forecasting, June 2008, http://www.eia.doe .gov/oiaf/aeo/pdf/0383(2008).pdf (accessed July 2, 2008)

CHAPTER 4
COAL

A HISTORICAL PERSPECTIVE

Even though it had been a source of energy for centuries, coal was first used on a large scale during the Industrial Revolution in England. From the mid-eighteenth to the mid-nineteenth centuries, the sky was filled with billowing columns of black smoke. Soot covered the towns and cities, and workers breathed the thick coal dust swirling around them. Environmental issues, if they were considered at all, were far less important than the jobs the factories provided. Factory owners had little reason or incentive to control the smoke pouring out of their plants—the environmental and public health effects of pollution were not as well understood as they are today, so government imposed little, if any, regulation on manufacturing.

In the United States early colonists used wood to heat their homes because it was so plentiful. Coal was not as readily available and far more expensive. Before the Civil War (1861–1865), some industries used coal as a source of energy, but its use expanded greatly with the building of railroads across the country. In fact, coal became such a fundamental part of American industrialization that some historians call this era the coal age. As in England, Americans considered the development of industry a source of national pride. Photographs and postcards of the time proudly featured trains and steel mills belching dark smoke into gray skies.

The Energy Information Administration (EIA) notes in *Annual Energy Review 2007* (June 2008, http://www.eia.doe.gov/aer/pdf/aer.pdf) that by the early twentieth century coal had become the major fuel in the United States, accounting for nearly 75% of the nation's energy requirements. However, as oil—which was much cleaner—became a favored fuel for heating homes and offices, and gasoline powered the growing number of cars, coal's dominance declined. By 1949 coal accounted for 37% of the energy consumed. It fell further out of favor in the 1950s

and 1960s until, in the early 1970s, coal provided as little as 17% of the nation's energy. By then it had been overtaken by concerns about pollution, along with the emergence of nuclear power as a promising energy source.

In 1973, however, the oil embargo by the Organization of Petroleum Exporting Countries made many Americans reconsider. The embargo clearly demonstrated the nation's heavy reliance on foreign sources of energy and the potentially crippling effect that dependence could have on the U.S. economy. Consequently, the nation revived its interest in domestic coal as a plentiful and economical energy source.

According to the article "Primary Sources: The President's Proposed Energy Policy" (2002, http://www.pbs.org/wgbh/amex/carter/filmmore/ps_energy.html), President Jimmy Carter (1924–) called for an increase in domestic coal production by two-thirds—to about 1 billion short tons (907 billion t) annually by 1985. He proposed a ten-year, $10 billion program to spark that production. He also asked utility companies and other large industries to convert their operations to coal. In 2007 more coal was produced in the United States than any other form of energy: 23.5 quadrillion British thermal units (Btu), or 33% of all energy produced. (See Table 1.1 and Figure 1.6 in Chapter 1.) Coal was the third-largest source of energy consumed in the United States in 2007, after petroleum and natural gas. (See Figure 1.7 in Chapter 1.)

WHAT IS COAL?

Coal is a black, combustible, mineral solid. It developed over millions of years as plant matter decomposed in an airless space under increased temperature and pressure. Coal beds, sometimes called seams, are found in the earth between beds of sandstone, shale, and limestone and range in thickness from less than an 1 inch (2.5 cm) to more than 100 feet (30 m). Approximately 5 to 10 feet (1.5 to 3 m) of ancient plant material were compressed to create each foot of coal.

Coal is used as a fuel and in the production of coal gas, water gas, many coal-tar compounds, and coke (the solid substance left after coal gas and coal tar have been extracted from coal). When coal is burned, its fossil energy—sunlight converted and stored by plants over millions of years—is released. One short ton (0.9 t) of coal produces 22 million Btu on average, about the same heating value as 22,000 cubic feet (623 cubic m) of natural gas, 160 gallons (606 L) of home heating oil, or a cord of seasoned firewood measuring 4 feet by 4 feet by 8 feet (1.2 by 1.2 by 2.4 m). (A short ton is 2,000 pounds [907 k].)

CLASSIFICATIONS OF COAL

There are four basic types of coal. Classifications, or coal ranks, are based on how much carbon, volatile matter, and heating value are contained in the coal:

- Anthracite (hard coal) is the highest-ranked coal. It is hard and jet-black, with a moisture content of less than 15%. It contains approximately 22 million to 28 million Btu per ton, with an ignition temperature of approximately 925° to 970° Fahrenheit (496° to 521° C). Anthracite, which is used for generating electricity and space heating, is mined mainly in northeastern Pennsylvania. (See Figure 4.1.)

- Bituminous (soft coal) is the most common. It is dense and black, with a moisture content of less than 20% and an ignition range of 700° to 900° Fahrenheit (371° to 482° C). With a heating value of 19 million to 30 million Btu per ton, bituminous coal is used to generate electricity, for space heating, and to produce coke. It is mined chiefly in the Appalachian and midwestern regions of the United States. (See Figure 4.1.)

- Subbituminous coal (black lignite) is dull black in color and generally contains 20% to 30% moisture. Used for generating electricity and for space heating, it contains 16 million to 24 million Btu per ton. Black lignite is mined primarily in the western United States. (See Figure 4.1.)

- Lignite, the lowest-ranked coal, is brownish-black in color and has a high moisture content. It tends to disintegrate when exposed to weather. Lignite contains about 9 million to 17 million Btu per ton and is used mainly to generate electricity. Most lignite is mined in North Dakota, Montana, Texas, California, and Louisiana. (See Figure 4.1.)

In 2007 domestic mines produced over 1.1 billion short tons (998 million t) of all types of coal. About 93% of it was bituminous (535 million short tons [485 million t]) and subbituminous (531 million short tons [482 million t]) coal. (See Table 4.1.) Lignite accounted for much of the remainder. Very little of the total was anthracite.

LOCATIONS OF COAL DEPOSITS

Coal is found in about 450,000 square miles (1.2 million sq km), or 13%, of the total land area of the United States. Figure 4.1 shows the coal-bearing areas of the United States. Geologists divide U.S. coalfields into the Appalachian, Interior, and Western regions. The Appalachian region is subdivided into three areas: Northern (Maryland, Ohio, Pennsylvania, and northern West Virginia), Central (eastern Kentucky, Tennessee, Virginia, and southern West Virginia), and Southern Appalachia (Alabama). The Interior region includes mines in Arkansas, Illinois, Indiana, Iowa, Kansas, western Kentucky, Louisiana, Missouri, Oklahoma, and Texas. The Western region is divided into the Northern Great Plains (northern Colorado, Montana, North and South Dakota, and Wyoming), the Rocky Mountains, the Southwest (Arizona, southern Colorado, New Mexico, and Utah), and the Northwest (Alaska and Washington).

Before 1999 most of the nation's coal was mined east of the Mississippi River. Miners had been digging deeper and deeper into the Appalachian Mountains for years before bulldozers began cutting open the rich coal seams of eastern Montana. In 1965 western mines produced 27.4 million short tons (24.9 million t), only 5% of the national total. By 1999, however, western production had increased more than twentyfold, to 570.8 million short tons (517.8 million t), or 52% of the total. (See Table 4.1.) The amount of coal mined east of the Mississippi that year was 529.6 million short tons (480.4 million t). In 2007 mines west of the Mississippi produced 668.4 million short tons (606.4 million t)—58% of the total—whereas eastern mines produced 477.2 million short tons (432.9 million t).

The growth in coal production in the western states resulted, in part, because of an increased demand for low-sulfur coal, which is concentrated there. Low-sulfur coal burns cleaner and is considered less dangerous to the environment. In addition, the coal is closer to the surface, so it can be extracted by surface mining, which is cheaper and more efficient. Improved rail service has also made it easier to deliver this low-sulfur coal to electric power plants located east of the Mississippi River.

COAL MINING METHODS

The method used to mine coal depends on the terrain and the depth of the coal. Before the early 1970s most coal was taken from underground mines. Since then, coal production has shifted to surface mines. (See Table 4.1 and Figure 4.2.)

Underground mining is required when the coal lies more than 200 feet (61 m) below ground. The depth of most underground mines is less than 1,000 feet (305 m), but a few are 2,000 feet (610 m) deep. In underground

FIGURE 4.1

Coal-bearing areas

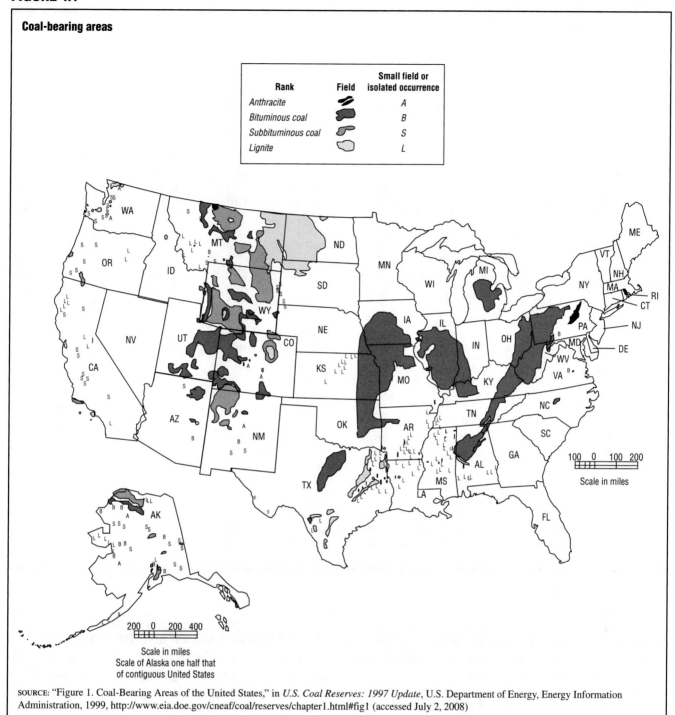

Rank	Field	Small field or isolated occurrence
Anthracite		A
Bituminous coal		B
Subbituminous coal		S
Lignite		L

SOURCE: "Figure 1. Coal-Bearing Areas of the United States," in *U.S. Coal Reserves: 1997 Update*, U.S. Department of Energy, Energy Information Administration, 1999, http://www.eia.doe.gov/cneaf/coal/reserves/chapter1.html#fig1 (accessed July 2, 2008)

mines, some coal must be left untouched to form pillars that prevent the mines from caving in.

Figure 4.3 shows three types of underground mines: a shaft mine, a slope mine, and a drift mine. In a shaft mine, elevators take miners and equipment up and down a vertical shaft to the coal deposit. By contrast, the entrance to a slope mine is an incline from the above-ground opening. In a drift mine, the mineshaft runs horizontally from the opening in the hillside. As Figure 4.3 shows, workers and equipment are moved externally up the side of a hill or mountain to the entry.

Surface mines are usually less than 200 feet (61 m) deep and can be developed in flat or hilly terrain. On large plots of relatively flat ground workers use a technique known as area surface mining. Rock and soil that lie above the coal—called overburden or spoil—are loosened by drilling and blasting and then dug away. Another technique, contour surface mining, follows coal deposits

TABLE 4.1

Coal production, selected years 1949–2007

[Million short tons]

Year	Rank Bituminous coal[a]	Rank Subbituminous coal	Rank Lignite	Rank Anthracite[a]	Mining method Underground	Mining method Surface[a]	Location East of the Mississippi[a]	Location West of the Mississippi[a]	Total[a]
1949	437.9	(b)	(b)	42.7	358.9	121.7	444.2	36.4	480.6
1950	516.3	(b)	(b)	44.1	421.0	139.4	524.4	36.0	560.4
1955	464.6	(b)	(b)	26.2	358.0	132.9	464.2	26.6	490.8
1960	415.5	(b)	(b)	18.8	292.6	141.7	413.0	21.3	434.3
1965	512.1	(b)	(b)	14.9	338.0	189.0	499.5	27.4	527.0
1970	578.5	16.4	8.0	9.7	340.5	272.1	567.8	44.9	612.7
1971	521.3	22.2	8.7	8.7	277.2	283.7	509.9	51.0	560.9
1972	556.8	27.5	11.0	7.1	305.0	297.4	538.2	64.3	602.5
1974	545.7	42.2	15.5	6.6	278.0	332.1	518.1	91.9	610.0
1976	588.4	64.8	25.5	6.2	295.5	389.4	548.8	136.1	684.9
1978	534.0	96.8	34.4	5.0	242.8	427.4	487.2	183.0	670.2
1980	628.8	147.7	47.2	6.1	337.5	492.2	578.7	251.0	829.7
1982	620.2	160.9	52.4	4.6	339.2	499.0	564.3	273.9	838.1
1984	649.5	179.2	63.1	4.2	352.1	543.9	587.6	308.3	895.9
1986	620.1	189.6	76.4	4.3	360.4	529.9	564.4	325.9	890.3
1988	638.1	223.5	85.1	3.6	382.2	568.1	579.6	370.7	950.3
1990	693.2	244.3	88.1	3.5	424.5	604.5	630.2	398.9	1,029.1
1992	651.8	252.2	90.1	3.5	407.2	590.3	588.6	409.0	997.5
1994	640.3	300.5	88.1	4.6	399.1	634.4	566.3	467.2	1,033.5
1996	630.7	340.3	88.1	4.8	409.8	654.0	563.7	500.2	1,063.9
1998	640.6	385.9	85.8	5.3	417.7	699.8	570.6	547.0	1,117.5
1999	601.7	406.7	87.2	4.8	391.8	708.6	529.6	570.8	1,100.4
2000	574.3	409.2	85.6	4.6	373.7	700.0	507.5	566.1	1,073.6
2002	572.1	438.4	82.5	1.4	357.4	736.9	492.9	601.4	1,094.3
2003	541.5	442.6	86.4	1.3	352.8	719.0	469.2	602.5	1,071.8
2004	561.5	465.4	83.5	1.7	367.6	744.5	484.8	627.3	1,112.1
2005	571.2	474.7	83.9	1.7	368.6	762.9	493.8	637.7	1,131.5
2006	R561.6	R515.3	84.2	1.5	R359.0	R803.7	R490.8	672.0	R1,162.7
2007	E534.9	E530.6	E78.5	E1.6	E351.3	E794.3	E477.2	E668.4	P1,145.6

[a]Beginning in 2001, includes a small amount of refuse recovery.
[b]Included in "bituminous coal."
R = Revised.
P = Preliminary.
E = Estimate.
Note: Totals may not equal sum of components due to independent rounding.

SOURCE: Adapted from "Table 7.2. Coal Production, Selected Years, 1949–2007 (Million Short Tons)," in *Annual Energy Review 2007*, U.S. Department of Energy, Energy Information Administration, Office of Energy Markets and End Use, June 2008, http://www.eia.doe.gov/aer/pdf/aer.pdf (accessed June 28, 2008)

along hillsides. (See Figure 4.3.) Open pit mining—a combination of area and contour mining—is used to mine thick, steeply inclined coal deposits.

The growth of surface mining and the closure of non-productive mines led to increases in coal mining productivity through the 1980s and 1990s. (See Figure 4.4.) Because surface mines are easier to work, they average up to three times the productivity of underground mines. According to the EIA, in *Annual Energy Review 2007*, the productivity for surface mines was 10.2 short tons (9.3 t) of coal per miner hour in 2007, whereas productivity for underground mines was 3.4 short tons (3.1 t) per miner hour. In 2000 the combined average productivity for both mining methods reached an all-time high of 6.9 short tons (6.3 t) per miner hour. In 2007 combined average productivity was 6.3 short tons (5.7 t) per miner hour.

COAL MINING SAFETY AND HEALTH RISKS

Mining safety in the United States is overseen by the Mine Safety and Health Administration (MSHA), which was formed in 1978 after Congress passed the Federal Mine Safety and Health Act of 1977. The law established mandatory health and safety standards for mines and required that mine operators and miners comply with them. It also provided assistance to states to develop and enforce effective state mine health and safety programs and expanded research and development aimed at preventing accidents and diseases associated with mining occupations.

Throughout its history, coal mining has been a physically challenging and dangerous occupation, with a recognized risk for injury or disease. As early as 1822 the term *miner's asthma* was used to describe the breathing difficulties and coughing often experienced by mine workers.

FIGURE 4.2

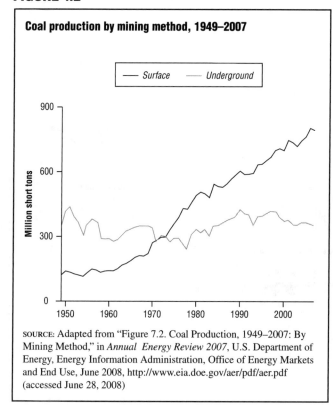

Coal production by mining method, 1949–2007

SOURCE: Adapted from "Figure 7.2. Coal Production, 1949–2007: By Mining Method," in *Annual Energy Review 2007*, U.S. Department of Energy, Energy Information Administration, Office of Energy Markets and End Use, June 2008, http://www.eia.doe.gov/aer/pdf/aer.pdf (accessed June 28, 2008)

In addition, mine accidents can occur without warning, including cave-ins, fires, underground floods, equipment failures, and gas explosions. (Flammable gases, notably methane, are found naturally in coal mines.) In underground mines these accidents carry the additional risk of trapping miners in the mine without air, water, or food.

Fatalities

The MSHA states in "Coal Fatalities for 1900 through 2007" (2008, http://www.msha.gov/stats/centurystats/coalstats.asp) that a total of 104,655 people were killed in coal mining accidents from 1900 through 2007. In "Coal Mining Disasters" (April 18, 2008, http://www.cdc.gov/niosh/mining/statistics/discoal.htm), the National Institute for Occupational Safety and Health (NIOSH) finds that in records dating back to 1839, 13,819 fatalities in the United States have resulted from 616 coal mine disasters; a mine disaster is a mine accident that claims five or more lives. The number of disasters peaked during the period 1901 through 1925, when 297 large accidents occurred. The most deadly event in U.S. history occurred when explosions in the Monongah mines in Monongah, West Virginia, claimed 362 lives in December 1907. The MSHA shows that 1907 was, in fact, the deadliest year on record, with 3,242 fatalities. According to NIOSH, of the twenty-six U.S. disasters that caused one hundred or more fatalities, seventeen of them took place between 1901 and 1925.

With a death toll of 125 and more than 1,100 injured, the deadliest coal mining accident in recent decades was the massive Buffalo Creek flood in southern West Virginia in February 1972. The West Virginia Division of Culture and History notes in *Buffalo Creek* (2008, http://www.wvculture.org/hiStory/buffcreek/bctitle.html) that after several days of heavy rain, a dam burst that was holding mine wastewater in a series of hillside pools. Over 132 million gallons (500 million L) of water then poured out and rushed through the valley below in the form of a black wave that reached 15 to 20 feet (4.6 to 6.1 m) high. The power of the water smashed structures and moved whole houses and railroad cars downstream. Terrified residents ran up nearby hills to get above the water level. Within minutes several communities located along a 17-mile (27.4-km) stretch of Buffalo Creek were devastated, and the town of Saunders was completely destroyed.

Coal mining has dramatically increased its safety record since the early and mid-twentieth century. Tighter regulations, improvements in technology, and preventive programs are credited with lowering—though not eliminating—many of the risks undertaken by miners. NIOSH indicates that from 1981 through August 2007 there were thirteen coal mine disasters that killed five or more people. The worst accident during this period was a mine fire that claimed twenty-seven lives at the Wilberg Mine in Orangeville, Utah, in December 1984. According to the MSHA, in 2005 there were twenty-three fatalities, the fewest fatalities recorded between 1900 and 2007.

The January 2006 mine disaster at the Sago Mine in Tallmansville, West Virginia, was the worst mining disaster in the United States since thirteen miners were killed in 2001 in a mine in Brookwood, Alabama, and the worst in West Virginia since seventy-eight were killed at the Consol No. 9 mine in Farmington in 1968. Sago claimed the lives of twelve miners. One miner survived. The miners were trapped following an explosion of methane gas that may have been triggered by a lightning strike; investigators theorized that a buildup of gas over the holidays might have contributed to the disaster, as the blast occurred shortly after the first shift returned to work on January 2. The explosion disabled the mine's internal communication system, which interfered with rescue operations. Rescue was also delayed because the air in the mine contained high concentrations of carbon monoxide and methane, which made it unsafe for rescue workers. Of those who perished, one was believed to have been killed by the initial blast, and the others succumbed to carbon monoxide poisoning.

One of the most recent mine disasters was investigated by Congress, and possible criminal charges against the owners of the mine were discussed. On August 6, 2007, six miners were trapped when a portion of the Crandall Canyon Mine collapsed. Crandall Canyon is located about 140 miles (225 km) south of Salt Lake City, Utah. An owner of the mine said a small earthquake

FIGURE 4.3

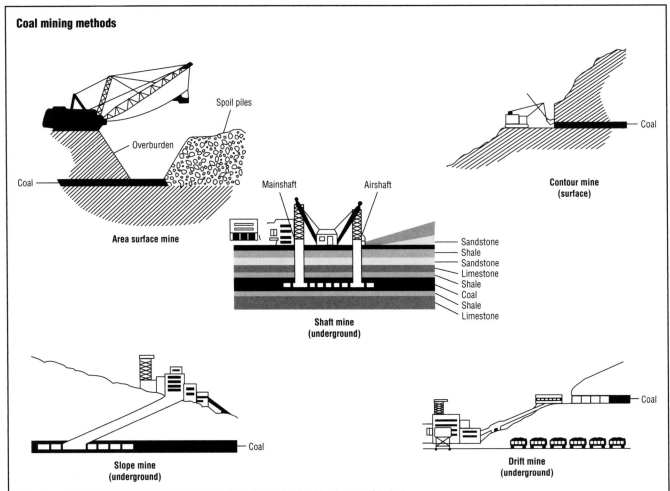

Coal mining methods

Note: The method of mining a coal deposit depends on the depth of the coal bed and the character of the land.

SOURCE: Adapted from "Figure 5. Coal Mining Methods," in *Coal Data: A Reference*, U.S. Department of Energy, Energy Information Administration, February 1995, http://tonto.eia.doe.gov/ftproot/coal/006493.pdf (accessed July 3, 2008)

FIGURE 4.4

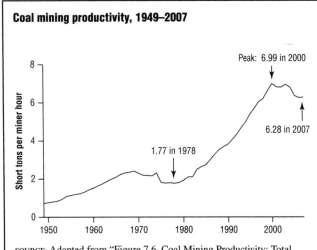

Coal mining productivity, 1949–2007

SOURCE: Adapted from "Figure 7.6. Coal Mining Productivity: Total, 1949–2007," in *Annual Energy Review 2007*, U.S. Department of Energy, Energy Information Administration, Office of Energy Markets and End Use, June 2008, http://www.eia.doe.gov/aer/pdf/aer.pdf (accessed June 28, 2008)

collapsed the mine, whereas others believed the recorded seismic activity was due to the tremendous force of the mine collapse. Eleven days into the rescue effort, three rescue workers were killed and seven injured when an additional collapse of the mine occurred. The bodies of the original six trapped miners were never recovered. U.S. House of Representatives and U.S. Senate committees and the U.S. Department of Labor all conducted independent investigations into the disaster and mining practices at Crandall Canyon. Investigations revealed that the mine collapse was likely due to retreat mining, a risky practice in which some coal is removed from the pillars that support the mine roof. These compromised pillars often collapse under the weight of the rock above. By May 2008 there were calls for the U.S. Department of Justice to open a criminal investigation into the tragedy.

Long-Term Health Risks

Besides the risk of injury or death, coal miners face a wide range of long-term health concerns, including muscle

FIGURE 4.5

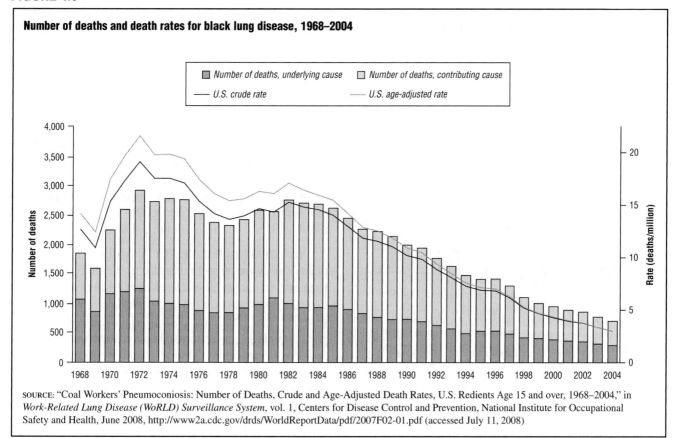

Number of deaths and death rates for black lung disease, 1968–2004

Legend:
- Number of deaths, underlying cause
- Number of deaths, contributing cause
- U.S. crude rate
- U.S. age-adjusted rate

SOURCE: "Coal Workers' Pneumoconiosis: Number of Deaths, Crude and Age-Adjusted Death Rates, U.S. Redients Age 15 and over, 1968–2004," in *Work-Related Lung Disease (WoRLD) Surveillance System*, vol. 1, Centers for Disease Control and Prevention, National Institute for Occupational Safety and Health, June 2008, http://www2a.cdc.gov/drds/WorldReportData/pdf/2007F02-01.pdf (accessed July 11, 2008)

and joint conditions, hearing loss brought on by excessive noise, and respiratory illnesses associated with dust, fumes, and chemical exposure. One serious illness associated with mining is coal workers' pneumoconiosis, also known as black lung disease, which results from repeated inhalation of coal dust. However, this risk has been drastically reduced through the use of dust masks and respirators, by covering the walls of mine tunnels and shafts with pulverized white rock to lower the level of the dust, and by spraying water to settle the dust.

Deaths from pneumoconiosis as an underlying cause have decreased dramatically from a peak of about 1,250 deaths in 1972 to about 250 deaths in 2004. (See Figure 4.5.) The age-adjusted death rate from pneumoconiosis was approximately 22 deaths per 1 million people aged fifteen and over in 1972 and dropped to about 3 deaths per 1 million in 2004.

COAL IN THE DOMESTIC MARKET
Overall Production and Consumption

In *Annual Energy Review 2007*, the EIA indicates that the nation consumed 625.3 million short tons (567.3 million t) of coal in 1977. Thirty years later, in 2007, consumption had grown to more than 1.1 billion short tons (998 million t)—nearly twice as much. Increases in consumption were in the electric power sector, as existing

power plants switched to coal from more expensive oil and natural gas and many new coal-fired power plants were constructed. Consumption of coal in the residential, commercial, and industrial sectors decreased from 1949 to 2007. (See Figure 4.6.)

Coal Consumption by Sector

In the electric power sector, coal is pulverized and burned to heat boilers that produce steam, which drives generators that create electricity. Each ton of coal used to drive a generator produces about 2,000 kilowatt-hours (kWh) of electricity. In household terms, each pound of coal produces enough electricity to light ten 100-watt lightbulbs for one hour.

In the twenty-first century, electric power companies are by far the largest consumers of coal today. (See Figure 4.6 and Figure 4.7.) They accounted for 93% of domestic coal consumption, or slightly more than 1 billion short tons (907.2 million t), in 2007. According to the EIA, in *Annual Energy Review 2007*, coal-fired plants produced 2 trillion kWh of electricity, or 49% of U.S. electricity net generation, in 2007. Net generation refers to the power available to the system—it does not include power used at the generating plant, but it does include power that may be lost during transmission and distribution.

FIGURE 4.6

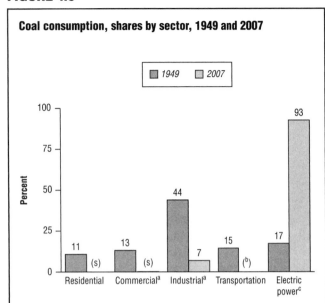

Coal consumption, shares by sector, 1949 and 2007

[Legend: ■ 1949 ■ 2007]

Percent

	Residential	Commercial[a]	Industrial[a]	Transportation	Electric power[c]
1949	11	13	44	15	17
2007	(s)	(s)	7	(b)	93

[a]Includes combined-heat-and-power (CHP) plants and a small number of electricity-only plants.
[b]For 1978 forward, small amounts of transportation sector use are included in "Industrial."
[c]Electricity-only and combined-heat-and-power (CHP) plants whose primary business is to sell electricity, or electricity and heat, to the public.
(s) = Less than 0.5.

SOURCE: Adapted from "Figure 7.3. Coal Consumption by Sector: Sector Shares, 1949 and 2007," in *Annual Energy Review 2007*, U.S. Department of Energy, Energy Information Administration, Office of Energy Markets and End Use, June 2008, http://www.eia.doe.gov/aer/pdf/aer.pdf (accessed June 28, 2008).

The industrial sector was the second-largest consumer of coal in 2007, accounting for 7% of coal use, or 79.2 million short tons (71.9 million t). (See Figure 4.6 and Figure 4.7.) Coal is used in many industrial applications, including the chemical, cement, paper, synthetic fuels, metals, and food-processing industries.

Coal was once a significant fuel source in the residential and commercial sectors. (See Figure 4.6.) In 1949 these sectors together used 116.5 million short tons (105.7 million t) of coal, or 24% of all coal consumption. After the 1940s, however, coal was replaced by oil, natural gas, and electricity, which are cleaner and more convenient. The EIA notes that by 1970 only 16.1 million short tons (14.6 million t) of coal were used in the residential and commercial sectors. Since then, residential and commercial coal use has continued to decline, falling to 3.3 million short tons (3 million t) in 2007, or far less than 1% of total coal use.

The Price of Coal

In 2007 the average price of a short ton of coal was $21.23 in real dollars (i.e., adjusted for inflation), which was slightly higher than the all-time low of $16.78 in 2000 and 2003, and only 42% of the all-time high of $50.92 per short ton in real dollars in 1975. (See Table 4.2.) On a per-Btu basis, coal remains the least expensive fossil fuel. According to the EIA, in *Annual Energy Review 2007*, in 2007 the average cost of coal was $1.62 per million Btu, compared to $9.92 per million Btu for natural gas and $23.92 per million Btu for retail electricity.

COAL AND THE ENVIRONMENT
Problems

In 1306 King Edward I (1239–1307) of England so objected to the noxious smoke from London's coal-burning fires that he banned the use of coal by everyone except blacksmiths. Since then, the potential for pollution has multiplied exponentially, given the amount of fossil fuels, such as coal, that are burned worldwide.

THE GREENHOUSE EFFECT. Coal-fired electric power plants emit gases that are considered harmful to the environment. Scientists have learned that burning huge quantities of fossil fuels causes a greenhouse effect, in which gases released from the fuels trap heat in the earth's atmosphere, raising temperatures. Manav Tanneeru reports in "Global Warming: A Natural Cycle or Human Result?" (CNN.com, April 8, 2008) that according to the National Research Council, the earth has warmed about 1° Fahrenheit (0.6° C) in the past one hundred years. Some of the effects of the added heat are immediate, whereas others happen over long periods of time.

Much of the gas that causes the greenhouse effect is carbon dioxide. In 2006 the combustion of coal in the United States produced 2.1 billion metric tons (2.3 million short tons) of carbon dioxide, or 36% of the total carbon dioxide emissions from all fossil fuels used in the United States. (See Figure 4.8.)

ACID RAIN. Acid rain is any form of precipitation that contains a greater-than-normal amount of acid. In many parts of the world it has caused significant damage to forests and lakes.

Even nonpolluted rain is slightly acidic: rainwater combines with the carbon dioxide normally found in the air to produce a weak acid called carbonic acid. However, pollutants in the air can increase the acidity of rain and other forms of precipitation, such as snow and fog. Chemicals such as oxides of sulfur and nitrogen, which are released during the combustion of fossil fuels, create highly acidic precipitation. The amount of these oxides in the air is directly related to the amount and content of automobile exhaust and industrial and power plant emissions.

COMMUNITY HEALTH ISSUES. Emissions from coal-fired power plants include mercury, sulfur oxides, and nitrogen oxides. Mercury can reach humans when they eat fish contaminated by mercury that, after being emitted into the air, settles in lakes and streams. Mercury can cause birth defects in newborns exposed to it in the

FIGURE 4.7

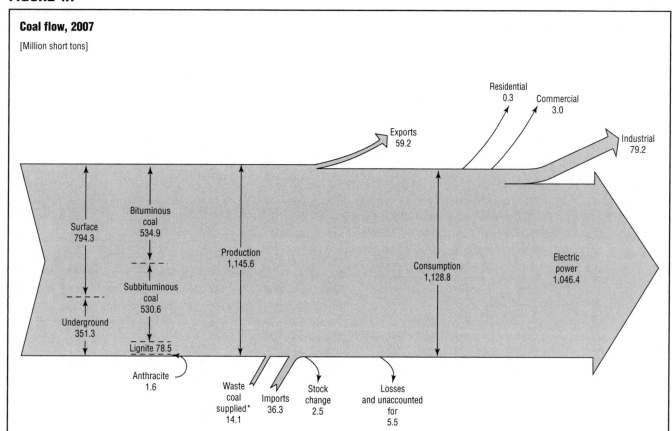

Coal flow, 2007

[Million short tons]

*Includes fine coal, coal obtained from a refuse bank or slurry dam, anthracite culm, bituminous gob, and lignite waste that are consumed by the electric power industrial sectors.
Notes: Production categories are estimated; other data are preliminary. Values are derived from source data prior to rounding for publication. Totals may not equal sum of components due to independent rounding.

SOURCE: "Diagram 4. Coal Flow, 2007 (Million Short Tons)," in *Annual Energy Review 2007*, U.S. Department of Energy, Energy Information Administration, Office of Energy Markets and End Use, June 2008, http://www.eia.doe.gov/aer/pdf/aer.pdf (accessed June 28, 2008)

womb. Sulfur oxides and nitrogen oxides contribute to air pollution, which is known to cause respiratory impairments. (See Table 4.3.)

Solutions

THE CLEAN COAL TECHNOLOGY PROGRAM. In 1984 Congress established the Clean Coal Technology program, which directed the U.S. Department of Energy to administer projects that would demonstrate that coal could be used in environmentally and economically efficient ways. The cost of the projects was to be shared by industry and government.

CLEAN COAL TECHNOLOGY AND THE CLEAN AIR ACT. The stated goal of both Congress and the Department of Energy has been to develop cost-effective ways to burn coal more cleanly, both to control acid rain and air pollution and to reduce the nation's dependence on imported fuels. One strategy is a slow, phased-in approach that allows utility companies and states to reduce their emissions in stages.

The burning of coal can be made cleaner by using physical or chemical methods. Scrubbers, a common phys-

ical method used to reduce sulfur dioxide emissions, filter coal emissions by spraying a lime or calcium compound and water across the emission stream before it leaves the smokestack. The sulfur dioxide bonds to the spray and settles as a mudlike substance that can be pumped out for disposal. However, scrubbers are expensive to operate, so mechanical and fabric particulate collectors are the most common emissions cleaners. Even though they are cheaper to operate than scrubbers, they are less effective. Some utilities use cooling towers to reduce the heat in emissions before they are released into the atmosphere and to reduce some pollutants. Chemical cleaning, a relatively new technology, uses biological or chemical agents to clean emissions.

The Clean Air Act of 1990 placed restrictions on sulfur dioxide and nitrogen oxide emissions; the restrictions first took effect in 1995 and were tightened in 2000. Each round of regulation requires utilities to find lower-sulfur coal or to install cleaner technology, such as scrubbers. The first Clean Air Act, passed in 1970, sought to change air-quality standards at new generating stations while exempting existing coal-fired plants. Under the 1990 act, older plants are also bound by the 1970 regulations. In addition, plants with coal-fired boilers must be built to reduce sulfur emissions

TABLE 4.2

Coal prices, selected years 1949–2007

[Dollars per short ton]

Year	Bituminous coal		Subbituminous coal		Lignite[a]		Anthracite		Total	
	Nominal	Real[b]	Nominal	Real[b]	Nominal	Real[b]	Nominal	Real[b]	Nominal	Real[b]
1949	[c]4.90	[c]29.97	(c)	(c)	2.37	14.49	8.90	54.43	5.24	32.05
1950	[c]4.86	[c]29.40	(c)	(c)	2.41	14.58	9.34	56.50	5.19	31.40
1955	[c]4.51	[c]24.06	(c)	(c)	2.38	12.70	8.00	42.68	4.69	25.02
1960	[c]4.71	[c]22.38	(c)	(c)	2.29	10.88	8.01	38.07	4.83	22.96
1965	[c]4.45	[c]19.75	(c)	(c)	2.13	9.45	8.51	37.76	4.55	20.19
1970	[c]6.30	[c]22.88	(c)	(c)	1.86	6.76	11.03	40.06	6.34	23.03
1971	[c]7.13	[c]24.66	(c)	(c)	1.93	6.68	12.08	41.78	7.15	24.73
1972	[c]7.78	[c]25.79	(c)	(c)	2.04	6.76	12.40	41.11	7.72	25.59
1974	[c]16.01	[c]46.11	(c)	(c)	2.19	6.31	22.19	63.90	15.82	45.56
1975	[c]19.79	[c]52.08	(c)	(c)	3.17	8.34	32.26	84.89	19.35	50.92
1976	[c]20.11	[c]50.03	(c)	(c)	3.74	9.30	33.92	84.39	19.56	48.66
1978	[c]22.64	[c]49.48	(c)	(c)	5.68	12.41	35.25	77.04	21.86	47.77
1980	29.17	53.98	11.08	20.50	7.60	14.06	42.51	78.66	24.65	45.61
1982	32.15	51.25	13.37	21.31	9.79	15.61	49.85	79.47	27.25	43.44
1984	30.63	45.27	12.41	18.34	10.45	15.45	48.22	71.27	25.61	37.85
1986	28.84	40.48	12.26	17.21	10.64	14.93	44.12	61.92	23.79	33.39
1988	27.66	36.54	10.45	13.81	10.06	13.29	44.16	58.34	22.07	29.16
1990	27.43	33.62	9.70	11.89	10.13	12.42	39.40	48.29	21.76	26.67
1992	26.78	31.00	9.68	11.21	10.81	12.51	34.24	39.64	21.03	24.34
1994	25.68	28.45	8.37	9.27	10.77	11.93	36.07	39.96	19.41	21.50
1996	25.17	26.82	7.87	8.39	10.92	11.64	36.78	39.19	18.50	19.71
1998	24.87	25.78	6.96	7.21	11.08	11.49	42.91	44.48	17.67	18.32
2000	24.15	24.15	7.12	7.12	11.41	11.41	40.90	40.90	16.78	16.78
2002	26.57	25.50	7.34	7.05	11.07	10.63	47.78	45.86	17.98	17.26
2003	26.73	25.12	7.73	7.26	11.20	10.53	49.87	46.87	17.85	16.78
2004	30.56	[R]27.92	8.12	7.42	12.27	11.21	39.77	[R]36.33	19.93	18.21
2005	36.80	[R]32.57	8.68	[R]7.68	13.49	[R]11.94	41.00	[R]36.28	23.59	[R]20.88
2006	[R]39.32	[R]33.73	[R]9.95	[R]8.54	[R]14.00	[R]12.01	[R]43.61	[R]37.41	[R]25.16	[R]21.58
2007[E]	40.83	34.12	11.01	9.20	14.89	12.44	51.23	42.81	25.40	21.23

[a]Because of withholding to protect company confidentiality, lignite prices exclude Texas for 1955–1977 and Montana for 1974–1978. As a result, lignite prices for 1974–1977 are for North Dakota only.
[b]In chained (2000) dollars, calculated by using gross domestic product implicit price deflators.
[c]Through 1978, subbituminous coal is included in "bituminous coal."
R = Revised.
E = Estimate.
Note: Prices are free-on-board (F.O.B.) rail/barge prices, which are the F.O.B. prices of coal at the point of first sale, excluding freight or shipping and insurance costs.
Web pages: For all data beginning in 1949, see http://www.eia.doe.gov/emeu/aer/coal.html. For related information, see http://www.eia.doe.gov/fuelcoal.html.

SOURCE: Adapted from "Table 7.8. Coal Prices, Selected Years, 1949–2007 (Dollars per Short Ton)," in *Annual Energy Review 2007*, U.S. Department of Energy, Energy Information Administration, Office of Energy Markets and End Use, June 2008, http://www.eia.doe.gov/aer/pdf/aer.pdf (accessed June 28, 2008)

by 70% to 90%. When new plants that burn high-sulfur coal are built, about 30% of their construction costs are spent on pollution control equipment. Up to 5% of the plants' power output is used to operate this equipment. Research is under way to develop technology to lower these costs.

When President George W. Bush (1946–) took office in 2001, he promised to ease the regulations for older coal-burning plants to keep them up and running. His energy policy would have allowed the plants to modify their equipment and structures without adding pollution control measures, as long as they met certain conditions. Fifteen state governments and environmental and public health groups brought suit to stop this interpretation of the Clean Air Act. In April 2006 the Bush policy was rejected by the courts. In his 2008 State of the Union address, President Bush (January 28, 2008, http://www.whitehouse.gov/stateoftheunion/2008/initiatives/energy.html) urged the use of clean coal technology for generating electricity and the funding of new technologies that can produce power from coal with less carbon dioxide emissions.

THE CLEAN AIR INTERSTATE RULE AND THE CLEAN AIR MERCURY RULE. In March 2005 the U.S. Environmental Protection Agency (EPA) announced the Clean Air Interstate Rule (CAIR). It focused primarily on twenty-eight eastern states and the District of Columbia, where sulfur dioxide and nitrogen oxide emissions contributed significantly to fine particle and ozone pollution. Under the regulations, coal-burning power plants would have to install advanced pollution-control technologies, use coal that burned cleaner, or make other changes to reduce emissions of sulfur dioxide and nitrogen oxide that travel across state borders. The EPA expected the regulation, which would go into effect in 2009 and be fully implemented between 2020 and 2025, would reduce sulfur dioxide emissions by 70% and nitrogen oxide emissions by 60% from 2003 levels. However, the state

FIGURE 4.8

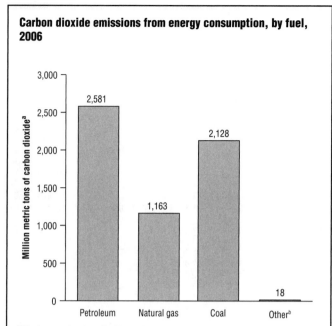

Carbon dioxide emissions from energy consumption, by fuel, 2006

[a]Metric tons of carbon dioxide can be converted to metric tons of carbon equivalent by multiplying by12/44.
[b]Coal coke net imports, the plastics component of municipal solid waste, and geothermal.

SOURCE: Adapted from "Figure 12.3. Carbon Dioxide Emissions from Energy Consumption by Sector by Energy Source, 2006: Total by Fuel," in *Annual Energy Review 2007*, U.S. Department of Energy, Energy Information Administration, Office of Energy Markets and End Use, June 2008, http://www.eia.doe.gov/aer/pdf/aer.pdf (accessed June 28, 2008)

TABLE 4.3

Air pollutants, health risks, and contributing sources

Pollutants	Health risks	Contributing sources
Ozone* (O_3)	Asthma, reduced respiratory function, eye irritation	Cars, refineries, dry cleaners
Particulate matter (PM-IO)	Bronchitis, cancer, lung damage	Dust, pesticides
Carbon monoxide (CO)	Blood oxygen carrying capacity reduction, cardiovascular and nervous system impairments	Cars, power plants, wood stoves
Sulphur dioxide (SO_2)	Respiratory tract impairment, destruction of lung tissue	Power plants, paper mills
Lead (Pb)	Retardation and brain damage, esp. children	Cars, nonferrous smelters, battery plants
Nitrogen dioxide (NO_2)	Lung damage and respiratory illness	Power plants, cars, trucks

*Ozone refers to tropospheric ozone which is hazardous to human health.

SOURCE: Fred Seitz and Christine Plepys, "Table 1. Criteria Air Pollutants, Health Risks and Sources," in *Healthy People 2000: Statistical Notes*, no. 9, Centers for Disease Control and Prevention, National Center for Health Statistics, September 1995, http://www.cdc.gov/nchs/data/statnt/statnt09.pdf (accessed July 3, 2008)

of North Carolina and some companies that produce electric power had opposed the rule and filed suit, contending that the EPA had overstepped its authority. In July 2008 a federal appeals court struck down CAIR, agreeing with the plaintiffs and stating, in addition, that it had found several flaws in the regulation.

In March 2005 the EPA also announced the Clean Air Mercury Rule (CAMR). The EPA expected mercury emissions from electric power plants to be reduced by nearly 70% from 1999 levels when the rule was fully implemented. The state of New Jersey challenged the legality of the rule because its provisions were not stringent enough to meet the standards of the Clean Air Act. In February 2008 a federal appeals court struck down CAMR, agreeing that the EPA failed to fulfill its obligations under the Clean Air Act by allowing utilities to make mercury cuts from some coal-fired units and not others. In March 2008 the EPA asked the court to reexamine its decision. In May 2008 the court refused.

CARBON DIOXIDE CAPTURE. In "Germany Leads 'Clean Coal' Pilot" (BBC News, September 3, 2008), Roger Harrabin reports that in September 2008 the first coal-fired plant that captures and stores its own carbon dioxide emissions began operations in northern Germany. The Schwarze Pump power station is a pilot project that will help determine whether the new technology used in the plant is economically and practically feasible. The European Union expects to build ten to twelve full-scale power plants using the clean coal technology within the next few years if the pilot experiment is successful.

COAL EXPORTS

Since 1950 the United States has produced more coal than it has consumed, allowing it to become a significant exporter. However, exports of this energy source have declined dramatically since 1991, when the United States exported 109 million short tons (98.9 million t) of coal. (See Table 4.4.) In 2007 the U.S. exported 59.2 million short tons (53.7 million t).

The EIA reports in *Annual Energy Review 2007* that coal made up 28% of all U.S. energy exports in 2007. The countries that bought the most U.S. coal from the United States were Canada, Japan, Italy, Germany, the Netherlands, and Brazil, respectively. (See Table 4.4.)

INTERNATIONAL COAL PRODUCTION AND CONSUMPTION

In *Annual Energy Review 2007*, the EIA reports that slightly more than 6.8 billion short tons (6.1 billion t) of coal were produced worldwide in 2006, and accounted for 122.5 quadrillion Btu (27%) of the world energy production in 2005. (See Table 1.4 in Chapter 1.) In 2006 China produced the most coal—more than 2.6 billion short tons (2.4 billion t)—followed by the United States, which mined almost 1.2 billion short tons (1.1 billion t). (See Figure 4.9.) Other major coal producers in order of amount produced

TABLE 4.4

Coal exports by country of destination, selected years 1960–2007

[Million short tons]

Year	Canada	Brazil	Europe											Japan	Other	Total
			Belgium[a]	Denmark	France	Germany[b]	Italy	Netherlands	Spain	Turkey	United Kingdom	Other	Total			
1960	12.8	1.1	1.1	0.1	0.8	4.6	4.9	2.8	0.3	NA	—	2.4	17.1	5.6	1.3	38.0
1961	12.1	1.0	1.0	.1	.7	4.3	4.8	2.6	.2	NA	—	2.0	15.7	6.6	1.0	36.4
1962	12.3	1.3	1.3	(s)	.9	5.1	6.0	3.3	.8	NA	(s)	1.8	19.1	6.5	1.0	40.2
1964	14.8	1.1	2.3	(s)	2.2	5.2	8.1	4.2	1.4	NA	—	2.6	26.0	6.5	1.1	49.5
1966	16.5	1.7	1.8	(s)	1.6	4.9	7.8	3.2	1.2	NA	(s)	2.5	23.1	7.8	1.0	50.1
1968	17.1	1.8	1.1	—	1.5	3.8	4.3	1.5	1.5	NA	—	1.9	15.5	15.8	.9	51.2
1970	19.1	2.0	1.9	—	3.6	5.0	4.3	2.1	3.2	NA	(s)	1.8	21.8	27.6	1.2	71.7
1972	18.7	1.9	1.1	—	1.7	2.4	3.7	2.3	2.1	NA	2.4	1.1	16.9	18.0	1.2	56.7
1974	14.2	1.3	1.1	—	2.7	1.5	3.9	2.6	2.0	NA	1.4	.9	16.1	27.3	1.8	60.7
1976	16.9	2.2	2.2	(s)	3.5	1.0	4.2	3.5	2.5	NA	.8	2.1	19.9	18.8	2.1	60.0
1978	15.7	1.5	1.1	—	1.7	.6	3.2	1.1	.8	NA	.4	2.2	11.0	10.1	2.5	40.7
1980	17.5	3.3	4.6	1.7	7.8	2.5	7.1	4.7	3.4	NA	4.1	6.0	41.9	23.1	6.0	91.7
1982	18.6	3.1	4.8	2.8	9.0	2.3	11.3	5.9	5.6	1.6	2.0	6.0	51.3	25.8	7.5	106.3
1984	20.4	4.7	3.9	.6	3.8	.9	7.6	5.5	2.3	1.5	2.9	3.9	32.8	16.3	7.2	81.5
1986	14.5	5.7	4.4	2.1	5.4	.8	10.4	5.6	2.6	2.4	2.9	5.9	42.6	11.4	11.4	85.5
1988	19.2	5.3	6.5	2.8	4.3	.7	11.1	5.1	2.5	2.0	3.7	6.4	45.1	14.1	11.3	95.0
1990	15.5	5.8	8.5	3.2	6.9	1.1	11.9	8.4	3.8	2.1	5.2	7.4	58.4	13.3	12.7	105.8
1991	11.2	7.1	7.5	4.7	9.5	1.7	11.3	9.6	4.7	2.2	6.2	8.2	65.5	12.3	13.0	109.0
1992	15.1	6.4	7.2	3.8	8.1	1.0	9.3	9.1	4.5	2.0	5.6	6.6	57.3	12.3	11.4	102.5
1994	9.2	5.5	4.9	.5	2.9	.3	7.5	4.9	4.1	1.3	3.4	6.0	35.8	10.2	10.7	71.4
1996	12.0	6.5	4.6	1.3	3.9	1.1	9.2	7.1	4.1	2.2	6.2	7.7	47.2	10.5	14.2	90.5
1998	20.7	6.5	3.2	.3	3.2	1.2	5.3	4.5	3.2	1.6	5.9	5.3	33.8	7.7	9.4	78.0
2000	18.8	4.5	2.9	.1	3.0	1.0	3.7	2.6	2.7	1.8	3.3	3.9	25.0	4.4	5.8	58.5
2002	16.7	3.5	2.4	—	1.3	1.0	3.1	1.7	1.9	.6	1.9	1.8	15.6	1.3	2.6	39.6
2003	20.8	3.5	1.8	.3	1.3	.5	2.8	2.0	1.8	1.1	1.5	2.1	15.1	(s)	3.6	43.0
2004	17.8	4.4	1.7	.1	1.1	.6	2.1	2.5	1.5	1.3	2.0	2.3	15.2	4.4	6.2	48.0
2005	19.5	4.2	2.1	.1	1.3	.7	2.5	2.6	1.9	1.9	1.8	4.1	18.8	2.1	5.4	49.9
2006	19.9	4.5	2.2	.4	1.6	1.7	3.3	2.1	1.6	1.2	2.6	4.2	20.8	.3	4.1	49.6
2007[P]	18.4	6.5	2.1	.1	2.4	2.3	3.5	4.6	1.5	1.4	3.4	5.8	27.1	(s)	7.1	59.2

[a]Through 1999, includes Luxembourg.
[b]Through 1990, data for Germany are for the former West Germany only. Beginning in 1991, data for Germany are for the unified Germany, i.e., the former East Germany and West Germany.
P = Preliminary.
NA = Not Available.
— = No data reported.
(s) = Less than 0.05 million short tons.
Note: Totals may not equal sum of components due to independent rounding.

SOURCE: Adapted from "Table 7.4. Coal Exports by Country of Destination, 1960–2007 (Million Short Tons)," in *Annual Energy Review 2007*, U.S. Department of Energy, Energy Information Administration, Office of Energy Markets and End Use, June 2008, http://www.eia.doe.gov/aer/pdf/aer.pdf (accessed June 28, 2008)

included India, Australia, Russia, South Africa, Germany, and Indonesia.

The world consumption of coal in 2006 totaled nearly 6.8 billion short tons (6.2 billion t). China consumed the most, using nearly 2.6 billion short tons (2.4 billion t), followed by the United States, which used slightly more than 1.1 billion (997.9 million t) short tons. (See Figure 4.10.) Other major consumers in order of amount consumed included India, Germany, Russia, Japan, and South Africa.

FUTURE TRENDS IN THE COAL INDUSTRY

In *Annual Energy Outlook 2008* (June 2008, http://www.eia.doe.gov/oiaf/aeo/pdf/0383(2008).pdf), the EIA provides forecasts for domestic coal production. The *Annual Energy Outlook 2008* reference case represents the EIA's updated projections in 2008 after the Energy Independence and Security Act of 2007 was passed relat-

ing to the increased production of biofuels under the Renewable Fuel Standard mandate.

Coal production in the United States is expected to increase to 1.2 billion short tons (1.1 billion t) by 2015, to 1.4 billion short tons (1.3 billion t) by 2025, and to 1.5 billion short tons (1.4 billion t) by 2030. (See Table 4.5.) Domestic coal consumption is projected to surpass coal production in 2015, 2025, and 2030, with the gap widening at each benchmark. Electric power generation is expected to use most of the coal produced in 2015 (approximately 1.1 billion short tons [997.9 million t]), 2025 (approximately 1.3 billion short tons [1.2 billion t]), and 2030 (1.4 billion short tons [1.3 billion t]). The projections assume the provisions of the Clean Air Act are being enforced.

Coal minemouth prices (the price of coal at the mouth of the mine before transportation and other costs

FIGURE 4.9

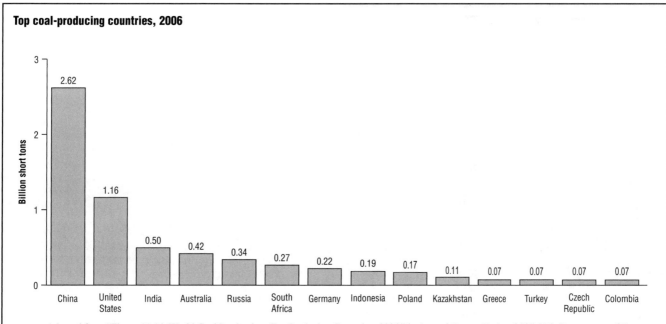

Top coal-producing countries, 2006

SOURCE: Adapted from "Figure 11.14. World Coal Production: Top Producing Countries, 2006," in *Annual Energy Review 2007*, U.S. Department of Energy, Energy Information Administration, Office of Energy Markets and End Use, June 2008, http://www.eia.doe.gov/aer/pdf/aer.pdf (accessed June 28, 2008)

FIGURE 4.10

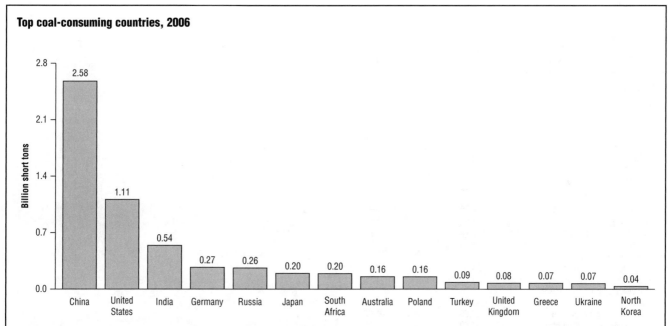

Top coal-consuming countries, 2006

SOURCE: Adapted from "Figure 11.15. World Coal Consumption: Top Consuming Countries, 2006," in *Annual Energy Review 2007*, U.S. Department of Energy, Energy Information Administration, Office of Energy Markets and End Use, June 2008, http://www.eia.doe.gov/aer/pdf/aer.pdf (accessed June 28, 2008)

are added) are projected to generally decrease during the projection period from $24.63 per short ton in 2006 to $23.38 in 2015, to $22.75 in 2025, and then rise slightly to $23.32 in 2030. (See Table 4.5.)

The EIA also predicts that U.S. coal exports—about 4% of the coal mined in 2006—will decline to only 2% of coal mined by 2030. (See Table 4.5.) All projections expect the United States to become a net importer of coal after 2015.

TABLE 4.5

Comparison of coal forecasts, 2015, 2025, and 2030

Projection	2006	AEO2008 reference case
		2015 forecast
Production	1,163	1,215
Consumption by sector		
Electric power	1,026	1,125
Coke plants	23	21
Coal-to-liquids	0	16
Other industrial/buildings	65	64
Total	**1,114**	**1,225**
Net coal exports	15.3	3.3
Exports	49.6	45.3
Imports	34.3	42.0
Minemouth price		
(2006 dollars per short ton)	24.63	23.38
(2006 dollars per million Btu)	1.21	1.17
Average delivered price to electricity generators		
(2006 dollars per short ton)	33.85	34.24
(2006 dollars per million Btu)	1.69	1.74
		2025 forecast
Production	1,163	1,363
Consumption by sector		
Electric power	1,026	1,303
Coke plants	23	20
Coal-to-liquids	0	46
Other industrial/buildings	65	62
Total	**1,114**	**1,431**
Net coal exports	15.3	−57.3
Exports	49.6	35.5
Imports	34.3	92.8
Minemouth price		
(2006 dollars per short ton)	24.63	22.75
(2006 dollars per million Btu)	1.21	1.16
Average delivered price to electricity generators		
(2006 dollars per short ton)	33.85	34.03
(2006 dollars per million Btu)	1.69	1.74
		2030 forecast
Production	1,163	1,455
Consumption by sector		
Electric power	1,026	1,401
Coke plants	23	18
Coal-to-liquids	0	64
Other industrial/buildings	65	62
Total	**1,114**	**1,545**
Net coal exports	15.3	−77.7
Exports	49.6	34.6
Imports	34.3	112.3
Minemouth price		
(2006 dollars per short ton)	24 63	23.32
(2006 dollars per million Btu)	1.21	1.19
Average delivered price to electricity generators		
(2006 dollars per short ton)	33.85	35.03
(2006 dollars per million Btu)	1.69	1.78

SOURCE: Adapted from "Table 13. Comparison of Coal Projections, 2015, 2025, and 2030 (Million Short Tons, Except Where Noted)," in *Annual Energy Outlook 2008*, U.S. Department of Energy, Energy Information Administration, Office of Integrated Analysis and Forecasting, June 2008, http://www.eia.doe.gov/oiaf/aeo/pdf/0383(2008).pdf (accessed July 2, 2008)

CHAPTER 5
NUCLEAR ENERGY

In the early 1970s many Americans favored the use of nuclear power to generate electricity. Reactors had been in operation since 1956, providing what appeared to be cleaner, more efficient energy than power plants that burned fossil fuels. In addition, the nation had plenty of uranium, the fuel used in U.S. reactors, so nuclear plants could help reduce U.S. dependence on foreign energy sources.

However, by the beginning of the twenty-first century opinion had turned: Voices were being raised in the United States—as well as around the world—in opposition to building additional nuclear power plants. In fact, some people wanted existing plants shut down. Two incidents—an accident in 1979 at the Three Mile Island nuclear power plant in Pennsylvania, in which the reactor core lost coolant and partially melted, and the 1986 catastrophe at Chernobyl in the Soviet Union, in which a reactor exploded and released huge amounts of radio-activity into the atmosphere—greatly increased concerns about the safety of nuclear power. Reports of design flaws, cracks, and leaks in other reactors fueled public fears. Furthermore, the safe disposal of radioactive waste, which is a by-product of nuclear energy, had become a scientific and political headache.

Supporters of nuclear power say it is as safe as any other form of energy production, as long as it is monitored properly. They point to the growing problems related to the use of fossil fuels: global warming, acid rain, and the damage caused by mining and transporting fossil fuels. This concern over fossil fuels has led some environmentalists who had previously opposed nuclear power to reconsider their position. Nonetheless, environmental, safety, and economic concerns have restrained growth in the nuclear industry since the mid-1970s. Figure 5.1 shows that from 1988 through 2007 nuclear energy's share of electricity production leveled off at about 19%.

HOW NUCLEAR ENERGY WORKS

In a nuclear power plant, fuel (uranium in the United States) in the core of the reactor generates a nuclear reaction (fission) that produces heat. In a pressurized water reactor, the heat from the reaction is carried away by water under high pressure, which heats a second water stream, producing steam. (See Figure 5.2.) The steam runs through a turbine, making the attached generator spin, which produces electricity. The large cooling towers associated with nuclear plants cool the steam after it has run through the turbines. A boiling water reactor works much the same way, except that the water surrounding the core boils and directly produces the steam, which is then piped to the turbine generator.

The challenges faced by those who operate a nuclear power reactor include finding fuel (uranium 235) that will sustain a chain reaction, maintaining the reaction at a level that yields heat but does not escalate out of control and explode, and coping with the radiation produced by the chain reaction.

Radioactivity

Radioactivity is the spontaneous emission of energy and/or high-energy particles from the nucleus of an atom. One type of radioactivity is produced naturally and is emitted by radioactive isotopes (or radioisotopes), such as radioactive carbon (carbon 14, or C-14) and radioactive hydrogen (H-3, or tritium). The energy and high-energy particles that radioactive isotopes emit include alpha rays, beta rays, and gamma rays.

Isotopes are atoms of an element that have the usual number of protons but different numbers of neutrons in their nuclei. For example, twelve protons and twelve neutrons make up the nucleus of the element carbon. One isotope of carbon, C-14, has twelve protons and fourteen neutrons in its nucleus.

FIGURE 5.1

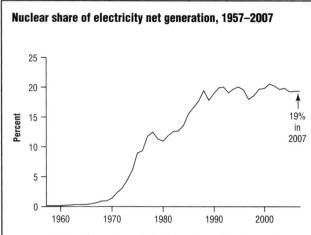

Nuclear share of electricity net generation, 1957–2007

SOURCE: Adapted from "Figure 9.2. Nuclear Power Plant Operations: Nuclear Share of Total Electricity Net Generation, 1957–2007," in *Annual Energy Review 2007*, U.S. Department of Energy, Energy Information Administration, Office of Energy Markets and End Use, June 2008, http://www.eia.doe.gov/aer/pdf/aer.pdf (accessed June 28, 2008)

FIGURE 5.2

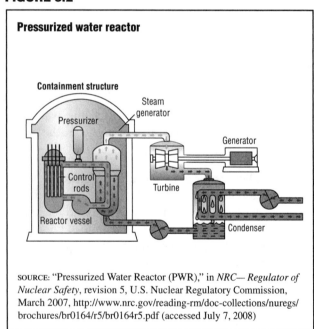

Pressurized water reactor

SOURCE: "Pressurized Water Reactor (PWR)," in *NRC— Regulator of Nuclear Safety*, revision 5, U.S. Nuclear Regulatory Commission, March 2007, http://www.nrc.gov/reading-rm/doc-collections/nuregs/brochures/br0164/r5/br0164r5.pdf (accessed July 7, 2008)

Radioisotopes (such as C-14) are unstable isotopes, and their nuclei decay (break apart) at a steady rate. Decaying radioisotopes produce other isotopes as they emit energy and/or high-energy particles. If the newly formed nuclei are radioactive as well, they emit radiation and change into other nuclei. The final products in this chain are stable, nonradioactive nuclei.

Radiation and radioisotopes reach our bodies daily, emitted from sources in outer space and from rocks and soil on earth. Figure 5.3 shows that radon is the largest source of radiation to which humans are exposed. This

FIGURE 5.3

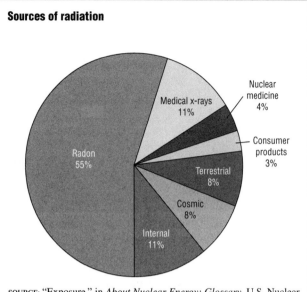

Sources of radiation

SOURCE: "Exposure," in *About Nuclear Energy: Glossary*, U.S. Nuclear Regulatory Commission, February 14, 2007, http://www.nrc.gov/reading-rm/basic-ref/glossary/exposure.html (accessed July 3, 2008)

gas is formed in rocks and soil from the radioactive decay of radium. Most prevalent in the northern half of the United States, radon can enter cracks in basement walls and remain trapped there. Prolonged exposure to high levels of radioactive radon is thought to lead to lung cancer. Other radioisotopes, in minute quantities, are used in medicine as diagnostic tools.

Radiation was discovered at the beginning of the twentieth century by Antoine Henri Becquerel (1852–1908), Marie Curie (1867–1934), and Pierre Curie (1859–1906). Decades later, other scientists determined that they could unleash energy by artificially breaking apart atomic nuclei. Such a process is called nuclear fission. Scientists discovered that they could produce the most energy by bombarding the nuclei of an isotope of uranium called uranium 235 (U-235). The fission of a U-235 atom releases several neutrons, which have the potential to penetrate other U-235 atomic nuclei and cause them to fission. In this way the fission of a single U-235 atom begins a cascading chain of nuclear reactions. (See Figure 5.4.) If this series of reactions is regulated to occur slowly, as it is in nuclear power plants, the energy emitted can be captured for a variety of uses, such as generating electricity. If this series of reactions is allowed to occur all at once, as in an atomic bomb, the energy emitted is explosive. (Plutonium 239 can also be used to generate a chain reaction similar to that of U-235.)

Mining Nuclear Fuel

In the United States, U-235 is used as nuclear fuel. Most of it is found in the form of ore in Wyoming and New Mexico, where it is mined using methods similar to those for other metal ores. The one difference is that uranium

FIGURE 5.4

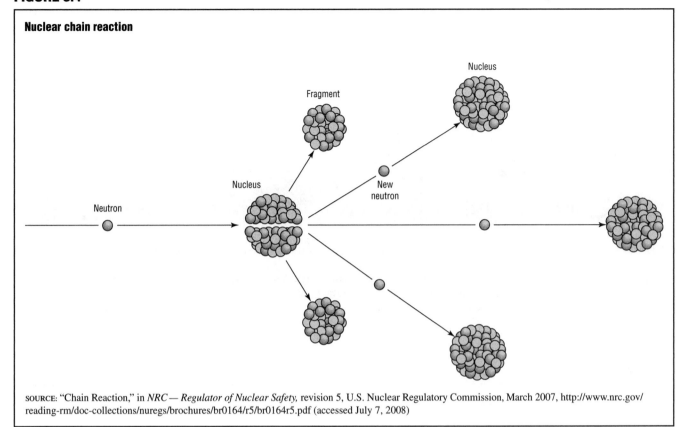

Nuclear chain reaction

Nucleus

Fragment

Nucleus

New
neutron

Neutron

SOURCE: "Chain Reaction," in *NRC — Regulator of Nuclear Safety,* revision 5, U.S. Nuclear Regulatory Commission, March 2007, http://www.nrc.gov/reading-rm/doc-collections/nuregs/brochures/br0164/r5/br0164r5.pdf (accessed July 7, 2008)

mining can expose workers to radioactivity. Uranium atoms split by themselves at a slow rate, causing radioactive substances such as radon to accumulate slowly in the deposits.

After it is mined, uranium must be concentrated, because uranium ore generally contains only 0.1% uranium metal by weight. To concentrate the uranium, it goes through a process called milling: the ore is first crushed, and then various chemicals are poured slowly through the crushed ore to dissolve the uranium. When the uranium—called yellowcake because of its color—is extracted from this chemical solution, it is 85% pure by weight. However, this uranium is 99.3% nonfissionable U-238 and only 0.7% fissionable U-235. Other processes are necessary to create enriched uranium, which has a higher percentage of fissionable uranium.

To enrich uranium, yellowcake is first converted into uranium hexafluoride (UF_6). Cylinders of this gas are sent to a gaseous diffusion plant, where the uranium is heated in a furnace (UF_6 vaporization). (See Figure 5.5.) The enriched uranium is then converted into oxide powder (UO_2), which is made into fingertip-sized fuel pellets. The pellets are less than 0.5 inches (1.3 cm) in diameter, but each one can produce as much energy as 120 gallons (454 L) of oil. The pellets are stacked in rods, which are tubes about 12 feet (3.7 m) long. Many rods (see "Control rods" in Figure 5.2) are bundled together in assemblies, and hundreds of these assemblies make up the core of a nuclear reactor.

DOMESTIC NUCLEAR ENERGY PRODUCTION

The percentage of U.S. electricity supplied by nuclear power grew considerably during the 1970s and early to mid-1980s and then leveled off. (See Figure 5.1.) According to the Energy Information Administration (EIA), in *Annual Energy Review 2007* (June 2008, http://www.eia.doe.gov/aer/pdf/aer.pdf), nuclear power supplied only 5% of the total electricity generated in the United States in 1973. In 2007 nuclear electricity net generation reached 806.5 billion kilowatt-hours (kWh), or 19% of the nation's electricity. Thirty-one states had 104 nuclear reactors in operation in 2005. Figure 5.6 shows that most of these reactors were located east of the Mississippi River.

No new nuclear power plants have been ordered since 1978, and some have closed. (See Table 5.1.) The number of operable nuclear generating units peaked in 1990 with 112 units; as of 2007, 104 units were operating. (See Figure 5.7.) The decline in nuclear power plants stems from several related issues. Financing is difficult to find, and construction has become more expensive, partly because of longer delays for licensing, but also because of regulations instituted following the Three Mile Island accident in 1979. Still, output of electricity at existing plants has increased, achieved largely through an increase

FIGURE 5.5

The nuclear fuel cycle

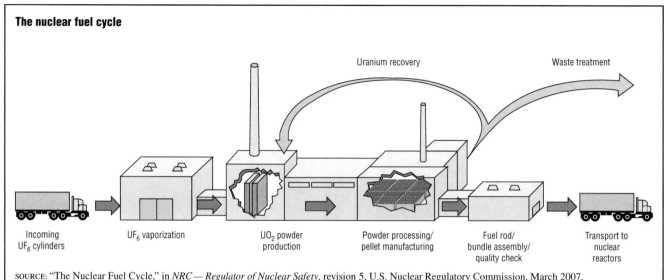

SOURCE: "The Nuclear Fuel Cycle," in *NRC — Regulator of Nuclear Safety*, revision 5, U.S. Nuclear Regulatory Commission, March 2007, http://www.nrc.gov/reading-rm/doc-collections/nuregs/brochures/br0164/r5/br0164r5.pdf (accessed July 7, 2008)

FIGURE 5.6

Operating nuclear reactors, June 2005

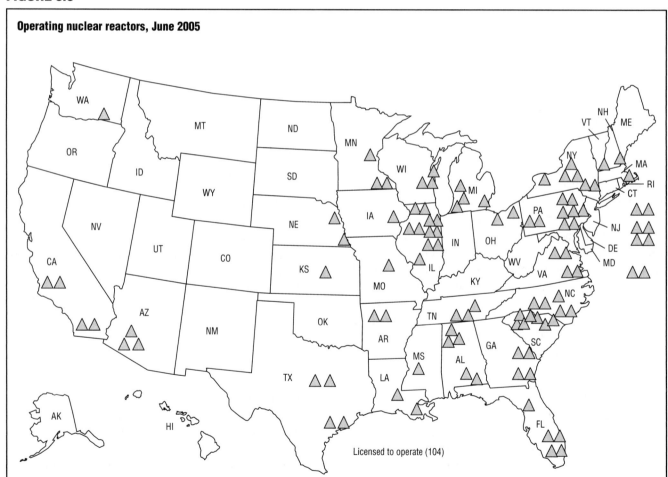

Note: Includes Browns Ferry Unit 1, which has no fuel loaded and requires commission approval to restart.

SOURCE: Adapted from "Figure 16. U.S. Operating Commercial Nuclear Power Reactors," in *Information Digest 2007–2008*, vol. 19, U.S. Nuclear Regulatory Commission, Division of Planning, Budget, and Analysis, Office of the Chief Financial Officer, August 2007, http://www.nrc.gov/reading-rm/doc-collections/nuregs/staff/sr1350/v19/sr1350v19.pdf (accessed July 3, 2008)

TABLE 5.1

Nuclear generating units, 1955–2007

Year	Original licensing regulations (10 CFR Part 50)[a]			Current licensing regulations (10 CFR Part 52)[a]			Permanent shutdowns[f]	Operable units[g]
	Construction permits issued[b, c]	Low-power operating licenses issued[c, d]	Full-power operating licenses issued[c, e]	Early site permits issued[c]	Combined license applications under review	Combined licenses issued[c]		
1955	1	0	0	0	0			
1956	3	0	0	—	—	—	0	0
1957	1	1	1	—	—	—	0	1
1958	0	0	0	—	—	—	0	1
1959	3	1	1	—	—	—	0	2
1960	7	1	1	—	—	—	0	3
1961	0	0	0	—	—	—	0	3
1962	1	7	6	—	—	—	0	9
1963	1	3	2	—	—	—	0	11
1964	3	2	3	—	—	—	1	13
1965	1	0	0	—	—	—	0	13
1966	5	1	2	—	—	—	1	14
1967	14	3	3	—	—	—	2	15
1968	23	0	0	—	—	—	2	13
1969	7	4	4	—	—	—	0	17
1970	10	4	3	—	—	—	0	20
1971	4	5	2	—	—	—	0	22
1972	8	6	6	—	—	—	1	27
1973	14	12	15	—	—	—	0	42
1974	23	14	15	—	—	—	2	55
1975	9	3	2	—	—	—	0	57
1976	9	7	7	—	—	—	1	63
1977	15	4	4	—	—	—	0	67
1978	13	3	4	—	—	—	1	70
1979	2	0	0	—	—	—	1	69
1980	0	5	2	—	—	—	0	71
1981	0	3	4	—	—	—	0	75
1982	0	6	4	—	—	—	1	78
1983	0	3	3	—	—	—	0	81
1984	0	7	6	—	—	—	0	87
1985	0	7	9	—	—	—	0	96
1986	0	7	5	—	—	—	0	101
1987	0	6	8	—	—	—	2	107
1988	0	1	2	—	—	—	0	109
1989	0	3	4	—	—	—	2	111
1990	0	1	2	—	—	—	1	112
1991	0	0	0	—	—	—	1	111
1992	0	0	0	—	—	—	2	109
1993	0	1	1	—	—	—	0	110
1994	0	0	0	—	—	—	1	109
1995	0	1	0	—	—	—	0	109
1996	0	0	1	—	—	—	1	109
1997	0	0	0	0	0	0	2	107
1998	0	0	0	0	0	0	3	104
1999–2006	0	0	0	0	0	0	0	104
2007	0	0	0	3	4	0	0	104
Total	**177**	**132**	**132**	**3**	**4**	**0**	**28**	**—**

[a]Data in columns 1–3 are based on the U.S. Nuclear Regulatory Commission (NRC) regulation 10 CFR Part 50. Data in columns 4–6 are based on the NRC regulation 10 CFR Part 52.
[b]Issuance by regulatory authority of a permit, or equivalent permission, to begin construction.
[c]Numbers reflect permits or licenses issued in a given year, not extant permits or licenses.
[d]Issuance by regulatory authority of license, or equivalent permission, to conduct testing but not to operate at full power.
[e]Issuance by regulatory authority of full-power operating license, or equivalent permission (note that some units receive full-power licenses the same year they receive low-power licenses). Units initially undergo low-power testing prior to commercial operation.
[f]Number of nuclear generating units, in a given year, ceasing operation permanently.
[g]Total of nuclear generating units holding full-power licenses, or equivalent permission to operate, at the end of the year (the number of operable units equals the cumulative number of units holding full-power licenses minus the cumulative number of permanent shutdowns).
— = Not applicable.
Web page: For related information, see http://www.eia.doe.gov/fuelnuclear.html.

SOURCE: Adapted from "Table 9.1. Nuclear Generating Units, 1955–2007," in *Annual Energy Review 2007*, U.S. Department of Energy, Energy Information Administration, Office of Energy Markets and End Use, June 2008, http://www.eia.doe.gov/aer/pdf/aer.pdf (accessed June 28, 2008). Non-U.S. governmental data from the Nuclear Energy Institute *Historical Profile of U.S. Nuclear Power Development*, 1988, and various utility, Federal, and contractor officials.

in average capacity factor. The capacity factor is the proportion of electricity produced to what could have been produced at full-power operation. The EIA reveals that in 2007 the average capacity factor for U.S. nuclear power plants was 92%, an all-time high. Better training for operators, longer operating cycles between refueling, and control-system improvements contributed to increased plant performance.

FIGURE 5.7

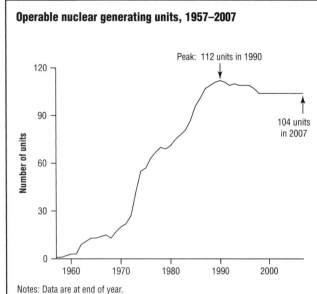

Operable nuclear generating units, 1957–2007

Peak: 112 units in 1990

104 units
in 2007

Number of units

120

90

60

30

0

1960   1970   1980   1990   2000

Notes: Data are at end of year.
Units holding full-power operating licenses, or equivalent permission to operate, at the end of the year.

SOURCE: Adapted from "Figure 9.1. Nuclear Generating Units: Operable Units, 1957–2007," in *Annual Energy Review 2007*, U.S. Department of Energy, Energy Information Administration, Office of Energy Markets and End Use, June 2008, http://www.eia.doe.gov/aer/pdf/aer.pdf (accessed June 28, 2008)

OUTLOOK FOR DOMESTIC NUCLEAR ENERGY

In *Annual Energy Outlook 2008* (2008, http://www.eia.doe.gov/oiaf/aeo/pdf/0383(2008).pdf), the EIA predicts that the capacity of nuclear power plants will increase from 100.2 gigawatts in 2006 to 114.9 gigawatts in 2030. About 17 gigawatts of capacity will come from new plants and 2.7 gigawatts from power uprates (an increase in the power output of a nuclear power plant accomplished by adding a more highly enriched uranium fuel to the existing fuel). The plant must be able to operate safely at the higher power level. These increases will be partially offset by 4.5 gigawatts of retirements. A power uprate is accomplished by adding a more highly enriched uranium fuel to the existing fuel. The plant must be able to operate safely at the higher power level.

Electricity generation from nuclear power plants is predicted to grow from 787 billion kWh in 2006 to 917 billion kWh in 2030. The share that nuclear power contributes to electricity generation in the United States is expected to decrease slightly from 19% in 2007 to 18% in 2030.

INTERNATIONAL PRODUCTION

At 2.6 trillion kWh, nuclear power provided about 15% of the total 17.3 trillion kWh of electricity produced in the world during 2005. (See Table 5.2.) The U.S. Nuclear Regulatory Commission (NRC) indicates in *2007–2008 Information Digest* (2007, http://www.nrc.gov/reading-rm/doc-collections/nuregs/staff/sr1350/v19/sr1350v19.pdf)

that as of December 31, 2006, electricity was being produced by 439 nuclear plants worldwide. Fifty-two other plants were under construction or on order.

In 2005 the United States led the world in nuclear power electricity generation with 782 billion kWh, followed by France (429 billion kWh) and Japan (278.4 billion kWh). (See Table 5.2.) Together, the three countries generated 57% of the world's nuclear electric power. About 80% of France's electrical power was produced by nuclear energy in 2005, followed by Belgium (56%), Sweden (45%), and Switzerland (38%). Japan produced 27% of its electricity by nuclear power generation in 2005, and the United States, 19%. Canada produced 14% of its electricity with nuclear power; the primary source for electricity generation in Canada is hydroelectric power.

Worldwide, the EIA projects in *International Energy Outlook 2008* (June 2008, http://www.eia.doe.gov/oiaf/ieo/) that nuclear generating capacity will increase slightly from 374 gigawatts in 2005 to 498 gigawatts in 2030. Some countries whose capacities are projected to increase are:

- Canada, from 13 gigawatts in 2005 to 18 gigawatts in 2030

- Japan, from 47 gigawatts in 2005 to 58 gigawatts by 2030

- China, from 7 gigawatts in 2005 to 52 gigawatts by 2030

- India, from 3 gigawatts in 2005 to 20 gigawatts by 2030

- United States, from 100 gigawatts in 2005 to 116 gigawatts in 2025, and then drop to 115 gigawatts by 2030

AGING NUCLEAR POWER PLANTS

At some point, the nuclear plants now operating worldwide may need to be retired. Most of them were designed to last about thirty years. Some plants showed serious levels of deterioration after as few as fifteen years; some have lasted well beyond their thirty-year expectations.

There are three methods of retiring, or decommissioning, a reactor. Safe enclosure, or mothballing, involves removing the fuel from the plant, monitoring any radioactive contamination (which is usually very low or nonexistent), and guarding the structure to prevent anyone from entering until eventual dismantling and decontamination activities occur. Entombment, which was used at Chernobyl, involves permanently encasing the structure in a long-lived material such as concrete. This procedure allows the radioactive material to remain safely on-site. Immediate dismantling involves decontaminating and tearing down the facility within a few months or years. This method is initially more expensive than the other options but removes the long-term costs of

TABLE 5.2

World net electric power generation by type, 1980, 1990, and 2005

[Billion kilowatthours]

Region and country	Fossil fuels			Nuclear electric power			Hydroelectric power[a]			Total[b]		
	1980	1990	2005[P]	1980	1990	2005[P]	1980	1990	2005[P]	1980	1990	2005[P]
North America	**1,880.1**	**2,292.0**	**3,238.4**	**287.0**	**648.9**	**879.7**	**546.9**	**606.5**	**651.1**	**2,721.6**	**3,624.0**	**4,888.4**
Canada	79.8	101.9	152.2	35.9	69.2	87.4	251.0	293.9	359.9	367.9	468.7	609.6
Mexico	46.0	85.7	175.2	.0	2.8	10.3	16.7	23.2	27.5	63.6	116.6	222.4
United States	1,753.8	2,103.8	2,910.0	251.1	576.9	782.0	279.2	289.4	263.8	2,289.6	3,038.0	4,055.4
Other	.5	.7	1.0	.0	.0	.0	.0	.0	.0	.5	.7	1.0
Central and South America	**99.8**	**114.8**	**253.3**	**2.2**	**9.0**	**16.3**	**201.5**	**365.1**	**613.2**	**308.2**	**497.2**	**908.7**
Argentina	22.2	20.9	59.5	2.2	7.0	6.4	17.3	20.2	33.9	41.8	48.3	101.1
Brazil	7.5	8.1	34.1	.0	1.9	9.9	128.4	204.6	334.1	138.3	219.6	396.4
Paraguay	(s)	(s)	(s)	.0	.0	.0	.7	27.2	50.7	.8	27.2	50.7
Venezuela	17.6	21.0	24.9	.0	.0	.0	14.4	36.6	74.3	32.0	57.6	99.2
Other	52.4	64.8	134.9	.0	.0	.0	40.6	76.4	120.2	95.3	144.4	261.4
Europe[c]	**[R]1,453.3**	**[R]1,441.0**	**1,837.7**	**229.6**	**761.3**	**957.3**	**458.0**	**474.5**	**539.6**	**[R]2,154.7**	**[R]2,696.4**	**3,494.7**
Belgium	38.3	25.0	33.0	11.9	40.6	45.2	.3	.3	.3	50.8	66.5	80.8
Czech Republic	—	—	50.8	—	—	23.5	—	—	2.4	—	—	77.4
Finland	22.0	22.8	22.0	6.6	18.3	22.1	10.1	10.8	13.6	38.7	51.8	67.1
France	118.0	44.3	57.2	63.4	298.4	429.0	68.3	52.8	51.2	250.8	397.6	543.6
Germany	390.3	358.9	362.3	55.6	145.1	154.9	18.8	17.2	19.4	469.9	526.0	579.4
Italy	125.5	167.5	231.1	2.1	.0	.0	45.0	31.3	33.3	176.4	202.1	278.5
Netherlands	58.0	63.2	81.8	3.9	3.3	3.8	.0	.1	.1	62.9	67.7	94.3
Norway	.1	.2	.5	.0	.0	.0	82.7	119.9	134.4	82.9	120.4	135.8
Poland	111.1	125.0	142.1	.0	.0	.0	2.3	1.4	2.2	113.8	126.7	146.2
Romania	51.4	49.7	31.6	.0	.0	5.3	12.5	10.9	20.0	63.9	60.6	56.9
Spain	74.5	66.5	173.1	5.2	51.6	54.7	29.2	25.2	19.4	109.2	143.9	270.3
Sweden	10.1	3.2	3.7	25.3	64.8	68.6	58.1	71.8	72.1	94.3	141.5	153.2
Switzerland	.9	.6	1.0	12.9	22.4	22.2	32.5	29.5	30.9	46.4	53.0	56.1
Turkey	12.0	32.3	114.8	.0	.0	.0	11.2	22.9	39.2	23.3	55.2	154.2
United Kingdom	228.9	230.0	277.5	32.3	62.5	75.2	3.9	5.1	4.9	265.1	299.0	372.6
Other	[R]212.1	[R]251.6	255.3	10.3	54.4	52.9	83.2	75.4	96.3	[R]306.3	[R]384.3	428.2
Eurasia[d]	**1,037.1**	**1,204.1**	**843.6**	**72.9**	**201.3**	**235.8**	**184.0**	**230.7**	**244.7**	**1,294.0**	**1,636.1**	**1,327.3**
Kazakhstan	—	—	56.5	—	—	.0	—	—	7.8	—	—	64.2
Russia	—	—	588.4	—	—	140.2	—	—	172.9	—	—	904.4
Ukraine	—	—	79.7	—	—	83.3	—	—	12.4	—	—	175.4
Other	1,037.1	1,204.1	119.1	72.9	201.3	12.3	184.0	230.7	51.7	1,294.0	1,636.1	183.3
Middle East	**[R]81.8**	**[R]215.5**	**581.7**	**.0**	**.0**	**.0**	**9.6**	**9.6**	**21.0**	**[R]91.4**	**[R]225.1**	**602.7**
Iran	15.7	49.8	154.4	.0	.0	.0	5.6	6.0	15.9	21.3	55.9	170.4
Saudi Arabia	20.5	64.9	165.6	.0	.0	.0	.0	.0	.0	20.5	64.9	165.6
Other	[R]45.7	[R]100.7	261.7	.0	.0	.0	4.1	3.6	5.0	[R]49.7	[R]104.3	266.7
Africa	**128.8**	**243.6**	**430.3**	**.0**	**8.4**	**12.2**	**60.1**	**54.9**	**88.7**	**188.9**	**307.3**	**533.2**
Egypt	8.6	31.5	89.8	.0	.0	.0	9.7	9.9	12.1	18.3	41.4	102.5
South Africa	92.1	146.6	214.9	.0	8.4	12.2	1.0	1.0	.9	93.1	156.0	228.3
Other	28.2	65.5	125.7	.0	.0	.0	49.4	44.0	75.6	77.6	109.9	202.4

monitoring both the structure and the radiation levels. It also frees the site for other uses, including the construction of another nuclear power plant. Nuclear power companies are also seeking alternative uses for nuclear shells, including the conversion of old nuclear plants to gas-fired plants.

Paying for the closing, decontamination, or dismantling of nuclear plants has become an issue of intense public debate. The industry contends that the cost of decommissioning retired plants and handling radioactive wastes will continue to escalate, causing serious financial problems for electric utilities.

A NEW GENERATION OF NUCLEAR PLANTS

In 2001 the Generation IV International Forum (July 14, 2005, http://gif.inel.gov/roadmap/), a group of nuclear nations, agreed to work together to create a new generation of nuclear reactors. Their intent was to develop new systems by 2030 that "present significant improvements in economics, safety and reliability and sustainability over currently operating reactor technologies." As of September 2008, its members included Argentina, Brazil, Canada, the European Atomic Energy Community, France, Japan, the Republic of Korea, the Republic of South Africa, Switzerland, the United Kingdom, and the United States.

The group chose six nuclear power technologies for development:

- *Gas-cooled fast reactor*—this technology would provide a closed system, helium-cooled reactor that minimizes long-lived radioactive waste by recycling it.

- *Very-high-temperature reactor (VHTR)*—with core outlet temperatures reaching 1,832° Fahrenheit (1,000° C),

TABLE 5.2

World net electric power generation by type, 1980, 1990, and 2005 [CONTINUED]

[Billion kilowatthours]

Region and country	Fossil fuels			Nuclear electric power			Hydroelectric power[a]			Total[b]		
	1980	1990	2005[P]	1980	1990	2005[P]	1980	1990	2005[P]	1980	1990	2005[P]
Asia and Oceania[c]	**907.7**	**1,626.8**	**4,270.2**	**92.7**	**279.9**	**524.3**	**262.7**	**404.1**	**735.3**	**1,268.0**	**2,333.0**	**5,589.1**
Australia	74.5	131.8	218.4	.0	.0	.0	12.8	14.0	15.5	87.7	146.4	236.7
China	227.9	465.2	1,922.1	.0	.0	50.3	57.6	125.1	397.0	285.5	590.3	2,371.8
India	69.7	198.9	539.2	3.0	5.6	15.7	46.5	70.9	99.0	119.3	275.5	661.6
Indonesia	10.6	35.3	103.4	.0	.0	.0	2.2	6.7	10.7	12.8	43.0	120.3
Japan	381.6	524.0	645.5	78.6	192.2	278.4	87.8	88.4	77.4	549.1	817.3	1,024.6
South Korea	29.8	45.5	222.7	3.3	50.2	139.4	1.5	4.6	3.6	34.6	100.4	366.2
Taiwan	31.3	43.6	164.5	7.8	31.6	38.0	2.9	8.2	7.8	42.0	83.3	210.2
Thailand	12.3	38.7	115.7	.0	.0	.0	1.3	4.9	5.7	13.6	43.7	124.6
Other	70.1	143.8	338.6	(s)	.4	2.4	50.0	81.2	118.5	123.5	233.2	472.9
World	**5,588.5**	**7,137.9**	**11,455.3**	**684.4**	**1,908.8**	**2,625.6**	**1,722.9**	**2,145.4**	**2,893.5**	**8,026.9**	**R11,319.2**	**17,344.0**

[a]Excludes pumped storage, except for the United States.
[b]Wood, waste, geothermal, solar, wind, batteries, chemicals, hydrogen, pitch, purchased steam, sulfur, and miscellaneous technologies are included in total.
[c]Excludes countries that were part of the former U.S.S.R.
[d]Includes only countries that were part of the former U.S.S.R.
P = Preliminary.
— = Not applicable.
(s) = Less than 0.05 billion kilowatthours.
Note: Totals may not equal sum of components due to independent rounding.
web page: For related information, see http://www.eia.doe.gov/international.

SOURCE: "Table 11.16. World Net Generation of Electricity by Type, 1980, 1990, and 2005 (Billion Kilowatthours)," in *Annual Energy Review 2007*, U.S. Department of Energy, Energy Information Administration, Office of Energy Markets and End Use, June 2008, http://www.eia.doe.gov/aer/pdf/aer.pdf (accessed June 28, 2008)

the VHTR would be used to produce hydrogen and to meet specific high-temperature heating needs of the petrochemical industry and others.

- *Supercritical-water-cooled reactor (SCWR)*—the SCWR is a high-temperature, high-pressure water-cooled reactor that increases efficiency by operating above the thermodynamic critical point of water. Water under high pressure does not boil and turn to steam; the thermodynamic critical point of water refers to the temperature and pressure at which the liquid state ceases to exist and the liquid and gaseous forms become indistinguishable. For water, this point is 705° Fahrenheit (374° C).

- *Sodium-cooled fast reactor (SFR)*—intended for electricity generation, this system uses a sodium-cooled reactor and a closed fuel cycle to increase safety and reduce high-level radioactive waste.

- *Lead-cooled fast reactor (LFR)*—designed with small electricity grids and developing countries in mind, the LFR proposes a factory-built system that would need refueling only every fifteen to twenty years. It features a fast-spectrum lead or liquid metal-cooled reactor and a closed cycle for reducing waste.

- *Molten salt reactor*—in this system, the fuel is a liquid mixture of sodium, zirconium, and uranium fluorides, which eliminates the need for fuel production. By-products can be recycled back into the fuel mixture.

Each of the new technologies builds on the knowledge gained during the three other periods of nuclear reactor

development: Generation I—the experimental reactors developed in the 1950s and 1960s; Generation II—large, central-station nuclear power reactors, such as the 104 plants still operating in the United States, built in the 1970s and 1980s; and Generation III—the advanced light-water reactors built in the 1990s, primarily in East Asia, to meet that region's expanding electricity needs.

NUCLEAR SAFETY

Safety has been an issue from the beginning of the industry. For example, some plant sites, especially those near earthquake fault lines, have raised serious questions for governments, industry leaders, and environmentalists. Plants can be shut down for a variety of reasons. For example, in 1987 the NRC shut down the Peach Bottom nuclear plant in Delta, Pennsylvania, because control room operators were found sleeping on duty. The plant was not restarted until 1989, after reactor operators had been retrained and changes in management had occurred. In addition, many workers resigned, retired, or were demoted—a few were even fired. The plant, as well as some of the workers, was fined by the NRC. In February 2005 the Kewaunee Power Station in Carlton, Wisconsin, was shut down after it was discovered that emergency shutdown systems could be compromised by flooding from water storage tanks located in an adjacent part of the plant. Even though no flood actually occurred, operations at the plant were halted until the shutdown systems could be protected from a potential water threat. In November 2007 the Perry Nuclear Power Plant near

Cleveland, Ohio, automatically shut down when the system that supplies coolant water to the reactor malfunctioned. Nuclear plants shut down from time to time, but most safety questions have been focused by major accidents since the late 1970s.

Three Mile Island

On March 28, 1979, the Three Mile Island nuclear facility near Harrisburg, Pennsylvania, was the site of the worst nuclear accident in U.S. history. Information released several years after the accident revealed that Unit 2, one of the reactors operating at the site, came much closer to meltdown than either the NRC or the industry had previously indicated. Temperatures inside the reactor, which were first said to have reached 3,500° Fahrenheit (1,927° C), are now known to have reached at least 4,800° Fahrenheit (2,649° C). The temperature needed to melt uranium dioxide fuel is 5,080° Fahrenheit (2,804° C). When meltdown occurs, an uncontrolled explosion may result, unlike the controlled nuclear reaction of normal operation.

The emergency system at Three Mile Island was designed to dump water on the hot core of the reactor and spray water into the reactor building to stop the production of steam. During the accident, however, the valves leading to the emergency water pumps closed. Another valve was stuck in the open position, drawing water away from the core, which then became partially uncovered and began to melt.

The accident resulted in no deaths or injuries to plant workers or the nearby community. On average, area residents were exposed to less radiation than that of a chest X-ray. Nevertheless, the incident raised concerns about nuclear safety, which resulted in more rigorous safety standards in the nuclear power industry and at the NRC. Antinuclear sentiment was fueled as well, heightening Americans' wariness of nuclear power as an energy source.

The nuclear reactor in Unit 2 at Three Mile Island has been in monitored storage since it underwent cleanup. Operation of the reactor in Unit 1 resumed in 1985.

Chernobyl

On April 26, 1986, the most serious nuclear accident ever occurred at Chernobyl, a nuclear plant in what is now Ukraine (then part of the Soviet Union). At least thirty-one people died and hundreds were injured when one of the four reactors exploded during a badly run test. Millions of people were exposed to some levels of radiation when radioactive particles were released into the atmosphere. About 350,000 people were eventually evacuated from the area, including residents of what are now the neighboring nations of Belarus and the Russian Federation, who were endangered by fallout carried by the prevailing winds.

The cleanup was a huge project. Helicopters dropped tons of limestone, sand, clay, lead, and boron on the smoldering reactor to stop the radiation leakage and reduce the heat. Workers built a giant steel and cement sarcophagus to entomb the remains of the reactor and contain the radioactive waste.

The International Atomic Energy Agency (IAEA) indicates in *Chernobyl's Legacy: Health, Environmental, and Socio-economic Impacts* (April 2006, http://www.iaea.org/Publications/Booklets/Chernobyl/chernobyl.pdf) that about one thousand people involved in the initial cleanup, including emergency workers and the military, received high doses of radiation. Eventually, over six hundred thousand people would be involved in decontamination and containment activities. The long-term effects of whatever exposure they received are being monitored. According to the IAEA, the most measurable effect of the radiation has been the incidence of thyroid cancer in children. At least four thousand children—which is considered a very large number, given the size of the population—have been treated for the cancer.

Even though some of the evacuated land has been declared fit for habitation again, several areas that received heavy concentrations of radiation are expected to be closed for decades. The three remaining nuclear reactors at Chernobyl continue to operate. The site itself is off-limits to all but official personnel.

An International Agreement on Safety

In September 1994 forty nations, including the United States, signed the International Convention on Nuclear Safety, an agreement that requires them to shut down nuclear power plants if necessary safety measures cannot be guaranteed. In "Summary Report of the 4th Review Meeting of the Contracting Parties to the Convention on Nuclear Safety" (June 2008, http://www-ns.iaea.org/downloads/ni/safety_convention/summary-report-april2008-final.pdf), the IAEA states that as of April 14, 2008, sixty countries and one regional organization had had ratified the agreement. The agreement applies to land-based civil nuclear power plants and seeks to avert accidents such as the 1986 explosion at Chernobyl. Ukraine, which inherited the Chernobyl plant after the collapse of the Soviet Union, signed the agreement. Signers must submit reports on atomic installations and, if necessary, make improvements to upgrade safety at the sites. Neighboring countries may call for an urgent study if they are concerned about a reactor's safety and the potential fallout that could affect their own population or crops.

RADIOACTIVE WASTE

Working in a laboratory in Chicago, Illinois, in 1942, the physicist Enrico Fermi (1901–1954) assembled enough uranium to cause a nuclear fission reaction. His discovery transformed both warfare and energy production. The experiment also produced a small packet of radioactive waste material that may remain dangerous for one hundred thousand years. That first radioactive waste lies buried under a foot of concrete and two feet of dirt on a hillside in Illinois.

Radioactive waste is produced at all stages of the nuclear fuel cycle, from the initial mining of the uranium to the final disposal of the spent fuel from the reactor. The term *radioactive waste* encompasses a broad range of material with widely varying characteristics. Some is barely radioactive and safe to handle, whereas other types are intensely hot and highly radioactive. Some waste decays to safe levels of radioactivity in a matter of days or weeks, whereas other types will remain dangerous for thousands of years. The U.S. Department of Energy and the NRC have defined the major types of radioactive waste.

Uranium Mill Tailings

Uranium mill tailings are sandlike wastes produced in uranium refining operations. Even though they emit low levels of radiation, their large volume (10 million to 15 million short tons [9.1 million to 13.6 million t] annually) poses a hazard, particularly from radon emissions and groundwater contamination. The dangers of uranium mill tailings were not realized until the early 1970s, so many miners and residents of the western United States were exposed to them. Cancer incidences are high among miners who worked before the 1970s. In addition, the World Information Source on Energy Uranium Project reports in "Health Impacts for Uranium Mine and Mill Residents—Science Issues" (April 9, 2008, http://www.wise-uranium.org/uhr.html) that those residing near uranium mills have shown increased risks of leukemia, lung and renal cancer, and birth defects.

Low-Level Waste

Low-level waste, which contains lesser levels of radioactivity, includes trash (such as wiping rags, swabs, and syringes), contaminated clothing (such as shoe covers and protective gloves), and hardware (such as luminous dials, filters, and tools). This waste comes from nuclear reactors, industrial users, government users (but not nuclear weapons sites), research universities, and medical facilities. In general, low-level waste decays relatively quickly (in ten to one hundred years).

High-Level Waste

Spent nuclear fuel (used reactor fuel) is high-level radioactive waste. Uranium fuel can be used for twelve to eighteen months, after which it is no longer as efficient in splitting its atoms and producing the heat needed to generate electricity. It must be removed from the reactor and replaced with fresh fuel. Some of the spent fuel is reprocessed to recover the usable uranium and plutonium,

but the radioactive material that remains is dangerous for thousands of years.

Transuranic Wastes

Transuranic wastes are eleven man-made radioactive elements with atomic numbers greater than that of uranium (ninety-two) and therefore beyond (*trans-*) uranium (*-uranic*) on the Periodic Table of the elements. Their half-lives (the time it takes for half the radioisotopes present in a sample to decay to nonradioactive elements) are thousands of years. They are found in trash produced mainly by nuclear weapons plants and are therefore part of the nuclear waste problem but not directly the concern of nuclear power utilities.

Mixed Waste

Mixed waste is high-level, low-level, or transuranic waste that also contains hazardous nonradioactive waste. Such waste poses serious institutional problems, because the radioactive portion is regulated by the Department of Energy or the NRC under the Atomic Energy Act of 1954, whereas the U.S. Environmental Protection Agency (EPA) regulates the nonradioactive elements under the Resource Conservation and Recovery Act of 1976.

RADIOACTIVE WASTE DISPOSAL

Disposing of radioactive waste is unquestionably one of the major problems associated with the development of nuclear power; radioactive waste is also a by-product of nuclear weapons plants, hospitals, and scientific research. Even though federal policy is based on the assumption that radioactive waste can be disposed of safely, new storage and disposal facilities for all types of radioactive waste have frequently been delayed or blocked by concerns about safety, health, and the environment.

The highly toxic wastes must be isolated from the environment until the radioactivity decays to a safe level. In the case of plutonium, for example, the half-life is twenty-six thousand years. At that rate, it will take at least one hundred thousand years before radioactive plutonium is no longer dangerous. Any facilities built to store such materials must last at least that long.

Regulation of Radioactive Waste Disposal

As of January 2006 the NRC had entered into agreements with thirty-three states to regulate the management, storage, and disposal of certain nuclear waste within their borders.

Disposal of Uranium Mill Tailings

Mill tailings are usually deposited in large piles next to the mill that processed the ore. In 1978 Congress passed the Uranium Mill Tailing Radiation Control Act, which requires mill owners to follow EPA standards for the cleanup of uranium and thorium after milling operations have permanently closed. The companies must cover the mill tailings to control the release of radon gas for one thousand years.

Disposal of Low-Level Waste

According to the NRC, in *2007–2008 Information Digest*, as of June 2007 three low-level licensed nuclear waste facilities were operating in the United States: in Barnwell, South Carolina; in Hanford, Washington; and in Clive, Utah, where Energy Solutions accepts large amounts of mill tailings and low-level waste, such as contaminated soil or debris from demolished buildings. Four low-level radioactive waste facilities have been closed: in West Valley, New York (closed 1975); in Maxey Flats, Kentucky (closed 1977); in Sheffield, Illinois (closed 1978); and in Beatty, Nevada (closed 1993).

The design of a low-level waste facility is shown in Figure 5.8. Wastes are buried in shallow underground

FIGURE 5.8

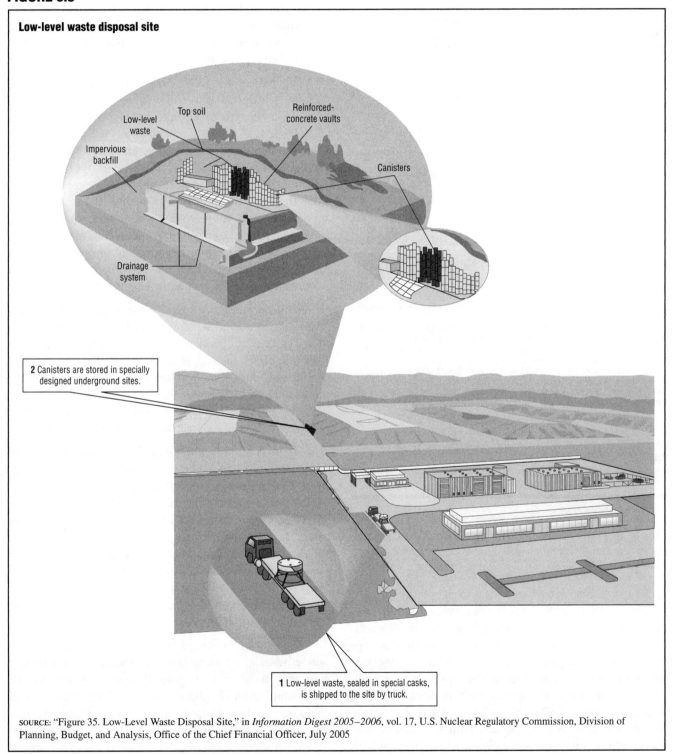

Low-level waste disposal site

Low-level waste

Top soil

Reinforced-concrete vaults

Impervious backfill

Canisters

Drainage system

2 Canisters are stored in specially designed underground sites.

1 Low-level waste, sealed in special casks, is shipped to the site by truck.

SOURCE: "Figure 35. Low-Level Waste Disposal Site," in *Information Digest 2005–2006*, vol. 17, U.S. Nuclear Regulatory Commission, Division of Planning, Budget, and Analysis, Office of the Chief Financial Officer, July 2005

TABLE 5.3

Low-level waste compacts, June 2007

Appalachian
Delaware
Maryland
Pennsylvania
West Virginia

Atlantic
New Jersey
South Carolina*

Central
Arkansas
Kansas
Louisiana
Nebraska
Oklahoma

Central Midwest
Illinois
Kentucky

Midwest
Indiana
Iowa
Minnesota
Missouri
Ohio
Wisconsin

Northwest
Alaska
Hawaii
Idaho
Montana
Oregon
Utah*
Washington*
Wyoming

Rocky Mountain
Colorado
Nevada
New Mexico

Southeast
Alabama
Florida
Georgia
Mississippi
Tennessee
Virginia

Southwestern
Arizona
California
North Dakota
South Dakota

Texas
Texas
Vermont

Unaffiliated
Maine
Massachusetts
Michigan
New Hampshire
New York
North Carolina
Rhode Island

*There are three active, licensed low-level waste disposal facilities located in agreement states.

Barnwell, located in Barnwell, South Carolina: Currently, Barnwell accepts waste from all U.S. generators. Beginning in 2008, Barnwell will only accept waste from the Atlantic Compact States (Connecticut, New Jersey, and South Carolina). Barnwell is licensed by the state of South Carolina to receive waste for classes A-C waste.

Energy Solutions, located in Clive, Utah: Energy Solutions accepts waste from all regions of the United States. It is licensed by the state of Utah for class A waste only.

Hanford, located in Hanford, Washington: Hanford accepts waste from the Northwest and Rocky Mountain compacts. Hanford is licensed by the state of Washington to receive waste for classes A-C waste.

SOURCE: "Table 15. U.S. Low-Level Waste Compacts," in *Information Digest 2007–2008*, vol. 19, U.S. Nuclear Regulatory Commission, Division of Planning, Budget, and Analysis, Office of the Chief Financial Officer, August 2007, http://www.nrc.gov/reading-rm/doc-collections/nuregs/staff/sr1350/v19/sr1350v19.pdf (accessed July 3, 2008)

sites in specially designed canisters. Underground storage may or may not include protection by concrete vaults.

The Low-Level Radioactive Waste Policy Amendments Act of 1985 encouraged states to enter into compacts, which are legal agreements among states for low-level radioactive waste disposal. Table 5.3 shows these compacts. Even though each compact is responsible for the development of disposal capacity for the low-level waste generated within the compact, new disposal sites have yet to be built. As Table 5.3 shows, two of the three operational low-level sites are located in the Northwest Compact and one is in the Atlantic Compact. Nuclear power facilities located in compacts without low-level waste disposal sites must petition

the compact to export their low-level radioactive waste to one of the three operating disposal sites.

Disposal of High-Level Waste

A major step toward shifting the responsibility for disposal of high-level radioactive wastes (spent fuel) from the nuclear power industry to the federal government was taken in 1982, when Congress passed the Nuclear Waste Policy Act. It established national policy, set a detailed timetable for the disposal and management of high-level nuclear waste, and authorized construction of the first high-level nuclear waste repository. A 1987 amendment to the Nuclear Waste Policy Act directed investigation of Yucca Mountain, about 100 miles (161 km) northwest of Las Vegas, Nevada, as a potential site.

The project was highly controversial, however, and Congress did not approve the Yucca Mountain site until July 2002. The state of Nevada challenged the decision, but in 2004 federal courts dismissed the challenge. In April 2006 the U.S. secretary of energy announced proposals to facilitate licensing and construction of the repository, which was expected to take about five years. In June 2008 the Department of Energy submitted a waste repository license application to the NRC—more than a decade after the repository was originally scheduled to open. Thus, by mid-2008, no long-term, permanent disposal repository for high-level waste existed, and construction of the Yucca Mountain Repository had not yet begun.

While waiting for the development of the Yucca Mountain site, as of September 2008 spent fuel was being stored at facilities away from the power plants that generated the waste, such as at the General Electric Company facility in Morris, Illinois. Alternately, spent fuel was being stored at the nuclear power plants that generated the waste. The map in Figure 5.9 notes the sites storing spent nuclear fuel and high-level radioactive waste as of June 2008.

Figure 5.10 shows the plan for the proposed Yucca Mountain high-level nuclear waste repository. Above-ground structures for handling and packaging nuclear waste would cover approximately 400 acres (162 hectares) and be surrounded by a 3-mile (4.8-km) buffer zone. Underground, about 1,400 acres (567 hectares) would be mined, with tunnels leading to areas where sealed metal containers would be placed. This type of deep geologic disposal is widely considered by governments, scientists, and engineers to be the best option for isolating highly radioactive waste.

The repository would be designed to contain radioactive material by using layers of man-made and natural barriers. Regulations require that a repository isolate waste until the radiation decays to a level that is about the same as that from a natural underground uranium deposit. This decay time was originally estimated to be about ten thousand years, but the National Academy of

FIGURE 5.9

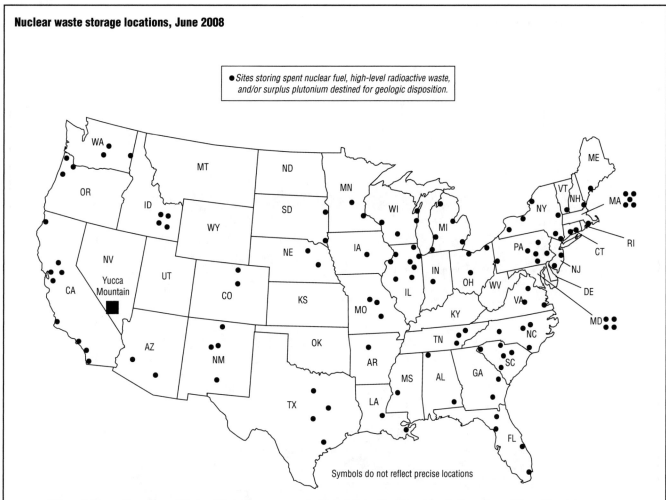

Nuclear waste storage locations, June 2008

● Sites storing spent nuclear fuel, high-level radioactive waste, and/or surplus plutonium destined for geologic disposition.

Symbols do not reflect precise locations

SOURCE: "Figure 2. Current Locations of Nuclear Waste Storage across the United States," in *The safety of a Repository at Yucca Mountain*, U.S. Department of Energy, Office of Civilian Radioactive Waste Management, June 2008, http://www.ocrwm.doe.gov/ym_repository/license/docs/Safety_ of _a_repository.pdf (accessed July 3, 2008)

Sciences has more recently recommended a higher standard of about three hundred thousand years.

After the repository has been filled to capacity, regulations require the Department of Energy to keep the facility open and to monitor it for at least fifty years from the fill date. Eventually, the repository shafts would be filled with rock and earth and sealed. At ground level, facilities would be removed and, as much as possible, the site returned to its original condition.

Scientists expect some of the man-made barriers in a repository to break down over thousands of years. Once that happens, natural barriers will be counted on to stop or slow the movement of radiation particles. The most likely way for particles to reach humans and the environment would be through water, which is why the low water tables at Yucca Mountain are so crucial. In addition, Yucca Mountain contains minerals called zeolites that will stick to the particles and slow their movement throughout the environment.

The long delay in providing disposal sites for spent nuclear fuel has been expensive for the industry. Several aging power plants are being maintained at a cost of $20 million per reactor per year simply because there is no place to send the waste once the plants are decommissioned. As of 2002, 47,023.4 metric tons (51,834.4 short tons) of nuclear uranium waste were sitting in spent fuel pools at the 104 operating and 28 permanently closed nuclear power plants. (See Table 5.4 and Table 5.1.)

Disposal of Transuranic Waste

The Waste Isolation Pilot Plant (WIPP) is the first disposal facility licensed to dispose of transuranic waste. It does not accept waste from commercial sources or electrical power plants, but disposes only of defense-related transuranic waste. It opened in March 1999 in southeastern New Mexico. Its disposal rooms were mined 2,150 feet (655 m) underground in a salt formation that is 2,000 feet (610 m) thick and that has been stable for over 200 million years. Beginning with one or two shipments

FIGURE 5.10

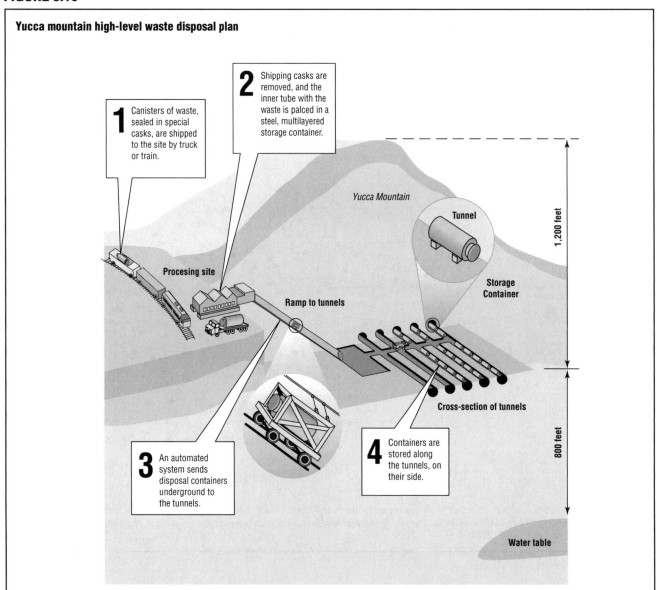

Yucca mountain high-level waste disposal plan

1 Canisters of waste, sealed in special casks, are shipped to the site by truck or train.

2 Shipping casks are removed, and the inner tube with the waste is palced in a steel, multilayered storage container.

Yucca Mountain

Tunnel

1,200 feet

Procesing site

Ramp to tunnels

Storage Container

3 An automated system sends disposal containers underground to the tunnels.

4 Containers are stored along the tunnels, on their side.

Cross-section of tunnels

800 feet

Water table

SOURCE: "Figure 32. The Yucca Mountain Disposal Plan," in *Information Digest 2007–2008*, vol. 19, U.S. Nuclear Regulatory Commission, Division of Planning, Budget, and Analysis, Office of the Chief Financial Officer, August 2007, http://www.nrc.gov/reading-rm/doc-collections/nuregs/staff/sr1350/v19/sr1350v19.pdf (accessed July 3, 2008). Data from: Department of Energy and Nuclear Energy Institute.

per week, operations grew over the years, expanding to an all-time high of thirty-three shipments received during a single week in February 2006. In September 2006 the plant received its five-thousandth shipment of transuranic waste and announced that thirteen sites around the country, most notably the Rocky Flats Environmental Technology site in Colorado, had been completely cleaned up by that time. As of August 25, 2008, WIPP (http://www.wipp.energy.gov/shipments.htm) had received 6,851 shipments from eight sites.

Disposal of Mixed Waste

Several commercial facilities in the United States accept mixed waste. However, only the Energy Solutions facility in Clive, Utah, is permitted to accept solid mixed waste. It stores the waste in aboveground, capped embank-ments designed to last at least one thousand years. The storage facility is located in an isolated area 20 miles (32 km) from the nearest water supply and more than 40 miles (64 km) from the nearest populated area. Containment efforts are supported by area soil and weather conditions, as well, with little permeability (the capacity of rock or soil to transmit water) in the clay soil and fewer than 6 inches (15 cm) of rain per year.

Sites in Florida, Tennessee, and Texas offer storage for liquid or sludge materials or use thermal or chemical processes to neutralize them. Among them, Diversified Scientific Services in Kingston, Tennessee, generates electrical power from liquid mixed waste through an industrial boiler system, and the Texas-based NSSI provides drum storage.

TABLE 5.4

Total commercial spent nuclear fuel discharges, 1968–2002

Reactor type	Number of assemblies		
	Stored at reactor sites	Stored at away-from-reactor facilities	Total
Boiling-water reactor	90,398	2,957	93,355
Pressurized-water reactor	69,800	491	70,291
High-temperature gas cooled reactor	1,464	744	2,208
Total	**161,662**	**4,192**	**165,854**
	Metric tonnes of uranium (MTU)		
Boiling-water reactor	16,153.60	554	16,707.60
Pressurized-water reactor	30,099.00	192.6	30,291.60
High-temperature gas cooled reactor	15.4	8.8	24.2
Total	**46,268.00**	**755.4**	**47,023.40**

Notes: A number of assemblies discharged prior to 1972, which were reprocessed, are not included in this table (no data is available for assemblies reprocessed before 1972). Totals may not equal sum of components because of independent rounding.

SOURCE: "Table 1. Total U.S. Commercial Spent Nuclear Fuel Discharges, 1968–2002," in *Spent Nuclear Fuel*, U.S. Department of Energy, Energy Information Administration, October 1, 2004, http://www.eia.doe.gov/cneaf/nuclear/spent_fuel/ussnfdata.html (accessed July 3, 2008)

CHAPTER 6
RENEWABLE ENERGY

WHAT IS RENEWABLE ENERGY?

Imagine energy sources that use no oil, produce no pollution, create no radioactive waste, cannot be affected by political events and cartels, and yet are economical. Even though this sounds impossible, some experts claim that technological advances could make wide use of renewable energy sources possible within a few decades. They may become substantially better energy sources than fossil fuels and nuclear power.

Renewable energy is naturally regenerated and virtually unlimited. Sources include the sun (solar), wind, water (hydropower), vegetation (biomass), and the heat of the earth (geothermal). Each of these alternative energy sources has advantages and disadvantages, and many observers hope that one or more of them may eventually provide a substantially better energy source than conventional fossil fuels, which are limited (nonrenewable) sources of energy. As the United States and the rest of the world continue to expand their energy needs—putting a strain on the environment and nonrenewable resources—alternative sources of energy continue to be explored.

A HISTORICAL PERSPECTIVE

Before the eighteenth century, most energy came from renewable sources. People burned wood for heat, used sails to harness the wind and propel boats, and installed water wheels on streams to run mills that ground grain. The large-scale shift to nonrenewable energy sources began in the 1700s with the Industrial Revolution, a period marked by the rise of factories, first in Europe and then in North America. As demand for energy grew, coal replaced wood as the main fuel. Coal was the most efficient fuel for the steam engine, which is considered to be one of the most important inventions of the Industrial Revolution.

Until the early 1970s most Americans were not concerned about the sources of the nation's energy. Supplies of coal and oil, which together provided more than 90% of U.S. energy, were believed to be plentiful. The decades preceding the 1970s were characterized by cheap gasoline and little public discussion of energy conservation.

That carefree approach to energy consumption ended in the 1970s. An oil crisis, caused in part by the devaluation of the dollar, but largely by an oil embargo by the Organization of Petroleum Exporting Countries, made Americans acutely aware of their dependence on foreign energy. Throughout the United States, people waited in line to fill their gas tanks—in some places gasoline was rationed—and lower heat settings for offices and homes were encouraged. In a country where mobility and convenience were highly valued, the oil crisis was a shock to the system. Developing alternative sources of energy to supplement and perhaps eventually replace fossil fuels suddenly became important. As a result, President Jimmy Carter (1924–) encouraged federal funding for research into alternative energy sources.

In 1978 Congress passed the Public Utilities Regulatory Policies Act, which was designed to help the struggling alternative energy industry. The act exempted small alternative producers from state and federal utility regulations and required existing local utilities to buy electricity from them. The renewable energy industries grew rapidly, gaining experience, improving technologies, and lowering costs. This law was the single most important factor in the development of the commercial renewable energy market.

In the 1980s President Ronald Reagan (1911–2004) favored private-sector financing, so he proposed the reduction or elimination of federal expenditures for alternative energy sources. Even though federal funds were severely cut, the U.S. Department of Energy continued to support some research and development. President Bill

Clinton (1946–) reemphasized the importance of renewable energy and increased funding in several areas. President George W. Bush (1946–) supported funding for research and development of renewable technologies and tax credits for the purchase of hybrid and alternative-fuel cars.

DOMESTIC RENEWABLE ENERGY USAGE

In 2007 the United States consumed approximately 6.8 quadrillion British thermal units (Btu) of renewable energy, nearly 7% of the nation's total energy consumption. (See Table 6.1 and Figure 6.1.) Biomass sources (wood, biofuels, and waste) contributed 3.6 quadrillion Btu, whereas hydroelectric power provided 2.5 quadril-lion Btu. Together, biomass and hydroelectric power provided 89% of renewable energy in 2007. Geothermal energy was the third-largest source, with about 0.4 quadrillion Btu. Wind provided 0.3 quadrillion Btu, and solar power contributed close to 0.1 quadrillion Btu.

BIOMASS ENERGY

The term *biomass* refers to organic material such as plant and animal waste, wood, seaweed and algae, fuel ethanol, and garbage. The use of biomass is not without environmental problems. Deforestation can occur from widespread use of wood, especially if forests are clear-cut, which can result in soil erosion and mudslides. Burning wood, like burning fossil fuels, also pollutes the

TABLE 6.1

Energy consumption by source, selected years 1949–2007

[Quadrillion Btu]

Year	Coal	Coal coke net imports[b]	Natural gas[c]	Petroleum[d]	Total	Nuclear electric power	Hydro-electric power[e]	Geothermal	Solar/PV	Wind	Biomass	Total	Electricity net imports[b]	Total
1949	11.981	−0.007	5.145	11.883	29.002	0.000	1.425	NA	NA	NA	1.549	2.974	0.005	31.982
1950	12.347	.001	5.968	13.315	31.632	.000	1.415	NA	NA	NA	1.562	2.978	.006	34.616
1955	11.167	−.010	8.998	17.255	37.410	.000	1.360	NA	NA	NA	1.424	2.784	.014	40.208
1960	9.838	−.006	12.385	19.919	42.137	.006	1.608	.001	NA	NA	1.320	2.929	.015	45.087
1965	11.581	−.018	15.769	23.246	50.577	.043	2.059	.004	NA	NA	1.335	3.398	(s)	54.017
1970	12.265	−.058	21.795	29.521	63.522	.239	2.634	.011	NA	NA	1.431	4.076	.007	67.844
1971	11.598	−.033	22.469	30.561	64.596	.413	2.824	.012	NA	NA	1.432	4.268	.012	69.289
1972	12.077	−.026	22.698	32.947	67.696	.584	2.864	.031	NA	NA	1.503	4.398	.026	72.704
1974	12.663	.056	21.732	33.455	67.906	1.272	3.177	.053	NA	NA	1.540	4.769	.043	73.991
1976	13.584	(s)	20.345	35.175	69.104	2.111	2.976	.078	NA	NA	1.713	4.768	.029	76.012
1978	13.766	.125	20.000	37.965	71.856	3.024	2.937	.064	NA	NA	2.038	5.039	.067	79.986
1980	15.423	−.035	20.235	34.202	69.826	2.739	2.900	.110	NA	NA	2.476	5.485	.071	78.122
1982	15.322	−.022	18.356	30.232	63.888	3.131	3.266	.105	NA	NA	2.664	6.034	.100	73.153
1984	17.071	−.011	18.394	31.051	66.504	3.553	3.386	.165	(s)	(s)	2.971	6.522	.135	76.714
1986	17.260	−.017	16.591	32.196	66.031	4.380	3.071	.219	(s)	(s)	2.932	6.223	.122	76.756
1988	18.846	.040	18.448	34.222	71.556	5.587	2.334	.217	(s)	(s)	3.016	5.568	.108	82.819
1990	19.173	.005	19.603	33.553	72.333	6.104	3.046	.336	.060	.029	2.735	6.206	.008	84.652
1992	19.122	.035	20.714	33.527	73.397	6.479	2.617	.349	.064	.030	2.933	5.993	.087	85.956
1994	19.909	.058	21.728	34.562	76.258	6.694	2.683	.338	.069	.036	3.030	6.155	.153	89.260
1996	21.002	.023	23.085	35.673	79.783	7.087	3.590	.316	.071	.033	3.159	7.168	.137	94.175
1998	21.656	.067	22.830	36.817	81.370	7.068	3.297	.328	.070	.031	2.931	6.657	.088	95.183
2000	22.580	.065	23.824	38.264	84.733	7.862	2.811	.317	.066	.057	3.013	R6.356	.075	96.375
2002	21.904	.061	23.558	38.227	83.750	8.143	2.689	.328	.064	.105	2.706	R5.893	.072	97.858
2003	22.321	.051	22.897	38.809	84.078	7.959	2.825	.331	.064	.115	2.817	R6.150	.022	98.209
2004	22.466	.138	22.931	40.294	85.830	8.222	2.690	.341	.065	.142	3.023	6.261	.039	100.351
2005	R22.797	.044	R22.583	40.393	R85.817	8.160	2.703	.343	.066	.178	R3.154	R6.444	.084	R100.506
2006	R22.447	.061	R22.191	R39.958	R84.658	R8.214	R2.869	R.343	R.072	R.264	R3.374	R6.922	R.063	R99.856
2007[P]	22.767	.025	23.638	39.818	86.248	8.415	2.463	.353	.080	.319	3.615	6.830	.107	101.600

[a]Most data are estimates.
[b]Net Imports equal imports minus exports. Minus sign indicates exports are greater than imports.
[c]Natural gas only; excludes supplemental gaseous fuels.
[d]Petroleum products supplied, including natural gas plant liquids and crude oil burned as fuel. Does not include the fuel ethanol portion of motor gasoline—fuel ethanol is included in "biomass."
[e]Conventional hydroelectric power.
R = Revised.
P = Preliminary.
NA = Not available.
(s) = Less than 0.0005 and greater than −0.0005 quadrillion Btu.
Note: Totals may not equal sum of components due to independent rounding.
Web page: For all data beginning in 1949, see http://www.eia.doe.gov/emeu/aer/overview.html.

SOURCE: Adapted from "Table 1.3. Primary Energy Consumption by Source, Selected Years, 1949–2007 (Quadrillion Btu)," in *Annual Energy Review 2007*, U.S. Department of Energy, Energy Information Administration, Office of Energy Markets and End Use, June 2008, http://www.eia.doe.gov/aer/pdf/aer.pdf (accessed June 28, 2008)

FIGURE 6.1

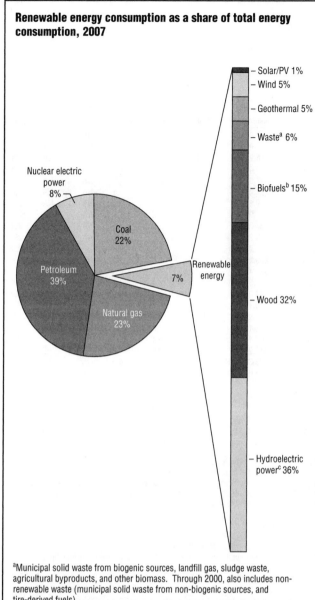

Renewable energy consumption as a share of total energy consumption, 2007

Solar/PV 1%
Wind 5%
Geothermal 5%
Waste[a] 6%
Biofuels[b] 15%
Renewable energy 7%
Wood 32%
Hydroelectric power[c] 36%

Nuclear electric power 8%
Coal 22%
Petroleum 39%
Natural gas 23%

[a]Municipal solid waste from biogenic sources, landfill gas, sludge waste, agricultural byproducts, and other biomass. Through 2000, also includes non-renewable waste (municipal solid waste from non-biogenic sources, and tire-derived fuels).
[b]Fuel ethanol and biodiesel consumption, plus losses and co-products from the production of fuel ethanol and biodiesel.
[c]Conventional hydroelectric power.

SOURCE: Adapted from "Figure 10.1. Renewable Energy Consumption by Major Sources: Renewable Energy As Share of Total Energy Consumption, 2007," in *Annual Energy Review 2007*, U.S. Department of Energy, Energy Information Administration, Office of Energy Markets and End Use, June 2008, http://www.eia.doe.gov/aer/pdf/aer .pdf (accessed June 28, 2008)

environment. Biomass can be burned directly or converted to biofuel by thermochemical and biochemical conversion.

Direct Burning

Direct combustion is the easiest and most commonly used method of using biomass as fuel. Materials such as dry wood or agricultural wastes are chopped and burned to produce steam, electricity, or heat for industries, util-

ities, and homes. Industrial-sized wood boilers operate throughout the country. The burning of agricultural wastes is also becoming more widespread. In Florida, sugarcane producers use the residue from harvested cane to generate much of their energy. The Energy Information Administration (EIA) reports in *Annual Energy Review 2007* (June 2008, http://www.eia.doe.gov/aer/pdf/aer.pdf) that residential use of wood as fuel generated 460 trillion Btu in 2007, about half of the 850 trillion to 1,010 trillion Btu generated in homes in the 1980s.

Thermochemical Conversion

Thermochemical conversion involves heating biomass in an oxygen-free or low-oxygen atmosphere, which transforms the material into simpler substances that can be used as fuels. Products such as charcoal and methanol are produced this way.

Biochemical Conversion

Biochemical conversion uses enzymes, fungi, or other microorganisms to convert high-moisture biomass into either liquid or gaseous fuels. Bacteria convert manure, agricultural wastes, paper, and algae into methane, which is used as fuel. Sewage treatment plants have used anaerobic (oxygen-free) digestion for many years to generate methane gas. Small-scale digesters have been used on farms, primarily in Europe and Asia, for hundreds of years. Biogas pits (a biomass-based technology) are a significant source of energy in China.

Another type of biochemical conversion, fermentation, uses yeast to decompose carbohydrates, yielding ethyl alcohol (ethanol), a colorless, nearly odorless, flammable liquid, and carbon dioxide. Most of the ethanol manufactured for use as fuel in the United States is derived from corn, wood, and sugar. Ethanol is mixed with gasoline to create gasohol, which is sold in three blends: 10% gasohol, which is a mixture of 10% ethanol and 90% gasoline; 7.7% gasohol, which is at least 7.7% ethanol but less than 10%; and 5.7% gasohol, which is at least 5.7% ethanol but less than 7.7%. In "Estimated Use of Gasohol–2004" (April 2006, http://www.fhwa.dot.gov/policy/ohim/hs04/pdf/mf33e.pdf), the Federal Highway Administration estimates that in 2004 Americans used about 25.9 billion gallons (98 billion L) of 10% gasohol and 18.1 billion gallons (68.5 billion L) of less-than-10% gasohol.

The Energy Policy Act of 2005 required fuel suppliers to nearly double their use of ethanol by 2012 to reduce the nation's dependence on foreign fuel sources. Automobiles can be built to run directly on ethanol or on any mixture of gasoline and ethanol, such as ethanol-85 (E-85), which is a blend of 85% ethanol and 15% unleaded gasoline. Dan Hartzell reports in "All Fueled up with No Place to Fuel" (*Morning Call* [Allentown, Pennsylvania], May 23, 2008) that in 2008 there were approximately 6.5 million automobiles on U.S. roads capable of using E-85 as a fuel. Such vehicles are called flex-fuel vehicles because they can run on E-85, gasohol, or gasoline.

Methanol (methyl alcohol) fuels have also been tested successfully. Using methanol instead of diesel fuel virtually eliminates sulfur emissions and reduces other environmental pollutants usually emitted from trucks and buses.

Municipal Waste Recovery

Each year millions of tons of garbage are buried in landfills and city dumps. This method of disposal is becoming increasingly costly, and many landfills across the nation are near capacity. Some communities discovered that they could solve both problems—cost and capacity—by constructing waste-to-energy plants. Not only is the garbage burned and reduced in volume by 90% but also energy in the form of steam or electricity is generated in a cost-effective way.

The use of municipal waste (including landfill gas, sludge waste, tires, and agricultural by-products) as fuel has increased steadily since the 1980s through 2000, when it reached an all-time high of 23.1 billion kilowatt-hours (kWh) of electricity generation. (See Table 6.2.) In 2002 electricity generation from waste dropped to 15 billion kWh but rose again to 16.9 billion kWh in 2007.

MASS BURN SYSTEMS. Most waste-to-energy plants in the United States use the mass burn system (also called direct combustion). Because the waste does not have to be sorted or prepared before burning—except for removing obviously noncombustible, oversized objects—the system eliminates expensive sorting, shredding, and transportation machinery that may be prone to break down. The waste is simply carried to the plant in trash trucks and dropped into a storage pit. Overhead cranes lift the garbage into a hopper that controls the amount of waste that is fed into the furnace. The burning waste produces heat, which is used to produce steam. The steam can be used directly for industrial needs or can be sent through a turbine to power a generator to produce electricity.

REFUSE-DERIVED FUEL SYSTEMS. At refuse-derived fuel plants, waste is first processed to remove noncombustible objects and to create homogeneous and uniformly sized fuel. Large items such as bedsprings, dangerous materials, and flammable liquids are removed by hand. The trash is then shredded and screened to remove glass, rocks, and other material that cannot be burned. The remaining material is usually sifted a second time with an air separator to yield fluff, which is placed in storage bins. It can also be compressed into pellets or briquettes for long-term storage. This fuel can be used alone or with other fuels, such as coal or wood.

TABLE 6.2

Electricity net generation by renewables, selected years 1949–2007

[Billion kilowatthours]

| Year | Conventional hydroelectric power | Renewable energy | | | | | |
| | | Biomass | | Geo-thermal | Solar/PV[c] | Wind | Total |
		Wood[a]	Waste[b]				
1949	94.8	0.4	NA	NA	NA	NA	95.2
1950	100.9	.4	NA	NA	NA	NA	101.3
1955	116.2	.3	NA	NA	NA	NA	116.5
1960	149.4	.1	NA	(s)	NA	NA	149.6
1965	197.0	.3	NA	.2	NA	NA	197.4
1970	251.0	.1	.2	.5	NA	NA	251.8
1971	269.5	.1	.2	.5	NA	NA	270.4
1972	275.9	.1	.2	1.5	NA	NA	277.7
1974	304.2	.1	.2	2.5	NA	NA	306.9
1976	286.9	.1	.2	3.6	NA	NA	290.8
1978	283.5	.2	.1	3.0	NA	NA	286.8
1980	279.2	.3	.2	5.1	NA	NA	284.7
1982	312.4	.2	.1	4.8	NA	NA	317.5
1984	324.3	.5	.4	7.7	(s)	(s)	332.9
1986	294.0	.5	.7	10.3	(s)	(s)	305.5
1988	226.1	.9	.7	10.3	(s)	(s)	238.1
1990	292.9	32.5	13.3	15.4	.4	2.8	357.2
1992	253.1	36.5	17.8	16.1	.4	2.9	326.9
1994	260.1	37.9	19.1	15.5	.5	3.4	336.7
1996	347.2	36.8	20.9	14.3	.5	3.2	423.0
1998	323.3	36.3	22.4	14.8	.5	3.0	400.4
2000	275.6	37.6	23.1	14.1	.5	5.6	356.5
2002	264.3	38.7	15.0	14.5	.6	10.4	343.4
2003	275.8	37.5	15.8	14.4	.5	11.2	355.3
2004	268.4	37.6	15.5	14.8	.6	14.1	351.0
2005	270.3	38.7	15.5	14.7	.6	17.8	357.5
2006	R289.2	R38.6	R16.1	R14.6	.5	R26.6	R385.7
2007[P]	248.3	38.5	16.9	14.8	.6	32.1	351.3

[a]Wood and wood-derived fuels.
[b]Municipal solid waste from biogenic sources, landfill gas, sludge waste, agricultural byproducts, and other biomass. Through 2000, also includes non-renewable waste (municipal solid waste from non-biogenic sources, and tire-derived fuels).
[c]Solar thermal and photovoltaic energy.
R = Revised.
P = Preliminary.
NA = Not available.
(s) = Less than 0.05 billion killowatthours.
Note: Totals may not equal sum of components due to independent rounding.

SOURCE: Adapted from "Table 8.2a. Electricity Net Generation: Total (All Sectors), Selected Years, 1949–2007 (Sum of Tables 8.2b and 8.2d; Billion Kilowatthours)," in Annual Energy Review 2007, U.S. Department of Energy, Energy Information Administration, Office of Energy Markets and End Use, June 2008, http://www.eia.doe.gov/aer/pdf/aer.pdf (accessed June 28, 2008)

DISADVANTAGES OF WASTE-TO-ENERGY PLANTS. The major problem with increasing the use of municipal waste-to-energy plants is their effect on the environment. The emission of particles into the air is partially controlled by electrostatic precipitators, and many gases can be eliminated by proper combustion techniques. However, large amounts of dioxin (a dangerous air pollutant) and other toxins are often emitted from these plants. Noise from trucks, fans, and processing equipment can also be unpleasant for nearby residents.

Landfill Gas Recovery

Landfills contain a large amount of biodegradable matter that is compacted and covered with soil. Methanogens,

FIGURE 6.2

Landfill gas energy sites and candidate landfills, April 2008

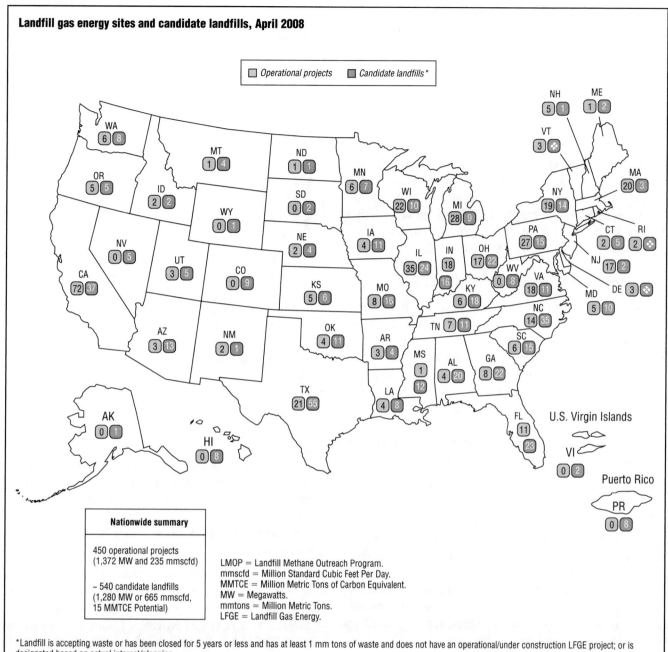

□ Operational projects   ■ Candidate landfills*

Nationwide summary

450 operational projects
(1,372 MW and 235 mmscfd)

~ 540 candidate landfills
(1,280 MW or 665 mmscfd,
15 MMTCE Potential)

LMOP = Landfill Methane Outreach Program.
mmscfd = Million Standard Cubic Feet Per Day.
MMTCE = Million Metric Tons of Carbon Equivalent.
MW = Megawatts.
mmtons = Million Metric Tons.
LFGE = Landfill Gas Energy.

*Landfill is accepting waste or has been closed for 5 years or less and has at least 1 mm tons of waste and does not have an operational/under construction LFGE project; or is designated based on actual interest/planning.

SOURCE: "Landfill Gas Energy Projects and Candidate Landfills," U.S. Environmental Protection Agency, Landfill Methane Outreach Program, April 11, 2008, http://www.epa.gov/lmop/docs/map.pdf (accessed July 15, 2008)

which are anaerobic microorganisms, thrive in this oxygen-depleted environment. They metabolize the biodegradable matter in the landfill, producing methane gas and carbon dioxide as by-products. In the past, as landfills aged, these gases built up and leaked out, which prompted some communities to drill holes in landfills and burn off the methane to prevent dangerously large amounts from exploding.

The energy crisis of the 1970s made landfill methane gas an energy resource too valuable to waste. The first landfill gas recovery site was built in 1975 at the Palos Verdes Landfill in Rolling Hills Estates, California. Since then the number of landfill gas recovery sites (landfill gas energy sites) has skyrocketed. Figure 6.2 shows the number and location of the landfill gas energy sites and candidate landfills throughout the United States as of April 2008. The map shows the 450 sites that were operational in 2008 and the approximately 540 landfill sites identified for potential development as gas recovery/energy sites.

In a typical landfill gas energy site, garbage is allowed to decompose for several months. When a sufficient amount of methane gas has developed, it is piped to a generating plant, where it is used to create electricity. In its purest form, methane gas can be used like natural gas. Depending on the extraction rates, most sites can produce gas for about twenty years. Besides the energy provided, tapping the methane reduces landfill odors and the chances of explosions.

HYDROPOWER

In the past, flowing water turned waterwheels of mills to grind grain; in the twenty-first century, hydropower plants convert the energy of flowing water into mechanical energy, turning turbines to create electricity. Hydropower is the most widely used renewable energy source in the world. In the United States it provided 248.3 billion kWh, or 71% of all electricity produced from renewable sources in 2007. (See Table 6.2.)

Advantages and Disadvantages of Hydropower

In the twenty-first century, hydropower is the only means of storing large quantities of energy for almost instant use. Water is held in a large reservoir behind a dam, with a hydroelectric power plant below. The dam creates a height from which water can flow at a fast rate. When it reaches the power plant, it pushes the turbine blades attached to the electrical generator. Whenever power is needed, the valves are opened, the moving water spins the turbines, and the generator quickly produces electricity.

Nearly all the best sites for large hydropower plants are being used in the United States. Small hydropower plants are expensive to build but may eventually become economical because of their low operating costs. One of the disadvantages of small hydropower generators is their reliance on rain and melting snow to fill reservoirs; drought conditions can affect the water supply. Additionally, environmental groups strongly protest the construction of new dams, pointing to ruined streams, dried up waterfalls, and altered aquatic habitats.

The Future of Hydropower

The last federally funded hydropower dam, completed by the U.S. Army Corps of Engineers in 1986, was the Richard B. Russell Dam and Lake on the Savannah River, which forms the border between South Carolina and Georgia. Since then, local governments have been required to contribute half the cost of any new dam proposed in the United States. Even though expansion and efficiency improvements at existing dams offer significant potential for additional energy, hydropower's future contribution to U.S. energy generation should remain relatively constant, with increases in production offset by increases in consumption. (See Figure 6.3.) Additional supplies of hydroelectric power for the United States will likely come from Canada.

FIGURE 6.3

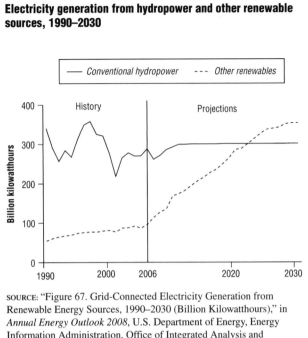

Electricity generation from hydropower and other renewable sources, 1990–2030

SOURCE: "Figure 67. Grid-Connected Electricity Generation from Renewable Energy Sources, 1990–2030 (Billion Kilowatthours)," in *Annual Energy Outlook 2008*, U.S. Department of Energy, Energy Information Administration, Office of Integrated Analysis and Forecasting, June 2008, http://www.eia.doe.gov/oiaf/aeo/pdf/0383 (2008).pdf (accessed July 2, 2008)

Most of the new development in hydropower is occurring in developing nations, which see it as an effective method of supplying power to growing populations. These massive public-works projects usually require huge amounts of money—most of it borrowed from the developed world. Hydroelectric dams are considered worth the cost and potential environmental threats because they bring cheap electric power to the citizenry.

The Chinese government (January 10, 2008, http://english.gov.cn/special/sanxia_index.htm) has constructed the world's largest dam, the Three Gorges Dam, on the Yangtze River in Hubei province, China. Five times the size of the Hoover Dam in the United States, the dam is 607 feet (185 m) tall and 7,575 feet (2,309 m) in length. One decade after the project was launched in 1993, the Three Gorges Dam began generating power. By 2007 the plant was generating 61.6 billion kWh of electricity. After installation of its twenty-six generators is completed at the end of 2008, the dam is expected to produce 84.7 billion kWh of electricity per year. Under an expansion plan, six more turbines will be added to the dam by 2012.

By November 2007 problems with the dam became evident that had been discussed in years prior as possibilities. Controversy over the dam heightened as water rose behind it and pollution, soil erosion, and landslides occurred. In response, Jim Yardley reports in "China to Address Issues around Dam" (*New York Times*, November 22, 2007) that the director of the Three Gorges Dam

FIGURE 6.4

Cross-section of the Earth showing source of geothermal energy

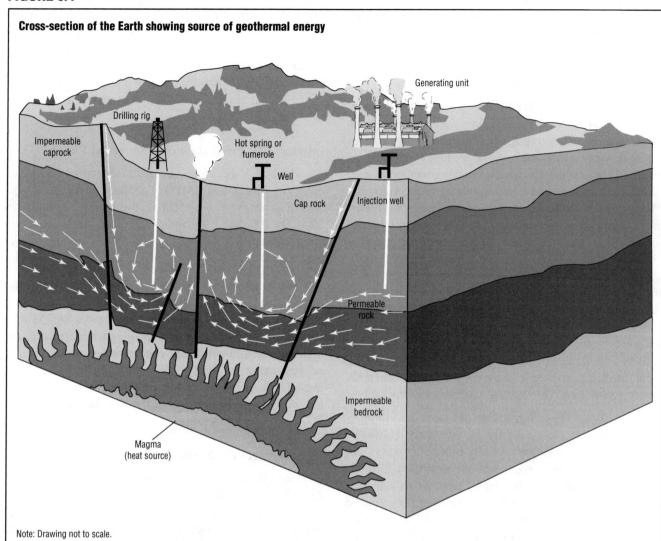

Note: Drawing not to scale.

SOURCE: "Figure A-4. Cross-Section of the Earth Showing Source of Geothermal Energy," in *Geothermal Energy in the Western United States and Hawaii: Resources and Projected Electricity Generation Supplies*, U.S. Department of Energy, Energy Information Administration, September 1991, http://www.osti.gov/energycitations/servlets/purl/5212047-gTiC1e/native/ (accessed July 30, 2008)

project announced measures that would be taken to lessen the environmental impact of the dam. On May 12, 2008, an earthquake measuring 7.9 on the Richter scale occurred near the dam, with the epicenter of the quake a few hundred miles to the east. No immediate problems were reported.

GEOTHERMAL ENERGY

Even though bubbling hot springs became public baths as early as ancient Rome, using hot water and underground steam to produce power is a relatively recent development. Electricity was first generated from natural steam in Italy in 1904. The world's first natural steam power plant was built in 1958 in a volcanic region of New Zealand. A field of twenty-eight geothermal power plants covering 30 square miles (78 sq km) in northern California was completed in 1960.

What Is Geothermal Energy?

Geothermal energy is the natural, internal heat of the earth trapped in rock formations deep underground. Only a fraction of it can be extracted, usually through large fractures in the earth's crust. Hot springs, geysers, and fumaroles (holes in or near volcanoes from which vapor escapes) are the most easily exploitable sources. (See Figure 6.4.) Geothermal reservoirs provide hot water or steam that can be used for heating buildings and processing food. Pressurized hot water or steam can also be directed toward turbines, which spin, generating electricity for residential and commercial customers.

Types of Geothermal Energy

Like most natural energy sources, geothermal energy is usable only when it is concentrated in one spot—in this case, in what is known as a thermal reservoir. There are four types of reservoirs: hydrothermal reservoirs, dry rock reservoirs, geopressurized reservoirs, and magma. Most of the known reservoirs for geothermal power in the United States are located west of the Mississippi River, and the highest-temperature geothermal resources occur for the most part west of the Rocky Mountains.

HYDROTHERMAL RESERVOIRS. Hydrothermal reservoirs are underground pools of hot water covered by a permeable formation through which steam escapes under pressure. Once at the surface, the steam is purified and piped directly to the electrical generating station. These systems are the cheapest and simplest form of geothermal energy. The Geysers thermal field, 90 miles (145 km) north of San Francisco, California, is the world's largest source of geothermal power. According to the Calpine Corporation (March 5, 2008, http://www.geysers.com/), which operates nineteen of the twenty-two power generating plants at the site, the Geysers generate enough electricity to satisfy the power needs of a city the size of San Francisco and provide nearly 60% of the electricity used in the region extending northward from the Golden Gate Bridge to the Oregon border. The remaining three facilities are operated by the Northern California Power Agency and the Western GeoPower Corporation.

DRY ROCK. These formations are the most common geothermal sources, especially in the West. However, reservoirs of this type are typically more than 6,000 feet (1,829 m) below the surface, which poses many difficulties. To tap them, water is injected into hot rock formations that have been fractured, and the resulting steam or water is collected. Hot dry rock technologies were developed and tested at the Fenton Hill plant, which operated between 1970 and 1996.

GEOPRESSURIZED RESERVOIRS. These sedimentary formations contain hot water and methane gas. Supplies of geopressurized energy remain uncertain, and drilling is expensive. Scientists are developing new technology to exploit the methane content in these reservoirs.

MAGMA. This molten or partially liquefied rock is found from 10,000 to 33,000 feet (3,048 to 10,058 m) below the earth's surface. Because magma is so hot, ranging from 1,650 to 2,200° Fahrenheit (899° to 1,204° C), it is a good geothermal resource. Extracting energy from magma is still in the experimental stages.

Domestic Production of Geothermal Energy

In 2007 geothermal energy produced 14.8 billion kWh of electricity, or 4% of the 351.3 billion kWh of electricity produced by renewable energy sources in the United States. (See Table 6.2.) According to the International Geothermal Association (IGA), in "Installed Generating Capacity" (July 29, 2008, http://iga.igg.cnr.it/geoworld/geoworld.php?sub=elgen), in 2005 the United States had 28% of the installed geothermal generating

capacity of the world and the largest installed generating capacity of any single country. However, most of the easily exploited geothermal reserves in the United States have already been developed. Continued growth in the U.S. market depends on the regulatory environment, oil price trends, who pays for the new plants, and the success of new technologies to exploit previously inaccessible reserves.

International Production of Geothermal Energy

The IGA indicates in "Installed Generating Capacity" that 7974.1 megawatts (MW) of geothermal electrical generating capacity was present in twenty-one countries in 2000. By 2005 the worldwide geothermal electrical generating capacity was 9,064.1 MW distributed among twenty-four countries.

This output is considered only a small fraction of the overall potential: many countries are believed to have more than 100,000 MW of geothermal energy available. As with other fuel sources, however, world geothermal reserves are unevenly distributed. They occur mostly in seismically active areas at the margins or borders of the planet's nine tectonic plates. Areas rich in geothermal reserves include the west coasts of North and South America, Japan, the Philippines, and Indonesia.

Disadvantages of Geothermal Energy

Geothermal plants, which are not very efficient, must be built near a geothermal source, so they are not accessible to many consumers. They also produce unpleasant odors when sulfur is released during processing and generate considerable noise. Environmental concerns have been raised about potentially harmful pollutants, such as ammonia, arsenic, boron, hydrogen sulfide, and radon, which are often found in geothermal waters. Other concerns are the collapse of the land from which the water is being drained and water shortages from massive withdrawals.

Geothermal Heating/Cooling Systems

The term *geothermal* is also used with a particular type of home heating/cooling system but has a much different meaning than is used in this section on geothermal energy. Geothermal heating/cooling systems for individual residences or other types of buildings use the constant temperature of the earth (approximately 55° Fahrenheit [13° C]) to help heat interiors in the winter and cool them in the summer. Such systems circulate water or a water/antifreeze solution in pipes located at least a few feet beneath the surface of the ground. As the liquid circulates within the underground pipes it becomes warmed in the winter and cooled in the summer. This water is used in conjunction with a special type of heat pump called a ground source heat pump. Heat pumps are machines used in heating and cooling applications.

WIND ENERGY

Winds are created by the uneven heating of the atmosphere by the sun, the irregularities of the earth's surface, and the rotation of the planet. They are strongly influenced by bodies of water, weather patterns, vegetation, and other factors. When "harvested" by turbines, wind can be used to generate electricity.

Early windmills produced mechanical energy to pump water and grind grain in mills. By the late 1890s, Americans had begun experimenting with wind power to generate electricity. Their early efforts produced enough electricity to light one or two modern lightbulbs.

Beginning in the late twentieth century, industrial and developing countries alike started using wind power on a significant scale to complement existing power sources and to bring electricity to remote regions. Wind turbines cost less to install per unit of kilowatt capacity than either coal or nuclear facilities. After installing a windmill, there are few additional costs.

Compared to the pinwheel-shaped farm windmills that still dot the rural parts of the United States, the twenty-first century's state-of-the-art wind turbines look more like airplane propellers. Their sleek fiberglass design allows them to generate an abundance of mechanical energy, which can be converted to electricity.

The most favorable locations for wind turbines are in mountain passes and along coastlines, where wind speeds are generally highest and most consistent. Of all the places in the world, Europe has the greatest coastal wind resources. In *International Energy Outlook 2007* (May 2007, http://www .eia.doe.gov/oiaf/archive/ieo07/pdf/0484(2007).pdf), the EIA indicates that at the end of 2006, European Union countries accounted for 65% of the world's total installed wind capacity.

Domestic Energy Production by Wind Turbines

The U.S. wind energy industry began in California in 1981 with the installation of 144 relatively small turbines with a combined capacity of 7 MW. During 1998 and 1999 wind farm activity expanded into other states, motivated by financial incentives (such as tax credits for wind-energy production), regulatory incentives, and state mandates (in Iowa and Minnesota). In 1999 Iowa, Minnesota, and Texas added capacity exceeding 100 MW each. At the end of 2007, the total installed generating capacity of the United States was 16,596 MW, and wind power plants operated in thirty-four states. (See Figure 6.5.) Twelve states—Texas (4,296 MW), California (2,439 MW), Minnesota (1,258 MW), Washington (1,163 MW), Iowa (1,115 MW), Colorado (1,067 MW), Oregon (885 MW), Illinois (733 MW), Oklahoma (689 MW), New Mexico (496 MW), New York (425 MW), and Kansas (364 MW)—contained 90% of the U.S. wind energy capacity.

In *Annual Energy Outlook 2008* (June 2008, http://www .eia.doe.gov/oiaf/aeo/pdf/0383(2008).pdf), the EIA projects that wind power capacity in the United States will nearly quintuple from 0.6% of total generation in 2006 to 2.4% in 2030. The EIA qualifies its forecast, however, suggesting that this projection is uncertain due to a variety of factors, which include fossil fuel costs, programs for renewable energy sources, improvements in technology, access to transmission grids, environmental concerns, and the future of the federal Production Tax Credit (PTC) program for renewable energy sources. The PTC has lapsed in the past and often gets renewed for only short periods of time.

International Development of Wind Energy

According to the Global Wind Energy Council (GWEC), in *Global Wind: 2007 Report* (May 2008, http://www.gwec .net/fileadmin/documents/test2/gwec-08-update_FINAL.pdf), global wind-power installed capacity was 94,123 MW in 2007, up 31% from 2006. Wind power was being used in more than seventy countries in 2007. The five countries with the highest installed wind capacity at the end of 2007 were Germany (22,247 MW), the United States (16,818 MW), Spain (15,145 MW), India (7,845), and China (5,906 MW). The GWEC predicted that by 2009 the United States would hold the top spot for installed wind capacity worldwide.

Interest in wind energy has been driven, in part, by the declining cost of capturing wind energy. In "Wind Power Set to Become World's Leading Energy Source" (June 25, 2003, http://www.earth-policy.org/Updates/ Update24_printable.htm), Lester R. Brown of the Earth Policy Institute explains that for new turbines at sites with strong winds, prices declined from more than $0.38 per kWh in the early 1980s to about $0.04 per kWh in 2003. Decreasing costs could make wind power competitive with gas and coal power plants, even before considering wind's environmental advantages.

Advantages and Disadvantages of Wind Energy

The main problem with wind energy is that the wind does not always blow. In addition, some people find the whirring noise of wind turbines annoying and object to clusters of wind turbines in mountain passes and along shorelines, where they interfere with scenic views. Environmentalists also point out that wind turbines are responsible for the loss of thousands of birds and bats that inadvertently fly into the blades. Birds frequently use windy passages in their travel patterns. However, wind farms do not emit climate-altering carbon dioxide and other pollutants, respiratory irritants, or radioactive waste. Furthermore, because wind farms do not require water to operate, they are especially well suited to semiarid and arid regions.

SOLAR ENERGY

Solar energy, which comes from the sun, is a renewable, widely available energy source that does not generate

FIGURE 6.5

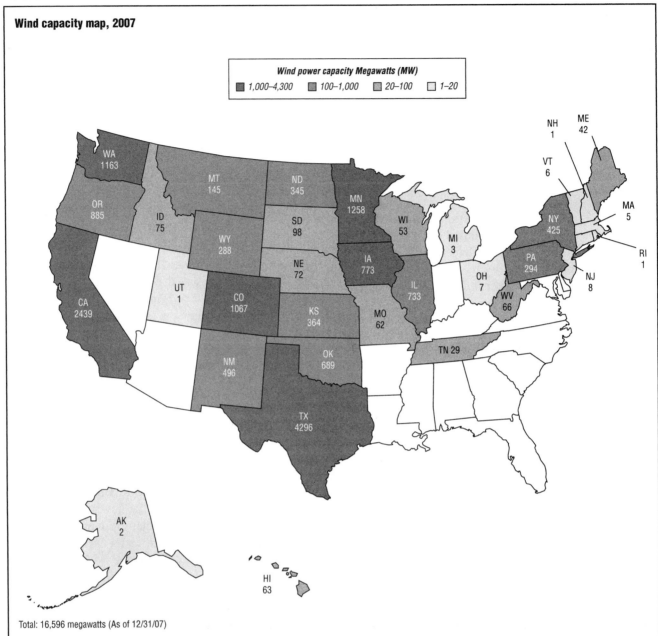

Wind capacity map, 2007

Wind power capacity Megawatts (MW)

■ *1,000–4,300* ■ *100–1,000* ■ *20–100* □ *1–20*

Total: 16,596 megawatts (As of 12/31/07)

SOURCE: "2007 Year End Wind Power Capacity (MW)," in *Wind Powering America*, U.S. Department of Energy, Wind and Hydropower Technologies Program, January 28, 2008, http://www.eere.energy.gov/windandhydro/windpoweringamerica/images/windmaps/installed_capacity_2007.jpg (accessed July 3, 2008). Data from the American Wind Energy Association (AWEA) and Global Energy Concepts (GEC) database.

huge amounts of pollution or radioactive waste. Solar-powered cars have competed in long-distance races, and solar energy has been used for many years to power space-craft. Even though many people consider solar energy a product of the space age, architectural researchers at the Massachusetts Institute of Technology built the first solar-heated house in 1939.

Solar radiation is nearly constant outside the Earth's atmosphere, but the amount of solar energy reaching any point on Earth varies with changing atmospheric conditions, such as clouds and dust, and the changing position of the earth relative to the sun. In the United States, exposure to the sun's rays is greatest in the Southwest, although almost all regions have some solar resources. Displaying nearly thirty years of averaged data, Figure 6.6 shows general trends in the amount of solar energy received in the United States.

Passive and Active Solar Systems

Passive solar energy systems, such as greenhouses or windows with a southern exposure, use heat flow, evaporation, or other natural processes to collect and transfer heat. (See Figure 6.7.) They are considered the least costly and least difficult solar systems to implement.

FIGURE 6.6

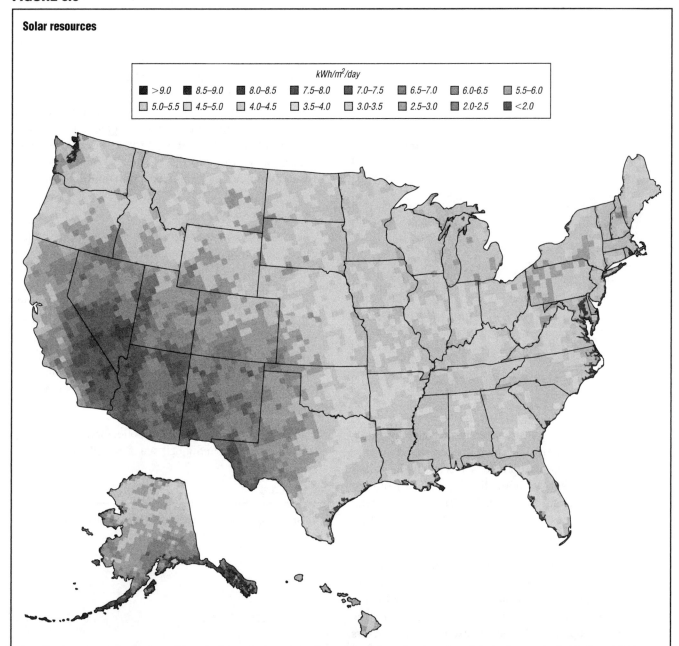

Solar resources

kWh/m²/day							
■ >9.0	■ 8.5–9.0	■ 8.0–8.5	■ 7.5–8.0	■ 7.0–7.5	■ 6.5–7.0	■ 6.0-6.5	■ 5.5–6.0
□ 5.0–5.5	□ 4.5–5.0	□ 4.0–4.5	□ 3.5–4.0	□ 3.0-3.5	■ 2.5–3.0	■ 2.0-2.5	■ <2.0

Note: Model estimates of monthly average daily total radiation using inputs derived from satellite and/or surface observations of cloud cover, aerosol optical depth, precipitable water vapor, albedo, atmospheric pressure and ozone resampled to 40km resolution.

SOURCE: "Direct Normal Solar Radiation (Two-Axis Tracking Concentrator)," in *Dynamic Maps, GIS Data, & Analysis Tools: Solar Maps*, National Renewable Energy Laboratory, May 2004, http://www.nrel.gov/gis/images/us_csp_annual_may2004.jpg (accessed July 15, 2008)

Active solar systems require collectors and storage devices as well as motors, pumps, and valves to operate the systems that transfer heat. (See Figure 6.7.) Collectors consist of an absorbing plate that transfers the sun's heat to a working fluid (liquid or gas), a translucent cover plate that prevents the heat from radiating back into the atmosphere, and insulation on the back of the collector panel to further reduce heat loss. Excess solar energy is transferred to a storage facility so it may provide power on cloudy days.

In both passive and active systems, the conversion of solar energy into a form of power is made at the site where it is used. The most common and least expensive active solar systems are used for heating water.

Solar Thermal Energy Systems

In a solar thermal energy system, mirrors or lenses constantly track the sun's position and focus its rays onto solar receivers that contain water or other fluids. The fluid is heated to more than 750° Fahrenheit (399° C);

FIGURE 6.7

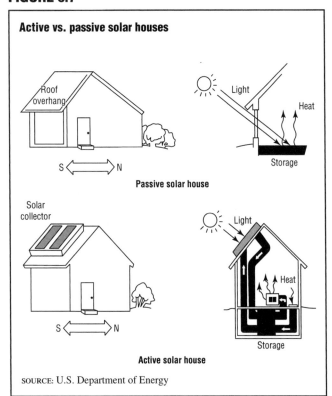

Active vs. passive solar houses

Passive solar house

Active solar house

SOURCE: U.S. Department of Energy

that heat is used to power an electric generator. In a distributed solar thermal system, the collected energy powers irrigation pumps, provides electricity for small communities, or captures normally wasted heat from the sun in industrial areas. In a central solar thermal system, the energy is collected at a central location and used by utility networks for many customers.

Other systems include solar ponds and trough systems. Solar ponds are pools filled with water and salt. Because saltwater is denser than freshwater, the saltwater on the bottom absorbs the heat, which is trapped by the freshwater on top. Trough systems use U-shaped mirrors to concentrate the sunshine on water or on oil-filled tubes.

Photovoltaic Conversion Systems

The photovoltaic cell system converts sunlight directly into electricity without the use of mechanical generators. Photovoltaic cells have no moving parts, are easy to install, require little maintenance, and can last up to twenty years. The cells are commonly used to power small devices, such as watches or calculators. On a larger scale they provide electricity for rural households, recreational vehicles, and businesses. Solar panels using photovoltaic cells have generated electricity for space stations and satellites for many years.

The cells produce the most power around noon, when sunlight is the most intense. They are usually connected to storage batteries that provide electricity during cloudy days and at night. A backup energy supply is usually required.

The use of photovoltaic cells is expanding around the world. Because they contain no turbines or other moving parts, operating costs are low and maintenance is minimal. Above all, the fuel source (sunshine) is free and plentiful. The main disadvantage of photovoltaic cell systems is the high initial cost, although prices have fallen considerably. Even though toxic materials are often used in the construction of the cells, researchers are investigating new materials, recycling, and disposal.

Solar Energy Usage

The use of solar energy is difficult to measure because it is rarely connected to any kind of metered grid. However, shipments of solar equipment can be used as an indicator of use. The EIA notes in *Annual Energy Review 2007* that the total shipments of solar thermal collectors peaked in 1981 at 21.1 million square feet (2 million sq m), fell to 6.6 million square feet (613,000 sq m) in 1991, and rose again to 11.6 million square feet (1.1 million sq m) in 2002. By 2006 the total shipments of solar thermal collectors had almost doubled to 20.7 million square feet (1.9 sq m). (See Figure 6.8.)

In 2006 most solar thermal collectors were sold for residential purposes in Sunbelt states, usually to heat water

FIGURE 6.8

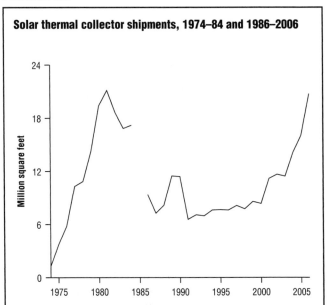

Solar thermal collector shipments, 1974–84 and 1986–2006

Million square feet

Notes: Shipments are for domestic and export shipments, and may include imports that subsequently were shipped to domestic or foreign customers. Data were not collected for 1985.

SOURCE: Adapted from "Figure 10.5. Solar Thermal Collector Shipments by Type, Price, and Trade: Total Shipments, 1974–1984 and 1986–2006," in *Annual Energy Review 2007*, U.S. Department of Energy, Energy Information Administration, Office of Energy Markets and End Use, June 2008, http://www.eia.doe.gov/aer/pdf/aer.pdf (accessed June 28, 2008)

FIGURE 6.9

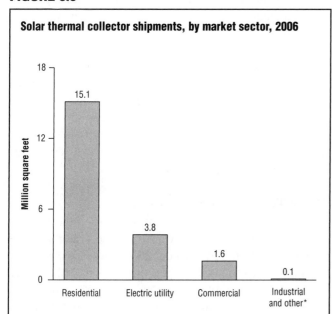

Solar thermal collector shipments, by market sector, 2006

*Other sectors, such as government, including the military but excluding space applications.
Notes: Data are for domestic and export shipments, and may include imports that subsequently were shipped to domestic or foreign customers.

SOURCE: Adapted from "Figure 10.6. Solar Thermal Collector Shipments by End Use, Market Sector, and Type, 2006: Market Sector," in *Annual Energy Review 2007*, U.S. Department of Energy, Energy Information Administration, Office of Energy Markets and End Use, June 2008, http://www.eia.doe.gov/aer/pdf/aer.pdf (accessed June 28, 2008)

FIGURE 6.10

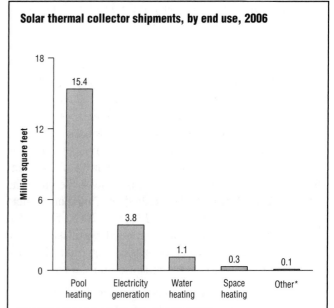

Solar thermal collector shipments, by end use, 2006

*Combined space and water heating, and space cooling.
Note: Data are for domestic and export shipments, and may include imports that subsequently were shipped to domestic or foreign customers.

SOURCE: Adapted from "Figure 10.6. Solar Thermal Collector Shipments by End Use, Market Sector, and Type, 2006: End Use," in *Annual Energy Review 2007*, U.S. Department of Energy, Energy Information Administration, Office of Energy Markets and End Use, June 2008, http://www.eia.doe.gov/aer/pdf/aer.pdf (accessed June 28, 2008)

for swimming pools. (See Figure 6.9 and Figure 6.10.) The market for solar energy space heating has virtually disappeared. Only a small proportion of solar thermal collectors are used for commercial purposes, although some state and municipal power companies have solar energy systems they can use for additional power during peak hours.

Solar Power as an International Rural Solution

Getting electricity to rural areas has always been more expensive than serving cities. In the United States most farmers did not receive electrical power until 1935, when the Rural Electrification Administration provided low-cost financing to rural electric cooperatives. In places such as western China, the Himalayan foothills, and the Amazon basin today, the cost of connecting new rural customers to electricity grids remains high.

Even though rural families may not have access to electrical grid systems, they do have sunlight: in most tropical countries, considerable sunlight falls on rooftops. Photovoltaic cells can be installed on them to run water pumps, lights, refrigerators, and communications equipment. Electricity produced by photovoltaic cells was initially extremely expensive, but prices have continually fallen, making solar energy a competitive choice in some areas.

Advantages and Disadvantages of Solar Energy

The primary advantage of solar energy is its inexhaustible supply. It is especially useful in rural or remote areas that cannot be easily connected to an electrical power grid. Michael Kanellos notes in "Shrinking the Cost for Solar Power" (CNET News, May 11, 2007) that even though solar power still costs two to three times as much as fossil fuel energy, utilities often turn to solar energy to provide peaking power on extremely hot or cold days. Building solar energy systems to provide peak power capacity is often cheaper than building the backup diesel generators that are often used.

Solar power's primary disadvantage is its reliance on a consistently sunny climate, which is possible in limited geographical areas. It also requires a large amount of land for the most efficient collection of solar energy by electricity plants.

POWER FROM THE OCEAN

Oceans are not as easily controlled as rivers or water directed through canals into turbines, so unlocking their potential power is far more challenging. Three ideas undergoing experimentation are tidal power, wave energy, and ocean thermal energy conversion.

Tidal Power

Tidal power plants use the movement of water as it ebbs and flows to generate power. A minimum tidal range of 9 to 15 feet (2.7 to 4.6 m) is generally considered necessary for an economically feasible plant. (The tidal range is the difference in height between consecutive high and low tides.)

The largest tidal facility in the world is the 240-MW plant at the La Rance estuary in northern France. Canada built a smaller 40-MW unit at the Bay of Fundy, which has a 45-foot (13.7-m) tidal range, the largest in the world. The Bay of Fundy is located northeast of Maine and is bordered by the Canadian provinces of New Brunswick and Nova Scotia. The Annapolis Tidal Generating Station is on the Nova Scotia side of the bay. The article "Tidal Power to be Studied in Canadian Waters off Maine" (Associated Press, May 27, 2008) notes that in May 2008 New Brunswick granted permission for a two-year feasibility study of eleven potential sites for another tidal power generating station on the bay.

Just months before this announcement, the British government announced the results of a two-year feasibility study on developing a tidal power facility in the Bristol Channel, which divides southwestern England from South Wales. This channel has a 42-foot (12.8-m) tidal range, second only to the Bay of Fundy. However, Erica Gies reports in "U.K. Debates a Barrier on the Severn" (*International Herald Tribune*, February 18, 2008) that the channel is home to an ecologically important estuary, making a tidal power facility at that location highly controversial. The world's first offshore tidal turbine, which is located in the ocean about 1 mile (1.6 km) from Devon, England, began producing energy in 2003.

Wave Energy

One type of wave power plant is the oscillating water column; the first significant examples were built at Toftestallen, on Norway's Atlantic coast, in 1985. In this system, the arrival of a wave forces water up a hollow 65-foot (19.8-m) tower, displacing the air in the tower. The air rushes out the top through a turbine, whose rotors spin, generating electricity. When the wave falls back and the water level falls, air is sucked back in through the turbine, again generating electricity. The Toftestallen plant was destroyed during a winter storm in 1988. Similar systems have been tested in China, India, Japan, Portugal, and Scotland.

A second type of wave power plant uses the overflow of high ocean waves. As the waves splash against the top of a dam, some of the water goes over and is trapped in a reservoir on the other side. The water is then directed through a turbine as it flows back to the sea.

A third and most recent type of significant wave power technology is the Pelamis wave energy converter, developed by a Scottish company. According to the article "Orkney to Get 'Biggest' Wave Farm" (BBC News, February 20, 2007), after successful testing at the European Marine Energy Centre in the Orkney Islands north of the

Scottish mainland beginning in 2004, the Scottish government announced financial support for adding wave energy converters to the site as well as testing of other wave power technologies there. Each wave energy converter consists of three cylindrical sections that are hinged together and float semi-submerged. As the waves bounce the sections up and down, the movement of the hinges drives generators that produce electricity. Pelamis Wave Power (2008, http://www.pelamiswave.com/content.php?id=149) notes, however, that Portugal developed the first wave farm using Pelamis wave energy converters in 2006.

Ocean Thermal Energy Conversion

Ocean thermal energy conversion uses the temperature difference between warm surface water and the cooler water in the ocean's depths to power a heat engine to produce electricity. The heat engine is placed between the higher temperature water and the lower temperature water. The water flows naturally from an area of higher temperature to an area of lower temperature. As this occurs, the engine captures some of the heat and uses this energy to produce electricity. Ocean thermal energy conversion systems can be installed on ships, barges, or offshore platforms with underwater cables that transmit electricity to shore.

HYDROGEN: A FUEL OF THE FUTURE?

Hydrogen, the lightest and most abundant chemical element, is the ideal fuel from an environmental point of view. Its combustion produces only water vapor, and it is entirely carbon free. Three-quarters of the mass of the universe is hydrogen, so in theory the supply is ample. However, the combustible form of hydrogen is a gas and is not found in nature. It must be made from other energy sources, such as fossil fuels. Hydrogen can be split from water, but the processes are either quite costly, require a great deal of energy, or both. Matthew W. Kanan and Daniel G. Nocera of the Massachusetts Institute of Technology report in "In Situ Formation of an Oxygen-Evolving Catalyst in Neutral Water Containing Phosphate and Co^{2+}" (*Science*, vol. 321, no. 5892, August 22, 2008) a new process for splitting water. This technique appears to be a breakthrough in water-splitting technologies, but the process is not yet ready to be used in commercial applications.

In hydrogen fuel cells, oxygen and hydrogen react to produce water and electricity. Alternatively, hydrogen can be burned in an engine, much like gasoline. BMW introduced its hydrogen-powered luxury vehicle the Hydrogen 7 in 2006. It burns either gasoline or hydrogen as fuel. The Hydrogen 7 was produced in limited quantities and will be used only by selected individuals worldwide.

Research into the use of hydrogen as a fuel got a boost when President Bush announced a hydrogen fuel initiative in his 2003 State of the Union Address. The

Department of Energy's Hydrogen Program (2008, http://www.hydrogen.energy.gov/budget.html) states that Congress appropriated $156.5 million for hydrogen and fuel cell research and development in fiscal year (FY) 2004; $221.7 million in FY 2005; $232.5 million in FY 2006; $269.2 million in FY 2007, and $283.5 in FY 2008. The budgetary request for FY 2009 was $267.5 million. Goals of the initiative include reducing the cost of hydrogen fuel to make it comparable to gasoline, resolving issues for safe in-vehicle storage of reserve fuel, and lowering the cost of hydrogen power systems to compete with internal combustion engines. In "President's Hydrogen Fuel Initiative: A Clean and Secure Energy Future" (2008, http://www.hydrogen.energy.gov/presidents_initiative.html), the Hydrogen Projects estimates that hydrogen fuel cell vehicles could reduce the U.S. demand for oil by about 11 million barrels per day—the amount the United States now imports—by 2040.

FUTURE TRENDS IN U.S. RENEWABLE ENERGY USE

In *Annual Energy Outlook 2008*, the EIA forecasts that total renewable fuel consumption, including ethanol for transportation, biodiesel, and diesel from biomass, will increase from 6.8 quadrillion Btu in 2006 to 13.7 quadrillion Btu in 2030. About 45% of the projected demand would be for electricity generation. Renewable fuel is expected to remain a small contributor to overall electricity generation through 2030.

The EIA notes that hydropower is expected to remain the largest single source of renewable electricity generation through 2030, but its share of total generation will fall from 7.1% in 2006 to 5.8% in 2030. The production of other renewables should increase steadily. (See Figure 6.3.) The largest source of renewable generation after hydropower was biomass in 2006, but wind is expected to overtake the second spot by 2010, and then biomass will retake its second position in 2020 and

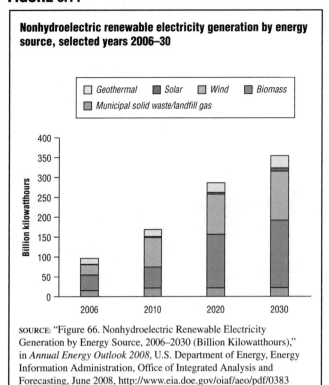

FIGURE 6.11

Nonhydroelectric renewable electricity generation by energy source, selected years 2006–30

SOURCE: "Figure 66. Nonhydroelectric Renewable Electricity Generation by Energy Source, 2006–2030 (Billion Kilowatthours)," in *Annual Energy Outlook 2008*, U.S. Department of Energy, Energy Information Administration, Office of Integrated Analysis and Forecasting, June 2008, http://www.eia.doe.gov/oiaf/aeo/pdf/0383 (2008).pdf (accessed July 2, 2008)

2030. (See Figure 6.11.) The EIA projects that wind power will increase from 0.6% of total generation in 2006 to 2.4% in 2030 and that biomass will increase from 1% of total generation in 2006 to 3.2% in 2030.

Energy production from municipal solid waste and landfill gas is expected to stay static from 2004 to 2030, remaining at 0.5% of total generation. Geothermal energy production will grow slightly from 0.4% of the total generation in 2006 to 0.6% of the total in 2030. Solar energy is not expected to contribute much to the total of centrally generated electricity.

CHAPTER 7
ENERGY RESERVES—OIL, GAS, COAL, AND URANIUM

Congress requires the U.S. Department of Energy to prepare estimates of the quantities of crude oil, natural gas, coal, and uranium that exist in the earth and can be used as fuel. These estimates, which include deposits in the United States and in other parts of the world, are considered essential to the development, implementation, and evaluation of national energy policies. The estimates are also important because these resources are nonrenewable, which means they can be used up—they are formed much more slowly than it takes to consume them.

The focus of the estimates is recoverable reserves. Proved reserves are deposits of fuel in known locations that, based on the geological and engineering data, can be recovered using existing technology. Drilling or mining for these fuels makes sense, given current economic conditions. By contrast, undiscovered recoverable resources are quantities of fuel that are thought to exist in favorable geologic settings. It would be feasible to retrieve these resources using existing technology, although it might not be feasible under current economic conditions.

CRUDE OIL

The Energy Information Administration (EIA) indicates in *U.S. Crude Oil, Natural Gas, and Natural Gas Liquids Reserves: 2006 Annual Report* (November 2007, http://www .eia.doe.gov/pub/oil_gas/natural_gas/data_publications/crude _oil_natural_gas_reserves/current/pdf/arr.pdf) that U.S. proved reserves of crude oil have declined over the decades. In the late 1970s proved reserves of crude oil were high, at about 30 billion barrels from 1977 to 1980. During the 1980s, proved reserves of oil averaged around 27 to 28 billion barrels. The decline continued through the 1990s and into the 2000s. On December 31, 2006, crude oil reserves totaled 20.9 billion barrels.

Together, Texas (4.9 billion barrels), Alaska (3.9 billion barrels), California (3.9 billion barrels), and offshore areas in the Gulf of Mexico (3.7 billion barrels) accounted

for 74% of U.S. proved reserves in 2006. (See Figure 7.1.) According to the EIA, all these regions reported a decrease in proved reserves from 2005 to 2006.

Proved reserves of crude oil rose in 1970 with the inclusion of Alaska's North Slope oil fields. However, as the oil has been extracted, the reserves have steadily declined. In *U.S. Crude Oil, Natural Gas, and Natural Gas Liquids Reserves 1996 Annual Report* (November 1997, ftp://ftp.eia .doe.gov/pub/oil_gas/natural_gas/data_publications/crude_oil _natural_gas_reserves/historical/1996/pdf/021696.pdf), the EIA notes that in 1995 Alaska's proved reserves totaled 5.6 billion barrels of crude oil. By 2006 the state had only 3.9 billion barrels. (See Figure 7.1.) The EIA explains that proved reserves of crude oil fell by 292 million barrels in Alaska from 2005 through 2006. The Gulf of Mexico federal offshore areas had nearly 3.7 billion barrels of proved reserves in 2006, down 387 million barrels from 2005.

NATURAL GAS

Figure 7.2 shows the distribution of U.S. proved reserves of dry natural gas in 2006, which totaled 211.1 trillion cubic feet (Tcf; 5.9 trillion cubic m), an increase of 6.7 billion cubic feet (189.7 billion cubic m) from 2005. The United States also had 8.5 billion barrels of natural gas liquids proved reserves, a 4% increase from the volume reported in 2005.

UNDISCOVERED RECOVERABLE OIL AND GAS RESOURCES

Other resources are believed to exist based on past geological experience, although they are not yet proved. The EIA estimates in *U.S. Crude Oil, Natural Gas, and Natural Gas Liquids Reserves 2006 Annual Report* that 130.2 billion barrels of crude oil, 724.8 Tcf (20.5 trillion cubic m) of dry natural gas, and 7.7 billion barrels of natural gas liquids remain undiscovered in the United States.

FIGURE 7.1

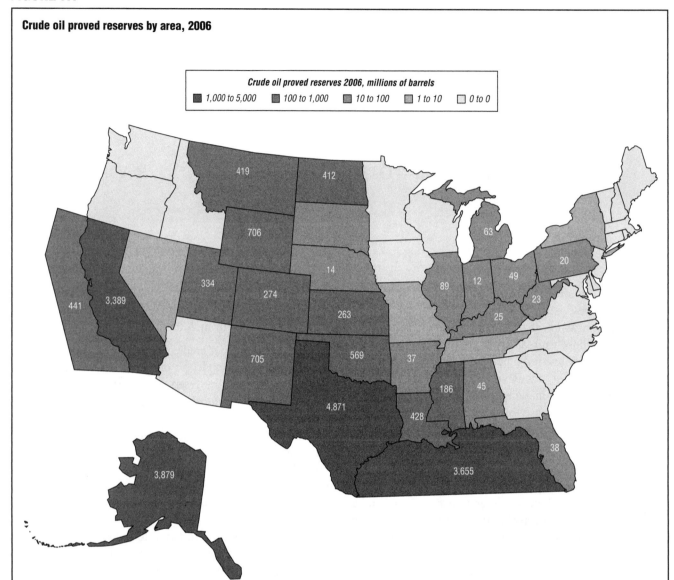

Crude oil proved reserves by area, 2006

Crude oil proved reserves 2006, millions of barrels

■ 1,000 to 5,000   ■ 100 to 1,000   ■ 10 to 100   ■ 1 to 10   □ 0 to 0

SOURCE: "Figure 16. Crude Oil Proved Reserves by Area, 2006," in *U.S. Crude Oil, Natural Gas, and Natural Gas Liquids Reserves 2006 Annual Report*, U.S. Department of Energy, Energy Information Administration, Office of Oil and Gas, November 2007, http://www.eia.doe.gov/pub/oil_gas/natural_gas/data_publications/crude_oil_natural_gas_reserves/current/pdf/arr.pdf (accessed July 3, 2008)

Looking for Oil and Gas

Finding oil and gas usually takes two steps. First, geological and geophysical exploration identifies areas where oil and gas are most likely to be found. Much of this exploration is seismic, using shock waves to determine the formations below the surface of the earth. Different rock formations transmit shock waves at different velocities, so they help determine if the geological features most often associated with oil and gas accumulations are present. After the seismic testing has been completed—and if it has been successful—exploratory wells are drilled to determine if oil or gas is present.

Drilling activity has declined dramatically since 1981, when 92,090 exploratory wells were drilled. (See Table 7.1.)

Nearly 70% of them found oil (43,887) and gas (20,250) deposits. In 2007 only 53,558 were attempted, but 88.5% were successful (oil, 14,477, and gas, 32,910). This number of wells drilled was up, however, from an all-time low of 18,939 in 1999.

In 1981 oil companies had 3,970 rotary rigs in operation. (See Figure 7.3.) By 2007 only 1,768 were operating, but this number was up from a low of 625 in 1999. According to the EIA, in *Annual Energy Review 2007* (June 2008, http://www.eia.doe.gov/aer/pdf/aer.pdf), of the 1,768 rotary rigs in operation in 2007, 297 rigs drilled for oil and 1,466 drilled for natural gas. There were 1,695 onshore rigs and 72 offshore rigs. The average depth of exploratory and development wells has steadily increased, from 3,635 feet

FIGURE 7.2

Dry natural gas proved reserves by area, 2006

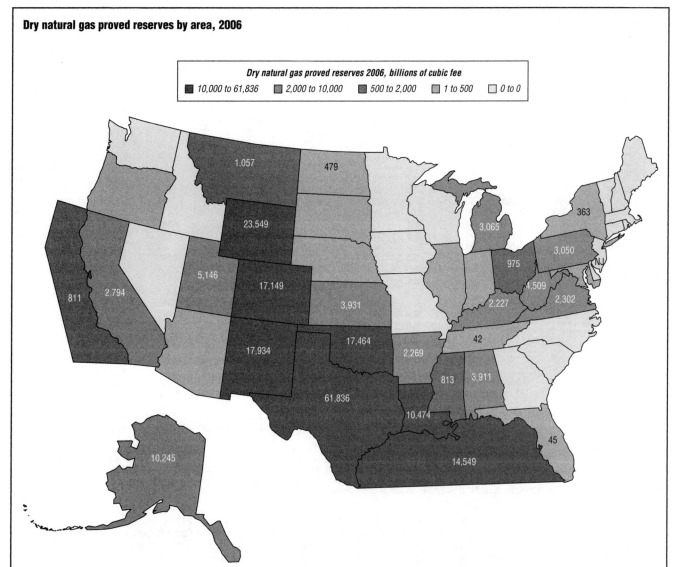

SOURCE: "Figure 19. Dry Natural Gas Proved Reserves by Area, 2006," in *U.S. Crude Oil, Natural Gas, and Natural Gas Liquids Reserves 2006 Annual Report*, U.S. Department of Energy, Energy Information Administration, Office of Oil and Gas, November 2007, http://www.eia.doe.gov/pub/oil_gas/natural_gas/data_publications/crude_oil_natural_gas_reserves/current/pdf/arr.pdf (accessed July 3, 2008)

(1,108 m) in 1949 to 6,401 feet (1,951 m) in 2007. (See Table 7.1.) Gas wells (averaging 6,927 feet [2,111 m] in 2007) are typically deeper than oil wells (averaging 5,532 feet [1,686 m] in 2007).

The Cost to Drill

In 2006 the average cost of drilling an oil or gas well was about $1.8 million in real dollars (i.e., adjusted for inflation), or about $324 per foot. (See Table 7.2.) Historically, it has cost more to drill a gas well than an oil well because gas wells are deeper. In 2006, however, the cost of drilling an average gas well ($1.9 million) was lower than the cost of drilling an oil well ($2.2 million) because the average cost per foot of drilling an oil well (about $402) was higher than that of drilling a foot of gas

well (about $348). Even though drilling costs have fluctuated over the years, it costs considerably more to drill a well today than it did in the 1960s and 1970s, not only because of inflation but also because all wells must now be drilled deeper.

The estimated expenditures on exploration for, and development of, oil and gas fields around the world by major U.S. companies peaked at $76.8 billion in 2000, which was a huge increase from each of the fifteen previous years. (See Table 7.3.) In 1984 the companies spent $65.3 billion, another high point. By 2006, however, expenditures had skyrocketed, with U.S. energy companies spending $157.1 billion on oil and gas exploration around the world; in the United States alone these companies spent $98 billion.

TABLE 7.1

Crude oil and natural gas exploratory and development wells, selected years 1949–2007

Year	Wells drilled (Number)				Successful wells (Percent)	Footage drilled (Thousand feet)				Average depth (Feet per well)			
	Crude oil	Natural gas	Dry holes	Total		Crude oil	Natural gas	Dry holes	Total	Crude oil	Natural gas	Dry holes	Total
1949	21,352	3,363	12,597	37,312	66.2	79,428	12,437	43,754	135,619	3,720	3,698	3,473	3,635
1950	23,812	3,439	14,799	42,050	64.8	92,695	13,685	50,977	157,358	3,893	3,979	3,445	3,742
1955	30,432	4,266	20,452	55,150	62.9	121,148	19,930	85,103	226,182	3,981	4,672	4,161	4,101
1960	22,258	5,149	18,212	45,619	60.1	86,568	28,246	77,361	192,176	3,889	5,486	4,248	4,213
1965	18,065	4,482	16,226	38,773	58.2	73,322	24,931	76,629	174,882	4,059	5,562	4,723	4,510
1970	12,968	4,011	11,031	28,010	60.6	56,859	23,623	58,074	138,556	4,385	5,860	5,265	4,943
1971	11,853	3,971	10,309	26,133	60.6	49,109	23,460	54,685	127,253	4,126	5,890	5,305	4,858
1972	11,378	5,440	10,891	27,709	60.7	49,269	30,006	58,556	137,831	4,330	5,516	5,377	4,974
1974	13,647	7,138	12,116	32,901	63.2	52,025	38,449	62,899	153,374	3,812	5,387	5,191	4,662
1976	17,688	9,409	13,758	40,855	66.3	68,892	49,113	68,977	186,982	3,895	5,220	5,014	4,577
1978	19,181	14,413	16,551	50,145	67.0	77,041	75,841	85,788	238,669	4,017	5,262	5,183	4,760
1980	32,959	17,461	20,785	71,205	70.8	125,262	92,106	99,575	316,943	3,801	5,275	4,791	4,451
1981	43,887	20,250	27,953	92,090	69.6	172,167	108,353	134,934	415,454	3,923	5,351	4,827	4,511
1982	39,459	19,076	26,379	84,914	68.9	149,674	107,149	123,746	380,569	3,793	5,617	4,691	4,482
1984	42,906	17,338	25,884	86,128	69.9	162,653	91,480	119,860	373,993	3,791	5,276	4,631	4,342
1986	19,213	8,599	12,799	40,611	68.5	76,825	45,039	60,961	182,825	3,999	5,238	4,763	4,502
1988	13,646	8,578	10,119	32,343	68.7	58,639	45,363	52,517	156,519	4,297	5,288	5,190	4,839
1990	12,445	11,126	8,496	32,067	73.5	55,269	56,775	44,160	156,204	4,441	5,103	5,198	4,871
1992	9,019	8,305	6,284	23,608	73.4	44,851	46,615	31,814	123,280	4,973	5,613	5,063	5,222
1994	7,001	9,739	5,515	22,255	75.2	37,270	61,576	30,293	129,139	5,324	6,323	5,493	5,803
1996	8,760	9,539	5,587	23,886	76.6	42,196	59,800	31,366	133,362	4,817	6,269	5,614	5,583
1998	6,979	11,127	4,805	22,911	79.0	34,340	67,789	29,008	131,137	4,920	6,092	6,037	5,724
1999	4,314	11,121	3,504	18,939	81.5	18,860	55,331	20,404	94,595	4,372	4,975	5,823	4,995
2000	7,585	16,242	4,046	27,873	85.5	33,777	79,605	23,193	136,575	4,453	4,901	5,732	4,900
2002	6,226	16,728	3,610	26,564	86.4	27,869	91,788	20,316	139,973	4,476	5,487	5,628	5,269
2003	7,465	19,522	3,688	30,675	88.0	35,220	112,990	20,968	169,178	4,718	5,788	5,685	5,515
2004ᴱ	ᴿ7,806	ᴿ21,816	ᴿ3,474	ᴿ33,096	ᴿ89.5	ᴿ36,691	ᴿ127,953	ᴿ20,056	ᴿ184,701	ᴿ4,700	ᴿ5,865	ᴿ5,773	ᴿ5,581
2005ᴱ	ᴿ9,668	ᴿ27,014	ᴿ4,063	ᴿ40,745	ᴿ90.0	ᴿ46,011	ᴿ159,778	ᴿ21,795	ᴿ227,584	ᴿ4,759	ᴿ5,915	ᴿ5,364	ᴿ5,586
2006ᴱ	12,339	31,587	5,581	49,507	88.7	60,494	194,504	29,533	284,531	4,903	6,158	5,292	5,747
2007ᴱ	14,477	32,910	6,171	53,558	88.5	80,086	227,968	34,753	342,807	5,532	6,927	5,632	6,401

R = Revised. E = Estimate.

Notes: Data are for exploratory and development wells combined. Service wells, stratigraphic tests, and core tests are excluded. For 1949–1959, data represent wells completed in a given year. For 1960–1969, data are for well completion reports received by the American Petroleum Institute during the reporting year. For 1970 forward, the data represent wells completed in a given year. The as-received well completion data for recent years are incomplete due to delays in the reporting of wells drilled. The Energy Information Administration (EIA) therefore statistically imputes the missing data. Totals may not equal sum of components due to independent rounding. Average depth may not equal average of components due to independent rounding.

SOURCE: Adapted from "Table 4.5. Crude Oil and Natural Gas Exploratory and Development Wells, Selected Years, 1949–2007," in *Annual Energy Review 2007*, U.S. Department of Energy, Energy Information Administration, Office of Energy Markets and End Use, June 2008, http://www.eia.doe.gov/aer/pdf/aer .pdf (accessed June 28, 2008). Non-U.S. governmental data from the Gulf Publishing Company, *World Oil*, "Forecast-Review" issue for the years 1949–65, and the American Petroleum Institute, *Quarterly Review of Drilling Statistics for the United States*, annual summaries and monthly reports, for the years 1966–69.

Drilling in the Arctic National Wildlife Refuge

Controversy has developed over opening part of the Arctic National Wildlife Refuge (ANWR) in Alaska to oil exploration. Oil fields in Prudhoe Bay, directly west of the refuge, supply about 60% of Alaska's oil and 20% of the country's domestic oil, although production is dropping steadily as the oil is extracted. In 1980 Congress passed the Alaska National Interest Lands Conservation Act, which set aside approximately 104 million acres (42.1 million hectares) for parks and wilderness areas, including 19 million acres (7.7 million hectares) for the wildlife refuge. The conservation act did not, however, include the coastal plain.

The U.S. Department of the Interior, in *Arctic National Wildlife Refuge, Alaska, Coastal Plain Resource Assessment: Report and Recommendation to the Congress of the United States and Final Legislative Environmental Impact Statement* (1987), recommended that the 1.5-million-acre (607,000-hectare) coastal plain be opened for exploration and extraction. It estimated that 3.2 billion barrels of recoverable oil exist in the area. It also predicted a 46% chance of recovering the oil, a high figure by industry standards. Vast quantities of natural gas are also likely to be found in the area.

Alaskan corporations supported the proposal because they wanted to share in the proceeds. Environmentalists strongly opposed the plan because of potential damage to the habitats and migration patterns of wildlife such as caribou, polar and grizzly bears, musk ox, wolves, arctic foxes, and millions of nesting birds.

The Department of the Interior did state that oil exploration could have a major effect on the migratory caribou herds, which number about 180,000 animals. Even though environmentalists estimated that 20% to 40% of the animals would be threatened, Department of Interior officials predicted the caribou would change their migratory habits.

FIGURE 7.3

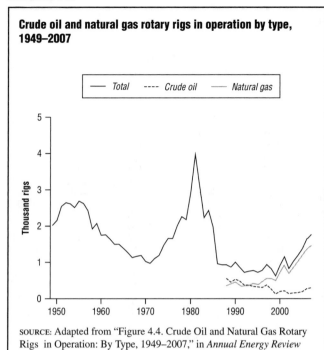

Crude oil and natural gas rotary rigs in operation by type, 1949–2007

SOURCE: Adapted from "Figure 4.4. Crude Oil and Natural Gas Rotary Rigs in Operation: By Type, 1949–2007," in *Annual Energy Review 2007*, U.S. Department of Energy, Energy Information Administration, Office of Energy Markets and End Use, June 2008, http://www.eia.doe.gov/aer/pdf/aer.pdf (accessed June 28, 2008)

If the coastal plain were opened to drilling and major oil reserves were found, oil companies could operate there for several decades. Debate over opening the region to oil drilling has continued for decades. In the press release "President Bush Discusses Energy" (June 18, 2008, http://www.whitehouse.gov/news/releases/2008/06/20080618.html), the White House notes that in June 2008 President George W. Bush (1946–) moved the debate forward by urging exploration in the ANWR with the goal of expanding U.S. production of oil.

COAL

The EIA estimates that on January 1, 2007, the United States had 491.1 billion short tons (445.5 billion t) in coal reserves. (A short ton is 2,000 pounds [907 k].) (See Table 7.4.) About 42% of this coal, 208.6 billion short tons (189.2 billion t), is underground bituminous coal. Montana (119.3 billion short tons [108.2 billion t]), Illinois (104.4 billion short tons [94.7 billion t]), and Wyoming (63.3 billion short tons [57.4 billion t]) have the largest reserves of all types of coal.

Besides untapped coal reserves, large stockpiles of coal are maintained by coal producers, distributors, and major consumers (such as electric utility companies and industrial plants) to compensate for possible interruptions in supply. Even though there is little seasonal change in demand for coal, supply can be affected by factors such as miners' strikes and bad weather. In *Annual Energy Review 2007*, the EIA states that coal stockpiles totaled 189.4 million short tons (171.8 million t) in 2007. Electric utilities held about 80% of this coal, whereas coal producers and distributors stocked 16%. The industrial sector stockpiled the remainder.

URANIUM

The United States has enough uranium to fuel existing nuclear reactors for more than forty years, so exploration for new reserves has been reduced. The EIA indicates in *Annual Energy Review 2007* that in 2003 uranium reserves totaled 1.4 billion pounds (635 million kg) of uranium oxide, mostly in Wyoming and New Mexico. In "Number of Uranium Mills and Plants Producing Uranium Concentrate" (August 5, 2008, http://www.eia.doe.gov/cneaf/nuclear/dupr/qupd_tbl2.pdf), the EIA notes that the number of uranium mills producing uranium concentrate dropped from eleven at the end of 1997 to two at the end of 2003, but then rose to six at the end of 2007.

INTERNATIONAL RESERVES
Crude Oil

Estimated world crude oil reserves totaled between 1.1 trillion and 1.3 trillion barrels as of January 1, 2007, with most of it located in the Middle East. (See Table 7.5, which provides two different sets of estimates—one from PennWell's *Oil & Gas Journal* and one from Gulf Publishing Company's *World Oil*.) Saudi Arabia, Iran, Iraq, Kuwait, the United Arab Emirates, Canada, Venezuela, and Russia had the largest reserves. The United States had 21 billion barrels of reserves, or about 1.7% of the world's total oil reserves.

Even though countries with large proved reserves have fewer incentives to find new fields, companies from many nations have turned their attention to areas where production has been limited or nonexistent, such as Azerbaijan, Kazakhstan, and other areas around the Caspian Sea; the northeastern Greenland Shelf; the Niger and Congo delta areas in Africa; and off Suriname in South America.

Natural Gas

Depending on the estimate, Russia had between 1,680 and 1,688.8 Tcf (47.6 and 47.8 trillion cubic m) and the Middle East had between 2,566 and 2,555.1 Tcf (72.7 and 72.4 trillion cubic m) of natural gas reserves on January 1, 2007. (See Table 7.5.) Russia has the largest natural gas reserves in the world, and Iran and Qatar possess the largest natural gas reserves in the Middle East. Large reserves (more than 100 Tcf [2.8 trillion cubic m]) are also located in Saudi Arabia, the United Arab Emirates, the United States, Nigeria, Algeria, Venezuela, and Iraq.

Coal

The EIA reports in *Annual Energy Review 2007* that worldwide recoverable reserves of coal were estimated at

TABLE 7.2

Costs of crude oil and natural gas wells drilled, selected years 1960–2006

Year	Thousand dollars per well					Dollars per foot				
	Crude oil	Natural gas	Dry holes	All		Crude oil	Natural gas	Dry holes	All	
	Nominal	Nominal	Nominal	Nominal	Real*	Nominal	Nominal	Nominal	Nominal	Real*
1960	52.2	102.7	44.0	54.9	261.1	13.22	18.57	10.56	13.01	61.83
1962	54.2	97.1	50.8	58.6	271.8	13.41	18.10	11.20	13.31	61.71
1964	50.6	104.8	48.5	55.8	252.2	13.12	18.57	10.64	12.86	58.11
1966	62.2	133.8	56.9	68.4	295.1	15.04	21.75	12.34	14.95	64.51
1968	79.1	148.5	66.2	81.5	327.0	18.63	24.05	12.88	16.83	67.56
1970	86.7	160.7	80.9	94.9	344.6	19.29	26.75	15.21	18.84	68.42
1972	93.5	157.8	94.9	106.4	352.8	20.77	27.78	17.28	20.76	68.82
1974	110.2	189.2	141.7	138.7	399.5	27.82	34.11	26.76	28.93	83.31
1976	151.1	270.4	190.3	191.6	476.7	37.35	49.78	36.94	40.46	100.66
1978	208.0	374.2	281.7	280.0	611.8	49.72	68.37	52.55	56.63	123.76
1980	272.1	536.4	376.5	367.7	680.4	66.36	95.16	73.70	77.02	142.52
1982	347.4	864.3	515.4	514.4	820.0	86.34	146.20	104.09	108.73	173.34
1984	262.1	489.8	329.2	326.5	482.5	66.32	88.80	67.18	71.90	106.27
1986	284.9	522.9	389.2	364.6	511.7	68.35	93.02	76.53	76.88	107.90
1988	279.4	460.3	366.4	354.7	468.6	62.28	84.65	66.96	70.23	92.78
1990	321.8	471.3	367.5	383.6	470.2	69.17	90.73	67.49	76.07	93.23
1992	362.3	426.1	357.6	382.6	442.9	69.50	72.83	67.82	70.27	81.35
1994	409.5	535.1	491.5	483.2	535.4	70.57	81.90	86.60	79.49	88.07
1996	341.0	616.0	541.0	496.1	528.6	70.60	98.67	95.74	88.92	94.74
1998	566.0	815.6	973.2	769.1	797.2	108.88	127.94	157.79	128.97	133.69
2000	593.4	756.9	1,075.4	754.6	754.6	125.96	138.39	181.83	142.16	142.16
2002	882.8	991.9	1,673.4	1,054.2	1,011.9	194.55	175.78	284.17	195.31	187.46
2003	1,037.3	1,106.0	2,065.1	1,199.5	1,127.4	221.13	189.95	345.94	216.27	203.25
2004	1,441.8	1,716.4	1,977.3	1,673.1	R1,528.5	298.45	284.78	327.91	292.57	R267.28
2005	1,920.4	1,497.6	2,392.9	1,720.7	R1,522.7	314.36	280.03	429.92	306.50	R271.24
2006	2,238.6	1,936.2	2,664.6	2,101.7	1,803.0	402.45	348.36	479.33	378.03	324.30

*In chained (2000) dollars, calculated by using gross domestic product implicit price deflators.
R = Revised.
Notes: The information reported for 1965 and prior years is not strictly comparable to that in more recent surveys. Average cost is the arithmetic mean and includes all costs for drilling and equipping wells and for surface-producing facilities. Wells drilled include exploratory and development wells; excludes service wells, stratigraphic tests, and core tests.
Web page: For related information, see http://www.api.org/statistics/accessapi/api-reports.cfm.

SOURCE: "Table 4.8. Costs of Crude Oil and Natural Gas Wells Drilled, 1960–2006," in *Annual Energy Review 2007*, U.S. Department of Energy, Energy Information Administration, Office of Energy Markets and End Use, June 2008, http://www.eia.doe.gov/aer/pdf/aer.pdf (accessed June 28, 2008). Data from the American Petroleum Institute, *2006 Joint Association Survey on Drilling Costs*, May 2008.

930.4 billion short tons (844.1 billion t) in 2005. The three countries with the most plentiful coal reserves in 2005 were the United States (264 billion short tons [239.5 billion t]), Russia (173 billion short tons [157 billion t]), and China (126 billion short tons [114.3 billion t]). (See Figure 7.4.)

Uranium

In "Supply of Uranium" (June 2008, http://www.world-nuclear.org/info/inf75.html?terms=uranium+reserves), the World Nuclear Association notes that the countries with the largest known recoverable reserves of uranium as of 2007 were Australia, Kazakhstan, Russia, South Africa, Canada, the United States, Brazil, Namibia, Niger, Ukraine, Jordan, and Uzbekistan. Australia had 1.2 million metric tons (1.3 million short tons), or 23% of the world total, and Kazakhstan had 817,000 metric tons (901,000 short tons, or 15%). The United States possessed 6% of the total world reserves of uranium, which were estimated at 342,000 metric tons (377,000 short tons).

TABLE 7.3

Major U.S. energy companies' expenditures for crude oil and natural gas exploration and development by region, 1974–2006

[Billion nominal dollars]

| Year | United States | | | Foreign | | | | | | | | Total |
	Onshore	Offshore	Total	Canada	Europe[a]	Eurasia[b]	Africa	Middle East	Other Eastern hemisphere[c]	Other Western hemisphere[d]	Total	
1974	NA	NA	8.7	NA	NA	NA	NA	NA	NA	NA	3.8	12.5
1975	NA	NA	7.8	NA	NA	—	NA	NA	NA	NA	5.3	13.1
1976	NA	NA	9.5	NA	NA	—	NA	NA	NA	NA	5.2	14.7
1977	6.7	4.0	10.7	1.5	2.5	—	.7	.2	.3	.4	5.6	16.3
1978	7.5	4.3	11.8	1.6	2.6	—	.8	.3	.4	.6	6.4	18.2
1979	13.0	8.3	21.3	2.3	3.0	—	.8	.2	.5	.8	7.8	29.1
1980	16.8	9.4	26.2	3.1	4.3	—	1.4	.2	.8	1.0	11.0	37.2
1981	19.9	13.0	33.0	1.8	5.0	—	2.1	.3	1.9	1.3	12.4	45.4
1982	27.2	11.9	39.1	1.9	6.3	—	2.1	.4	2.4	1.1	14.2	53.3
1983	16.0	11.1	27.1	1.6	4.3	—	1.7	.5	2.0	.6	10.7	37.7
1984	32.1	16.0	48.1	5.4	5.5	—	3.4	.5	2.0	.5	17.3	65.3
1985	20.0	8.5	28.5	1.9	3.7	—	1.6	.9	1.3	.7	10.1	38.6
1986	12.5	4.9	17.4	1.1	3.2	—	1.1	.3	1.2	.6	7.5	24.9
1987	9.7	4.5	14.3	1.9	3.0	—	.8	.4	2.8	.5	9.2	23.5
1988	12.9	8.1	21.0	5.4	4.3	—	.8	.4	1.4	.7	13.0	34.1
1989	9.0	6.0	15.0	6.3	3.5	—	1.0	.4	2.3	.6	14.1	29.1
1990	10.2	4.9	15.1	1.8	6.6	—	1.4	.6	2.4	.7	13.6	28.7
1991	9.6	4.6	14.2	1.7	6.8	—	1.5	.5	2.4	.7	13.7	27.9
1992	7.3	3.0	10.3	1.1	6.8	—	1.4	.6	2.4	.6	12.9	23.2
1993	7.2	3.7	10.9	1.6	5.5	.3	1.5	.7	2.5	.6	12.5	23.5
1994	7.8	4.8	12.6	1.8	4.4	.3	1.4	.4	2.8	.7	11.9	24.5
1995	7.7	4.7	12.4	1.9	5.2	.4	2.0	.4	2.4	.9	13.2	25.6
1996	7.9	6.7	14.6	1.6	5.6	.5	2.8	.5	4.1	1.6	16.6	31.3
1997	13.0	8.8	21.8	2.0	7.1	.6	3.0	.6	3.0	1.6	17.9	39.8
1998	13.5	11.0	24.4	4.8	8.6	1.3	3.1	.9	3.9	3.7	26.4	50.8
1999	6.6	6.9	13.5	2.1	4.1	.6	3.1	.4	3.4	3.8	17.5	31.0
2000	27.1	21.0	48.0	4.9	7.5	.9	2.7	.6	6.8	5.4	28.8	76.8
2001	24.2	9.6	33.9	15.3	5.4	.9	5.5	.7	5.0	3.1	35.9	69.8
2002	22.3	9.5	31.8	6.7	9.8	1.3	5.1	.8	6.2	1.6	31.4	63.2
2003	14.7	12.5	27.2	4.9	5.7	2.1	9.2	1.0	4.2	1.1	28.2	55.4
2004	21.9	10.5	32.4	5.3	4.4	2.0	6.9	1.3	3.8	1.6	25.3	57.7
2005	35.2	R11.3	R46.6	9.1	6.1	6.3	10.7	1.5	12.0	1.7	47.3	R93.8
2006	72.1	25.9	98.0	17.0	a9.0	b2.4	12.9	3.1	6.5	8.1	59.1	157.1

[a]Through 2005, includes Austria, Belgium, Denmark, Finland, France, Germany (the Federal Republic of), Greece, Ireland, Italy, Luxembourg, Netherlands, Norway, Portugal, Spain, Sweden, Switzerland, Turkey, and the United Kingdom. Beginning in 2006, includes all Europe except countries that were part of the former U.S.S.R.
[b]Through 2005, includes countries that were part of the former U.S.S.R. as well as Albania, Bosnia and Herzegovina, Bulgaria, Croatia, Czech Republic, Macedonia, Serbia and Montenegro, Slovakia, and Slovenia. Beginning in 2006, includes only countries that were part of the former U.S.S.R.
[c]This region includes areas that are eastward of the Greenwich prime meridian to 180° longitude and that are not included in other domestic or foreign classifications.
[d]This region includes areas that are westward of the Greenwich prime meridian to 180° longitude and that are not included in other domestic or foreign classifications.
R = Revised.
NA = Not available.
— = Not applicable.
Notes: "Major U.S. Energy Companies" are the top publicly-owned, U.S.-based crude oil and natural gas producers and petroleum refiners that form the Financial Reporting System (FRS).
Totals may not equal sum of components due to independent rounding.
Web page: For related information, see http://www.eia.doe.gov/emeu/finance.

SOURCE: "Table 4.10. Major U.S. Energy Companies' Expenditures for Crude Oil and Natural Gas Exploration and Development by Region, 1974–2006 (Billion Nominal Dollars)," in *Annual Energy Review 2007*, U.S. Department of Energy, Energy Information Administration, Office of Energy Markets and End Use, June 2008, http://www.eia.doe.gov/aer/pdf/aer.pdf (accessed June 28, 2008)

TABLE 7.4

Coal demonstrated reserve base, January 1, 2007

[Billion short tons]

| Region and state | Anthracite | Bituminous coal | | Subbituminous coal | | Lignite | Total | | |
		Underground	Surface	Underground	Surface	Surface[a]	Underground	Surface	Total
Appalachian	**7.3**	**70.0**	**22.5**	**0.0**	**0.0**	**1.1**	**73.9**	**27.0**	**100.9**
Alabama	.0	1.0	2.1	.0	.0	1.1	1.0	3.2	4.2
Kentucky, eastern	.0	1.1	9.3	.0	.0	.0	1.1	9.3	10.4
Ohio	.0	17.5	5.7	.0	.0	.0	17.5	5.7	23.2
Pennsylvania	7.2	19.3	.9	.0	.0	.0	23.1	4.3	27.4
Virginia	.1	1.0	.5	.0	.0	.0	1.1	.5	1.6
West Virginia	.0	29.0	3.7	.0	.0	.0	29.0	3.7	32.7
Other[b]	.0	1.1	.3	.0	.0	.0	1.1	.3	1.4
Interior	**.1**	**117.1**	**27.2**	**.0**	**.0**	**12.7**	**117.2**	**39.9**	**157.1**
Illinois	.0	87.9	16.5	.0	.0	.0	87.9	16.5	104.4
Indiana	.0	8.7	.7	.0	.0	.0	8.7	.7	9.4
Iowa	.0	1.7	.5	.0	.0	.0	1.7	.5	2.2
Kentucky, western	.0	15.8	3.6	.0	.0	.0	15.8	3.6	19.4
Missouri	.0	1.5	4.5	.0	.0	.0	1.5	4.5	6.0
Oklahoma	.0	1.2	.3	.0	.0	.0	1.2	.3	1.5
Texas	.0	.0	.0	.0	.0	12.3	.0	12.3	12.3
Other[c]	.1	.3	1.1	.0	.0	0.4	.4	1.5	1.9
Western	**(s)**	**21.5**	**2.4**	**121.3**	**58.5**	**29.4**	**142.8**	**90.3**	**233.1**
Alaska	.0	.6	.1	4.8	.6	(s)	5.4	.7	6.1
Colorado	(s)	7.6	.6	3.7	.0	4.2	11.3	4.8	16.1
Montana	.0	1.4	.0	69.6	32.5	15.8	71.0	48.3	119.3
New Mexico	(s)	2.7	.9	3.5	5.1	.0	6.2	6.0	12.2
North Dakota	.0	.0	.0	.0	.0	9.0	.0	9.0	9.0
Utah	.0	5.1	.3	(s)	.0	.0	5.1	.3	5.4
Washington	.0	.3	.0	1.0	.0	(s)	1.3	.0	1.3
Wyoming	.0	3.8	.5	38.7	20.3	.0	42.5	20.8	63.3
Other[d]	.0	.0	.0	(s)	(s)	.4	.0	.4	.4
U.S. total	**7.4**	**208.6**	**52.1**	**121.3**	**58.5**	**43.2**	**333.9**	**157.2**	**491.1**
States east of the Mississippi river	7.3	182.4	43.3	.0	.0	1.1	186.3	47.8	234.1
States west of the Mississippi river	.1	26.2	8.8	121.3	58.5	42.1	147.6	109.4	257.0

[a]Lignite resources are not mined underground in the United States.
[b]Georgia, Maryland, North Carolina, and Tennessee.
[c]Arkansas, Kansas, Louisiana, and Michigan.
[d]Arizona, Idaho, Oregon, and South Dakota.
(s)=Less than 0.05 billion short tons.
Notes: See *U.S. Coal Reserves: 1997 Update* on the web page for a description of the methodology used to produce these data. Data represent remaining measured and indicated coal resources, analyzed and on file, meeting minimum seam and depth criteria, and in the ground as of January 1, 2007. These coal resources are not totally recoverable. Net recoverability with current mining technologies ranges from 0 percent (in far northern Alaska) to more than 90 percent. Fifty-four percent of the demonstrated reserve base of coal in the United States is estimated to be recoverable. Totals may not equal sum of components due to independent rounding.
Web page: For related information, see http://www.eia.doe.gov/fuelcoal.html.

SOURCE: "Table 4.11. Coal Demonstrated Reserve Base, January 1, 2007 (Billion Short Tons)," in *Annual Energy Review 2007*, U.S. Department of Energy, Energy Information Administration, Office of Energy Markets and End Use, June 2008, http://www.eia.doe.gov/aer/pdf/aer.pdf (accessed June 28, 2008)

TABLE 7.5

World crude oil and natural gas reserves, Janurary 1, 2007

Region and country	Crude oil		Natural gas	
	Oil & Gas Journal	World Oil	Oil & Gas Journal	World Oil
	Billion barrels		Trillion cubic feet	
North America	**212.5**	**58.2**	**283.6**	**286.8**
Canada	179.2[a]	25.6[b]	57.9	56.8
Mexico	12.4	11.6	14.6	19.0
United States	21.0	21.0	211.1	211.1
Central and South America	**102.8**	**77.1**	**240.7**	**242.2**
Argentina	2.5	2.6	16.1	15.8
Bolivia	.4	.4	24.0	25.7
Brazil	11.8	12.3	10.8	12.3
Chile	.2	(s)	3.5	1.0
Colombia	1.5	1.4	4.0	6.7
Cuba	.1	.6	2.5	.6
Ecuador	4.5	4.9	NA	.3
Peru	.9	1.1	8.7	12.0
Trinidad and Tobago	.7	.6	18.8	16.7
Venezuela	80.0	52.9	152.4	151.1
Other[c]	.2	.2	(s)	(s)
Europe[d]	**15.8**	**14.5**	**180.3**	**175.7**
Austria	.1	.1	.6	.8
Croatia	.1	.1	1.1	1.0
Denmark	1.3	1.2	2.5	2.9
Germany	.4	.2	9.0	5.8
Hungary	(s)	.1	.3	2.0
Italy	.6	.4	5.8	3.7
Netherlands	.1	.2	50.0	50.8
Norway	7.8	7.1	82.3	81.3
Poland	.1	.3	5.8	4.9
Romania	.6	.5	2.2	4.5
Serbia	.1	NR	1.7	NR
United Kingdom	3.9	3.8	17.0	15.7
Other[c]	.8	.7	2.0	2.2
Eurasia[e]	**98.9**	**123.4**	**2,014.8**	**2,136.7**
Azerbaijan	7.0	NR	30.0	NR
Kazakhstan	30.0	NR	100.0	NR
Russia	60.0	74.4	1,680.0	1,688.8
Turkmenistan	.6	NR	100.0	NR
Ukraine	.4	NR	39.0	NR
Uzbekistan	.6	NR	65.0	NR
Other[c]	.3	48.9	.8	447.9
Middle East	**739.2**	**722.5**	**2,566.0**	**2,555.1**
Bahrain	.1	NR	3.3	NR
Iran	136.3	133.0	974.0	974.0
Iraq	115.0	125.1	112.0	90.0
Kuwait[f]	101.5	100.1	55.0	56.2
Oman	5.5	4.7	30.0	28.0
Qatar	15.2	20.4	910.5	905.5
Saudi Arabia[f]	262.3	262.3	240.0	252.5
Syria	2.5	2.9	8.5	12.8
United Arab Emirates	97.8	70.6	214.4	205.6
Yemen	3.0	2.8	16.9	17.0
Other[c]	(s)	.7	1.5	13.6
Africa	**114.1**	**111.7**	**484.4**	**500.7**
Algeria	12.3	11.9	161.7	161.2
Angola	8.0	9.3	2.0	4.1
Cameroon	.4	NR	3.9	NR
Congo (Brazzaville)	1.6	1.9	3.2	4.2
Egypt	3.7	3.6	58.5	67.4
Equatorial Guinea	1.1	1.8	1.3	3.4
Gabon	2.0	2.0	1.0	1.5
Libya	41.5	35.0	52.7	51.7
Mozambique	.0	.0	4.5	.0
Nigeria	36.2	37.2	181.9	184.5
Sudan	5.0	6.6	3.0	4.0
Tunisia	.4	.6	2.3	3.4
Other[c]	1.9	1.7	8.4	15.3

TABLE 7.5

World crude oil and natural gas reserves, Janurary 1, 2007

[CONTINUED]

Region and country	Crude oil		Natural gas	
	Oil & Gas Journal	World Oil	Oil & Gas Journal	World Oil
	Billion barrels		Trillion cubic feet	
Asia and Oceania[d]	**33.4**	**36.0**	**419.5**	**497.9**
Australia	1.6	4.3	30.4	153.0
Bangladesh	(s)	NR	5.0	NR
Brunei	1.1	1.2	13.8	11.5
Burma	.1	.2	10.0	16.0
China	16.0	16.3	80.0	60.9
India	5.6	3.8	38.0	27.2
Indonesia	4.3	4.8	97.8	93.0
Japan	.1	NR	1.4	NR
Malaysia	3.0	2.8	75.0	60.0
New Zealand	.1	.1	.9	1.8
Pakistan	.3	.3	28.0	30.5
Papua New Guinea	.2	.2	12.2	13.7
Thailand	.3	.5	14.8	11.7
Vietnam	.6	1.3	6.8	8.3
Other[c]	.1	.2	5.5	10.4
World	**1,316.7**	**1,143.4**	**6,189.4**	**6,395.0**

[a]Comprises 5.2 billion barrels of conventional crude oil and condensate and 174.0 billion barrels of bitumen in Alberta's oil sands.
[b]Includes 20.7 billion barrels of oil sands and bitumen. Excludes another 153 billion barrels claimed by Canadian authorities.
[c]Includes data for those countries not separately reported.
[d]Excludes countries that were part of the former U.S.S.R.
[e]Includes only countries that were part of the former U.S.S.R.
[f]Data for Kuwait and Saudi Arabia include one-half of the reserves in the neutral zone between Kuwait
NA = Not available.
NR = Not separately reported.
(s) = Less than 0.05 billion barrels.
Notes: • All reserve figures except those for Eurasia and natural gas reserves in Canada are proved reserves recoverable with present technology and prices at the time of estimation. Eurasia and Canadian natural gas figures include proved and some probable reserves.
• Totals may not equal sum of components due to independent rounding.
Web Page: For related information, see http://www.eia.doe.gov/international/oilreserves.html.

SOURCE: "Table 11.4. World Crude Oil and Natural Gas Reserves, January 1, 2007," in *Annual Energy Review 2007*, U.S. Department of Energy, Energy Information Administration, Office of Energy Markets and End Use, June 2008, http://www.eia.doe.gov/aer/pdf/aer.pdf (accessed June 28, 2008)

FIGURE 7.4

World recoverable reserves of coal in top reserves countries, 2005

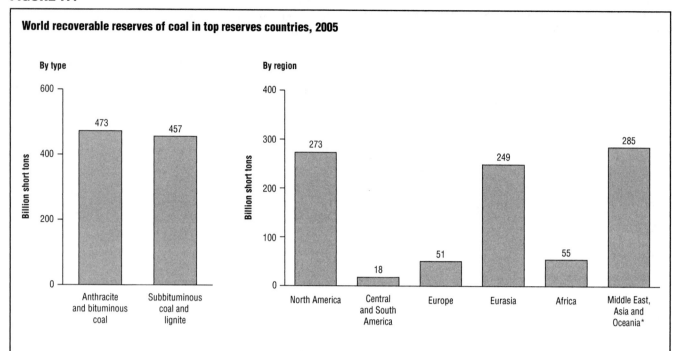

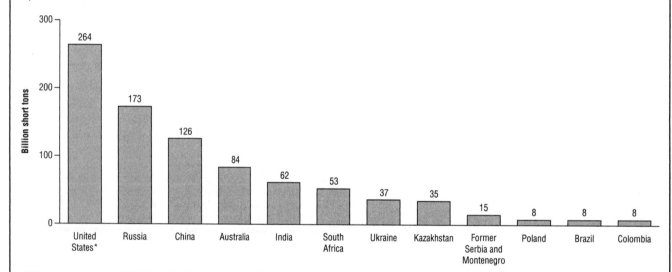

*U.S. reserves are at end of 2006, 1 year later than other data in this figure.
Notes: Data are at end of year.

SOURCE: Adapted from "Figure 11.13. World Recoverable Reserves of Coal, 2005: Top Reserves Countries," in *Annual Energy Review 2007*, U.S. Department of Energy, Energy Information Administration, Office of Energy Markets and End Use, June 2008, http://www.eia.doe.gov/aer/pdf/aer.pdf (accessed June 28, 2008)

CHAPTER 8
ELECTRICITY

Since 1879, when Thomas Alva Edison (1847–1931) flipped the first switch to light Menlo Park, New Jersey, the use of electrical power has become nearly universal in the United States.

WHAT IS ELECTRICITY?

Electricity is a form of energy resulting from the movement of charged particles, such as electrons (negatively charged subatomic particles) and protons (positively charged subatomic particles). For example, static electricity is caused by friction: when one material rubs against another, it transfers charged particles. The zap you might feel and the spark you might see when you drag your feet along the carpet and then touch a metal doorknob demonstrate static electricity—electrons being transferred between you and the doorknob.

Electric current is the flow of electric charge; it is measured in amperes (amps). Electrical power is the rate at which energy is transferred by electric current. A watt is the standard measure of electrical power, named after the Scottish engineer James Watt (1736–1819). The term *wattage* refers to the amount of electrical power required to operate a particular appliance or device. A kilowatt (kW) is a unit of electrical power equal to 1,000 watts, and a kilowatt-hour (kWh) is a unit of electrical work equal to that done by 1 kW acting for one hour.

Electrical Capacity

The generating capacity of an electrical power plant, which is measured in watts, indicates its ability to produce electrical power. A 1,000-kW generator running at full capacity for one hour supplies 1,000 kWh of power. That generator operating continuously for an entire year will produce nearly 8.8 million kWh of electricity (1,000 kW × 24 hours per day × 365 days per year). However, no generator can operate at 100% capacity during an entire year because of legal restrictions and downtime for routine maintenance and outages. On average, about one-fourth of the generating capacity of an electrical plant is not available at any given time.

Electricity demands vary daily and seasonally, so the continuous operation of electrical generators is usually not necessary. Utilities depend on steam, nuclear energy, and large hydroelectric plants to meet routine demand. Auxiliary gas, turbine, internal combustion, and smaller hydroelectric plants are used during short periods of high demand.

An Electric Power System

An electric power system has several components. Figure 8.1 illustrates a simple electric system. Generating units (power plants) produce electricity, transmission lines carry electricity over long distances, and distribution lines deliver the electricity to customers. Substations connect the pieces of the system together, and energy control centers coordinate the operation of all the components.

U.S. ELECTRICITY USAGE

In 2007 net generation of electricity totaled nearly 4.2 trillion kWh. Table 8.1 shows that electricity use in the United States—measured by the retail sales of utility companies—has increased nearly every year since 1949. In the thirty years between 1977 and 2007, retail sales of electricity nearly doubled, from 1.9 trillion kWh to 3.7 trillion kWh.

According to the Energy Information Administration (EIA), in *Annual Energy Review 2007* (June 2008, http://www.eia.doe.gov/aer/pdf/aer.pdf), coal has been and continues to be the most-used raw source for electricity production in the United States. It accounted for approximately 2 trillion kWh of electricity in 2007, supplying 49% of the net amount of 4.2 trillion kWh of electricity generated. (See Figure 8.2.) Natural gas was the second-largest source of net generation of electricity (893 billion kWh, or 21%), followed by nuclear power (807 billion kWh, or 19% of the

FIGURE 8.1

A simple electric system

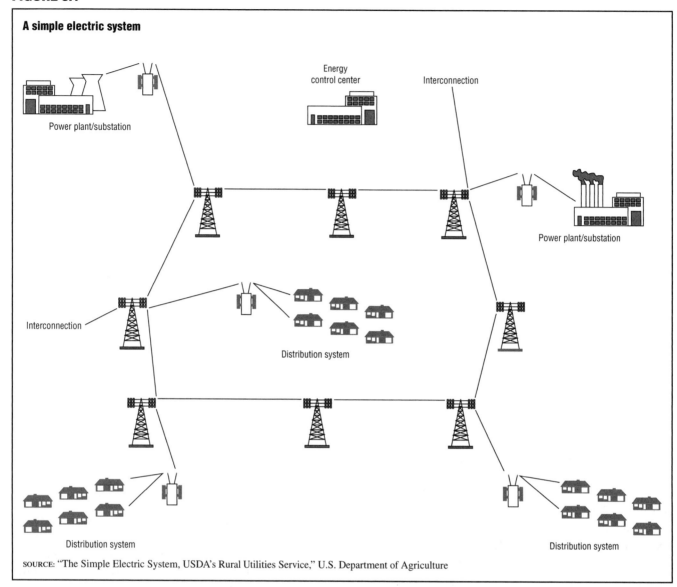

SOURCE: "The Simple Electric System, USDA's Rural Utilities Service," U.S. Department of Agriculture

total) and hydroelectric power, a renewable energy source (248 billion kWh, or 6%). Very little electricity (103 billion kWh, 2.5%) was generated by all other renewable sources combined, such as geothermal, solar, and wind power.

From 1949 to the early 1990s the industrial sector was the largest consumer of electricity in the United States. (See Table 8.2.) Since then sales to the residential sector have been higher. Beginning in 1998 sales in the commercial sector became higher than sales in the industrial sector. In 2007 about 1.4 trillion kWh went to residential users, 1.3 trillion kWh to commercial customers, and 1 trillion kWh to industrial users.

The consumption of electricity in general is growing because electricity is being used increasingly to perform tasks that were once done with coal, natural gas, or human muscle: manufacturing steel, assembling cars, and milking cows. Electricity is used extensively in technology fields, such as the computer industry, and residential and commer-cial customers need electricity to run appliances and machi-nery, such as air conditioners.

THE ELECTRIC BILL

The cost of electricity is affected by the amount of energy used to create the electricity and move it to the consumer. In 2007, for example, about 42.1 quadrillion British thermal units (Btu) of energy were consumed by U.S. utilities to generate 14.9 quadrillion Btu of electricity. (See Figure 8.3.) After accounting for energy used by the power plants themselves, only 14.2 quadrillion Btu were net generation—the amount available for transmission to customers. Almost 27.2 quadrillion Btu were lost when fuel was converted, and about 1.3 quadrillion Btu were lost during transmission and distribution (labeled "T & D losses" in Figure 8.3). In the end, for every three units of energy that were converted to create electricity in 2007, slightly less than one unit actually reached the end user.

TABLE 8.1

Electricity overview, selected years 1949–2007

[Billion kilowatthours]

Year	Net generation				Trade					T & D losses[e] and unaccounted for[f]	End use		
	Electric power sector[b]	Commercial sector[c]	Industrial sector[d]	Total	Imports[a]		Exports[a]		Net imports[a]				
					From Canada	Total	To Canada	Total	Total		Retail sales[g]	Direct use[h]	Total
1949	291	NA	5	296	NA	2	NA	(s)	2	43	255	NA	255
1950	329	NA	5	334	NA	2	NA	(s)	2	44	291	NA	291
1955	547	NA	3	550	NA	5	NA	(s)	4	58	497	NA	497
1960	756	NA	4	759	NA	5	NA	1	5	76	688	NA	688
1965	1,055	NA	3	1,058	NA	4	NA	4	(s)	104	954	NA	954
1970	1,532	NA	3	1,535	NA	6	NA	4	2	145	1,392	NA	1,392
1971	1,613	NA	3	1,616	NA	7	NA	4	4	150	1,470	NA	1,470
1972	1,750	NA	3	1,753	NA	10	NA	3	8	166	1,595	NA	1,595
1974	1,867	NA	3	1,870	NA	15	NA	3	13	177	1,706	NA	1,706
1976	2,038	NA	3	2,041	NA	11	NA	2	9	194	1,855	NA	1,855
1977	2,124	NA	3	2,127	NA	20	NA	3	17	197	1,948	NA	1,948
1978	2,206	NA	3	2,209	NA	21	NA	1	20	211	2,018	NA	2,018
1980	2,286	NA	3	2,290	NA	25	NA	4	21	216	2,094	NA	2,094
1982	2,241	NA	3	2,244	NA	33	NA	4	29	187	2,086	NA	2,086
									35	198	2,151	NA	2,151
1984	2,416	NA	3	2,419	NA	42	NA	3	40	173	2,286	NA	2,286
1986	2,487	NA	3	2,490	NA	41	NA	5	36	158	2,369	NA	2,369
1988	2,704	NA	3	2,707	NA	39	NA	7	32	161	2,578	NA	2,578
1990	2,901	6	131	3,038	16	18	16	16	2	203	2,713	125	2,837
1992	2,934	6	143	3,084	26	28	2	3	25	212	2,763	134	2,897
1994	3,089	8	151	3,248	45	47	1	2	45	211	2,935	146	3,081
1996	3,284	9	151	3,444	42	43	2	3	40	231	3,101	153	3,254
1998	3,457	9	154	3,620	40	40	12	14	26	221	3,264	161	3,425
2000	3,638	8	157	3,802	49	49	13	15	34	244	3,421	171	3,592
									16	22	202	3,394	163	3,557
2002	3,698	7	153	3,858	37	37	15	16	21	248	3,465	166	3,632
2003	3,721	7	155	3,883	29	30	24	24	6	228	3,494	168	3,662
2004	3,808	8	154	3,971	33	34	22	23	11	266	3,547	168	3,716
2005	3,902	8	145	4,055	43	45	19	20	25	R269	3,661	R150	R3,811
2006	R3,908	8	R148	R4,065	R42	R43	R23	R24	18	R266	R3,670	R147	R3,817
2007P	4,006	9	145	4,160	50	51	20	20	31	299	3,748	E144	3,892

[a]Electricity transmitted across U.S. borders. Net imports equal imports minus exports.
[b]Electricity-only and combined-heat-and-power (CHP) plants within the NAICS 22 category whose primary business is to sell electricity, or electricity and heat, to the public. Through 1988, data are for electric utilities only; beginning in 1989, data are for electric utilities and independent power producers.
[c]Commercial combined-heat-and-power (CHP) and commercial electricity-only plants.
[d]Industrial combined-heat-and-power (CHP) and industrial electricity-only plants. Through 1988, data are for industrial hydroelectric power only.
[e]Transmission and distribution losses (electricity losses that occur between the point of generation and delivery to the customer).
[f]Data collection frame differences and nonsampling error.
[g]Electricity retail sales to ultimate customers by electric utilities and, beginning in 1996, other energy service providers.
[8]Use of electricity that is 1) self-generated, 2) produced by either the same entity that consumes the power or an affiliate, and 3) used in direct support of a service or industrial process located within the same facility or group of facilities that house the generating equipment. Direct use is exclusive of station use.
R = Revised.
P = Preliminary.
E = Estimate.
NA = Not available.
(s) = Less than 0.5 billion kilowatthours.
Notes: Totals may not equal sum of components due to independent rounding.
Web pages: For all data beginning in 1949, see http://www.eia.doe.gov/emeu/aer/elect.html. For related information, see http://www.eia.doe.gov/fuelelectric.html.

SOURCE: Adapted from "Table 8.1. Electricity Overview, Selected Years, 1949–2007 (Billion Kilowatthours)," in *Annual Energy Review 2007*, U.S. Department of Energy, Energy Information Administration, Office of Energy Markets and End Use, June 2008, http://www.eia.doe.gov/aer/pdf/aer.pdf (accessed June 28, 2008). Non-U.S. governmental data from the National Energy Board of Canada for the years 1990–2007 and the California Independent System Operator for the years 2001–07.

Between 1960 and 1970 the price of electricity declined, but it began to increase during the 1970s because of an oil embargo by the Organization of the Petroleum Exporting Countries. (See Figure 8.4.) From the mid-1980s to 2002 the price of electricity dropped because prices of energy resources declined. After that time, electricity prices began to climb, and prices often varied by location. As Figure 8.5 shows, in 2006 electricity was the most expensive in Hawaii, Massachusetts, New York, Connecticut,

Rhode Island, New Hampshire, Alaska, and California, respectively. According to the EIA, in *Electric Power Annual 2006* (November 2007, http://www.eia.doe.gov/cneaf/electricity/epa/epa.pdf), the average price of electricity sold to the residential sector was 10.4 cents per kWh in 2006, whereas the commercial sector paid 9.4 cents per kWh. Industrial users paid only 6.1 cents per kWh because the huge amounts of electricity they use allowed them to receive volume discounts. The average

FIGURE 8.2

Electricity net generation by major sources, 1949–2007

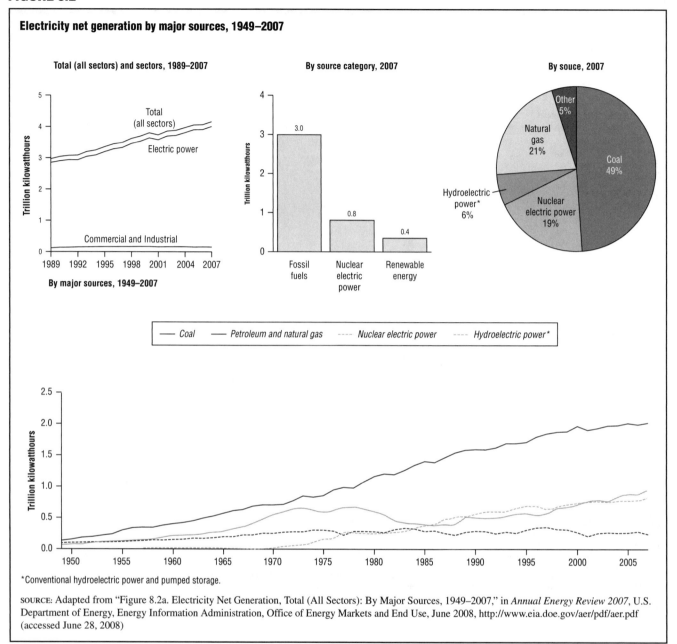

*Conventional hydroelectric power and pumped storage.

SOURCE: Adapted from "Figure 8.2a. Electricity Net Generation, Total (All Sectors): By Major Sources, 1949–2007," in *Annual Energy Review 2007*, U.S. Department of Energy, Energy Information Administration, Office of Energy Markets and End Use, June 2008, http://www.eia.doe.gov/aer/pdf/aer.pdf (accessed June 28, 2008)

price for all sectors across the United States in 2006 was 8.9 cents per kWh.

DEREGULATION OF ELECTRIC UTILITIES

Regulated by the government for decades, electric utilities in some states have passed through a controversial shift toward unregulated markets and increased competition. In 1978 Congress passed the Public Utilities Regulatory Policies Act, which required utilities to buy electricity from private companies when that would be cheaper than building their own power plants. The Energy Policy Act of 1992 gave other electricity generators greater access to the market, resulting in widespread debates about regulatory, economic, energy, and environmental policies. State public

utility commissions conducted proceedings and crafted rules related to competition.

California was a leader in deregulation. In the summer of 2000, however, the state experienced rolling electrical blackouts, and electricity bills doubled for many customers. Fearful of similar blackouts and price spikes, most other states had slowed or stopped their efforts to deregulate their electricity markets by the spring of 2001. At that time, twenty-four states and the District of Columbia had begun deregulation. Then, during an investigation of Enron Corporation, documents were found that showed how Enron's electricity traders had boosted profits with strategies that added to electricity costs and congestion on transmission lines. As a result, public confidence in power companies, in general, and deregulation,

TABLE 8.2

Electricity end use, selected years 1949–2007

[Billion kilowatthours]

Year	Retail sales[a]				Total retail sales[e]	Direct use[f]	Total end use[g]	Discontinued retail sales series	
	Residential	Commercial[b]	Industrial[c]	Transportation[d]				Commercial (old)[h]	Other (old)[i]
1949	67	E59	123	E6	255	NA	255	45	20
1950	72	E66	146	E7	291	NA	291	51	22
1955	128	E103	260	E6	497	NA	497	79	29
1960	201	E159	324	E3	688	NA	688	131	32
1965	291	E231	429	E3	954	NA	954	200	34
1970	466	E352	571	E3	1,392	NA	1,392	307	48
1971	500	E377	589	E3	1,470	NA	1,470	329	51
1972	539	E413	641	E3	1,595	NA	1,595	359	56
1974	578	E440	685	E3	1,706	NA	1,706	385	58
1976	606	E492	754	E3	1,855	NA	1,855	425	70
1978	674	E531	809	E3	2,018	NA	2,018	461	73
1980	717	559	815	3	2,094	NA	2,094	488	74
1982	730	609	745	3	2,086	NA	2,086	526	86
1984	780	664	838	4	2,286	NA	2,286	583	85
1986	819	715	831	4	2,369	NA	2,369	631	89
1988	893	784	896	5	2,578	NA	2,578	699	90
1990	924	838	946	5	2,713	125	2,837	751	92
1992	936	850	973	5	2,763	134	2,897	761	93
1994	1,008	913	1,008	5	2,935	146	3,081	820	98
1996	1,083	980	1,034	5	3,101	153	3,254	887	98
1998	1,130	1,078	1,051	5	3,264	161	3,425	979	104
2000	1,192	1,159	1,064	5	3,421	171	3,592	1,055	
2002	1,265	1,205	990	6	3,465	166	3,632	1,104	106
2003	1,276	1,199	1,012	7	3,494	168	3,662	—	—
2004	1,292	1,230	1,018	7	3,547	168	3,716	—	—
2005	1,359	1,275	1,019	8	3,661	R150	R3,811	—	—
2006	R1,352	R1,300	R1,011	R7	R3,670	R147	R3,817	—	—
2007[p]	1,392	1,343	1,006	8	3,748	E144	3,892	—	—

[a]Electricity retail sales to ultimate customers reported by electric utilities and, beginning in 1996, other energy service providers.
[b]Commercial sector, including public street and highway lighting, interdepartmental sales, and other sales to public authorities.
[c]Industrial sector. Through 2002, excludes agriculture and irrigation; beginning in 2003, includes agriculture and irrigation.
[d]Transportation sector, including sales to railroads and railways.
[e]The sum of "residential," "commercial," "industrial," and "transportation."
[f]Use of electricity that is 1) self-generated, 2) produced by either the same entity that consumes the power or an affiliate, and 3) used in direct support of a service or industrial process located within the same facility or group of facilities that house the generating equipment. Direct use is exclusive of station use.
[g]The sum of "total retail sales" and "direct use."
[h]"Commercial (old)" is a discontinued series—data are for the commercial sector, excluding public street and highway lighting, interdepartmental sales, and other sales to public authorities.
[i]"Other (old)" is a discontinued series—data are for public street and highway lighting, interdepartmental sales, other sales to public authorities, agriculture and irrigation, and transportation including railroads and railways.
R = Revised.
P = Preliminary.
E = Estimate.
NA = Not available.
— = Not applicable.
Note: Totals may not equal sum of components due to independent rounding.
Web pages: For all data beginning in 1949, see http://www.eia.doe.gov/emeu/aer/elect.html. For related information, see http://www.eia.doe.gov/fuelelectric.html.

SOURCE: Adapted from "Table 8.9. Electricity End Use, Selected Years, 1949–2007 (Billion Kilowatthours)," in *Annual Energy Review 2007*, U.S. Department of Energy, Energy Information Administration, Office of Energy Markets and End Use, June 2008, http://www.eia.doe.gov/aer/pdf/aer.pdf (accessed June 28, 2008)

in particular, eroded. As of February 2003, only seventeen states plus the District of Columbia were actively engaged in restructuring their utilities. (See Figure 8.6.) In addition, five states had delayed deregulation, and California had suspended its restructuring activities. Restructuring was not active in twenty-seven states.

By the last half of the first decade of the 2000s it was becoming widely known that the deregulation of electric utilities, which had occurred in some states as indicated in Figure 8.6, had done little to bring electric prices down. A comparison of Figure 8.5 and Figure 8.6 shows that many of the states in which restructuring and deregulation activity was active in 2003 were states in which electricity prices were the highest in 2006. John Funk reports in "Electric Deregulation: A Legacy of Problems; Consumers Never Got Expected Benefits" (*Plain Dealer* [Cleveland, Ohio], December 8, 2007) that by late 2007 only eleven states were still deregulated.

INTERNATIONAL ELECTRICITY USAGE
World Production
The EIA notes in *Annual Energy Review 2007* that in 2005 approximately 17.3 trillion kWh of electricity were

FIGURE 8.3

Electricity flow, 2007

[Quadrillion Btu]

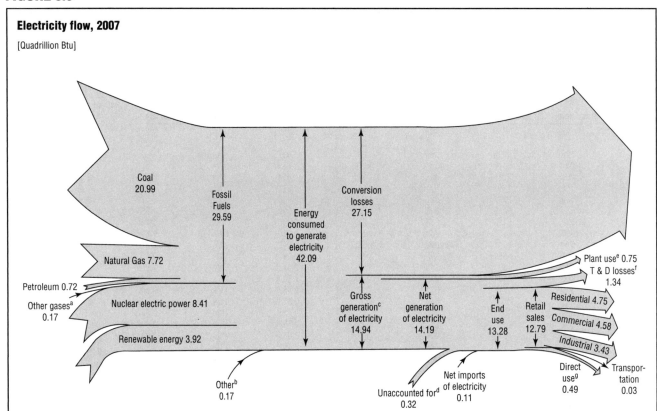

[a]Blast furnace gas, propane gas, and other manufactured and waste gases derived from fossil fuels.
[b]Batteries, chemicals, hydrogen, pitch, purchased steam, sulfur, miscellaneous technologies, and non-renewable waste (municipal solid waste from non-biogenic sources, and tire-derived fuels).
[c]Estimated as net generation divided by 0.95.
[d]Data collection frame differences and nonsampling error.
[e]Electric energy used in the operation of power plants, estimated as 5 percent of gross generation.
[f]Transmission and distribution losses (electricity losses that occur between the point of generation and delivery to the customer) are estimated as 9 percent of gross generation.
[g]Use of electricity that is 1) self-generated, 2) produced by either the same entity that consumes the power or an affiliate, and 3) used in direct support of a service or industrial process located within the same facility or group of facilities that house the generating equipment. Direct use in exclusive of station use.
Notes: Data are Preliminary. Values are derived from source data prior to rounding for publication.
Totals may not equal sum of components due to independent rounding.

SOURCE: "Diagram 5. Electricity Flow, 2007 (Quadrillion Btu)," in *Annual Energy Review 2007*, U.S. Department of Energy, Energy Information Administration, Office of Energy Markets and End Use, June 2008, http://www.eia.doe.gov/aer/pdf/aer.pdf (accessed June 28, 2008)

generated around the world: 11.5 trillion kWh from fossil fuels, 2.9 trillion kWh from hydroelectric power, 2.6 trillion kWh from nuclear power sources, and 0.4 trillion kWh from wood, waste, wind, and other sources. (See Figure 8.7.) The United States accounted for nearly 4.1 trillion kWh (23%); China, 2.4 trillion kWh (14%); Japan, 1 trillion kWh (6%); and Russia, 904 billion kWh (5%). Figure 8.8 shows net generation of electricity by the type of fuel used and by regions of the world.

World Consumption

In *International Energy Annual 2005* (October 2007, http://www.eia.doe.gov/iea/elec.html), the EIA explains that total world electricity consumption increased from 7.3 trillion kWh in 1980 to 15.7 trillion kWh in 2005. Asia and Oceania used 5.1 trillion kWh (32%) in 2005; North America, 4.5 trillion kWh (29%); Europe, 3.2 trillion (21%); and Eurasia, 1.1 trillion (7%). Central and South America used about 4%

of the world's electricity, and the Middle East and Africa each consumed about 3%.

TRENDS IN THE U.S. ELECTRICAL POWER INDUSTRY

In *Annual Energy Outlook 2008* (June 2008, http://www.eia.doe.gov/oiaf/aeo/pdf/0383(2008).pdf), the EIA predicts that from 2006 to 2030 total electricity consumption will grow at a rate of 1.1% annually. Even though demand will be high for products that use electricity, the efficiency of those products will be high, thereby tempering the demand. Population shifts to warmer climates are expected to increase the use of electricity for cooling.

The demand for electricity in the United States has always been related to economic growth. However, electricity use is expected to grow more slowly than the gross domestic product (a measure of economic growth). Figure 8.9 shows how

FIGURE 8.4

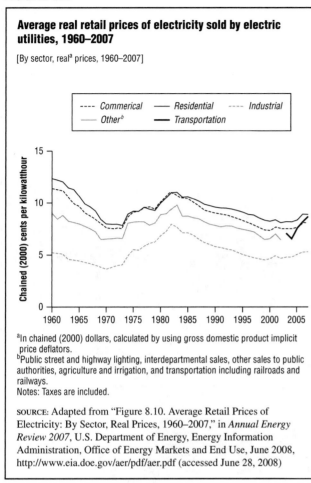

Average real retail prices of electricity sold by electric utilities, 1960–2007

[By sector, real[a] prices, 1960–2007]

[a]In chained (2000) dollars, calculated by using gross domestic product implicit price deflators.
[b]Public street and highway lighting, interdepartmental sales, other sales to public authorities, agriculture and irrigation, and transportation including railroads and railways.
Notes: Taxes are included.

SOURCE: Adapted from "Figure 8.10. Average Retail Prices of Electricity: By Sector, Real Prices, 1960–2007," in *Annual Energy Review 2007*, U.S. Department of Energy, Energy Information Administration, Office of Energy Markets and End Use, June 2008, http://www.eia.doe.gov/aer/pdf/aer.pdf (accessed June 28, 2008)

rience power shortages or losses. By contrast, excessive projections of the nation's needs may mean billions of dollars spent on unneeded equipment.

The EIA estimates that the United States will need 263 gigawatts (GW) of new generating capacity from 2007 to 2030 to meet growing demand for electricity and to replace aging power plants, most of it after 2015. From 2007 to 2030, 45 GW of capacity are expected to be taken out of production, mainly old fossil-fired plants that are not competitive with newer types of fossil-fired plants.

According to the EIA, the high cost of natural gas, petroleum, and coal as well as increasing prices for new electricity generating capacity led to a jump in electricity prices from 2000 through 2006. Furthermore, electricity prices are forecast to continue increasing through 2009. In 2009 electricity prices are expected to be at an annual average of 9.3 cents per kWh (in 2006 dollars). By 2015, however, as new sources of natural gas and coal are brought on line, electricity prices should fall to 8.5 cents per kWh. After 2015 natural gas and petroleum prices will rise, but electricity producers will rely more on coal and renewables for power generation. The result will be a slow rise in electricity prices to 8.8 cents per kWh in 2030.

Continued concerns about pollution and global warming could result in tightened environmental emission standards, which could, in turn, affect electrical utility expansion, supply, and prices. Advances in solar and wind turbine technology could make renewable sources of electrical power more economical. Some energy experts and environmentalists claim that increased efficiency and conservation efforts are the most sensible alternatives to new construction or to the burning of more fossil fuels in existing plants. Using this idea to its fullest, the former vice president and Nobel Peace Prize winner Al Gore Jr. (1948–) challenges the nation in "A Generational Challenge to Repower America" (July 17, 2008, http://blog.algore.com/2008/07/) to generate all electricity in the United States using only noncarbon-based renewable resources such as wind, solar, and geothermal power by 2018.

electricity sales are related more to economic growth than to population growth. Note that the phrase "five-year moving average" means that each point on the graph is an average for that year's data plus the previous four years' data. This type of averaging is used to determine long-term averages without the weight of cyclical influences such as the weather.

The rate of growth of consumption carries financial risks for electric companies. If the industry underestimates future needs for electricity, consumers may expe-

FIGURE 8.5

Average electricity rates by state, 2006

[U.S. total average price per kilowatthour is 8.90 cents]

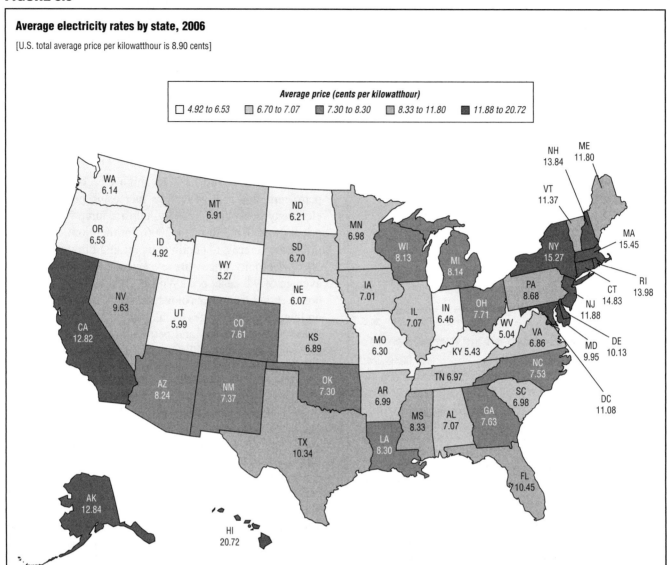

SOURCE: "Figure 7.4. Average Retail Price of Electricity by State, 2006," in *Electric Power Annual 2006*, U.S. Department of Energy, Energy Information Administration, Office of Coal, Nuclear, Electric and Alternate Fuels, November 2007, http://www.eia.doe.gov/cneaf/electricity/epa/epa.pdf (accessed July 3, 2008)

FIGURE 8.6

Status of state electric industry restructuring activity, as of February 2003

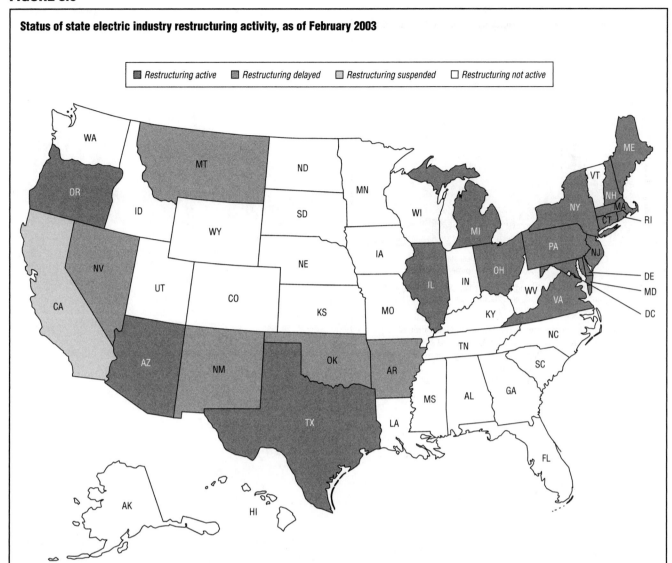

SOURCE: "Status of State Electric Industry Restructuring Activity as of February 2003," U.S. Department of Energy, Energy Information Administration, February 2003, http://www.eia.doe.gov/cneaf/electricity/chg_str/restructure.pdf (accessed July 17, 2008)

FIGURE 8.7

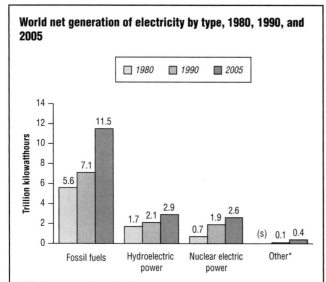

World net generation of electricity by type, 1980, 1990, and 2005

*Wood, waste, geothermal, solar, wind, batteries, chemicals, hydrogen, pitch, purchased steam, sulfur, and miscellaneous technologies.
(s) = Less than 0.05 trillion kilowatthours.

SOURCE: Adapted from "Figure 11.16. World Net Generation of Electricity: Net Generation by Type, 1980, 1990, and 2005," in *Annual Energy Review 2007*, U.S. Department of Energy, Energy Information Administration, Office of Energy Markets and End Use, June 2008, http://www.eia.doe.gov/aer/pdf/aer.pdf (accessed June 28, 2008)

FIGURE 8.8

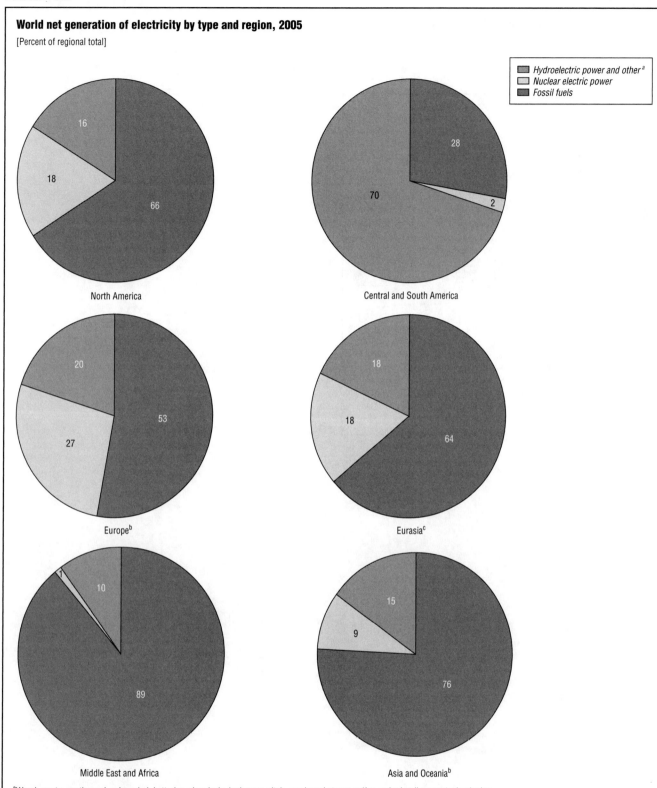

World net generation of electricity by type and region, 2005

[Percent of regional total]

Legend:
Hydroelectric power and other [a]
Nuclear electric power
Fossil fuels

North America

Central and South America

Europe[b]

Eurasia[c]

Middle East and Africa

Asia and Oceania[b]

[a]Wood, waste, geothermal, solar, wind, batteries. chemicals, hydrogen, pitch, purchased steam, sulfur, and miscellaneous technologies.
[b]Excludes countries that were part of the former U.S.S.R.
[c]Includes countries that were part of the former U.S.S.R.

SOURCE: Adapted from "Figure 11.16. World Net Generation of Electricity: Net Generation by Type by Region, 2005 (Percent of Regional Total)," in *Annual Energy Review 2007*, U.S. Department of Energy, Energy Information Administration, Office of Energy Markets and End Use, June 2008, http://www.eia.doe.gov/aer/pdf/aer.pdf (accessed June 28, 2008)

FIGURE 8.9

Population, gross domestic product, and electricity sales, 1965–2025

[Five-year moving average annual percent growth]

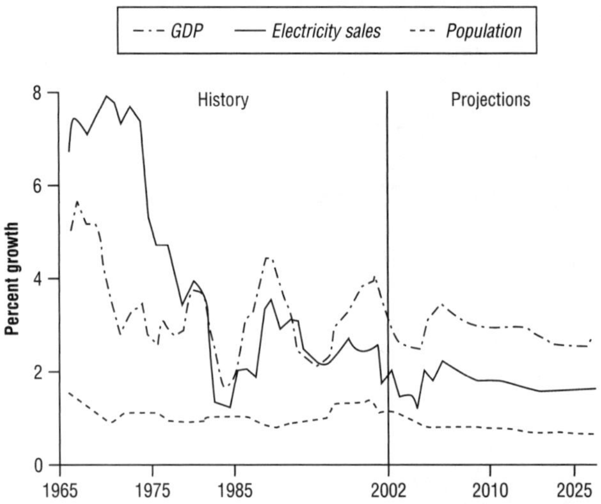

SOURCE: "Figure 67. Population, Gross Domestic Product, and Electricity Sales, 1965–2025 (5-Year Moving Average Annual Percent Growth)," in *Annual Energy Outlook 2004*, U.S. Department of Energy, Energy Information Administration, Office of Integrated Analysis and Forecasting, January 2004, http://www.eia.doe.gov/oiaf/archive/aeo04/pdf/0383(2004).pdf (accessed July 2, 2008)

CHAPTER 9
ENERGY CONSERVATION

ENERGY CONSERVATION AND EFFICIENCY

Energy conservation is the efficient use of energy, without necessarily curtailing the services that energy provides. Conservation occurs when societies develop efficient technologies that reduce energy needs. Environmental concerns, such as acid rain and the potential for global warming, have increased public awareness about the importance of energy conservation.

Energy efficiency can be measured by two indicators. The first is energy consumption per person (per capita) per year. Annual per person energy consumption in the United States was 214 million British thermal units (Btu) in 1949. (See Figure 9.1.) It topped out at 359 million Btu in 1978 and 1979; dropped to 313 million Btu by 1983; and then slowly rose until it reached 352 million Btu in 2000. It leveled off through 2007, when the annual rate of consumption per capita was 337 million Btu.

The second indicator of efficiency is energy consumption per dollar of gross domestic product (GDP; the total value of goods and services produced by a nation). When a country grows in its energy efficiency, it uses less energy to produce the same amount of goods and services. In 1949 Americans paid about $19.00 per 1,000 Btu of energy. (See Figure 9.2.) In 1970 this rate decreased to $17.99 per 1,000 Btu of energy, and by 2007 Americans paid $8.78 per 1,000 Btu of energy.

ENERGY CONSERVATION, PUBLIC HEALTH, AND THE ENVIRONMENT

People living in cities with high levels of pollution have higher risks of mortality from certain diseases than those living in less polluted cities. Energy-related emissions generate a vast majority of these polluting chemicals. (Table 4.3 in Chapter 4 shows some air pollutants and their sources.) According to the American Lung Association, air pollution has been related to diseases such as asthma, bronchitis, emphysema, and lung cancer. The association estimates the annual health costs of exposure to the most serious air pollutants to be in the billions. Clean and efficient energy technologies, it states, represent a cost-effective investment in public health.

Global warming is long-term climate change—a worldwide temperature increase—caused by the greenhouse effect. This occurs when heat is trapped within the atmosphere by high levels of carbon dioxide, methane, nitrogen oxide, hydrofluorocarbons, sulfur dioxides, and perfluorocarbons. Just as the glass of a greenhouse or the windows of a car trap heat, the greenhouse gases keep the earth warmer than it would be if the atmosphere contained only oxygen and nitrogen.

The Intergovernmental Panel on Climate Change

In 1988 the United Nations established the Intergovernmental Panel on Climate Change (IPCC), a group of two thousand of the world's leading scientists. The IPCC reported in *Climate Change 1995* that climate change, which includes temperature rise (global warming), sea-level rise, precipitation change, and extreme climatic events, is real, serious, and accelerating. (This and other IPCC assessment reports can be accessed at http://www.ipcc.ch/ipccreports/assessments-reports.htm.) The most likely cause, the IPCC said, is primarily the burning of coal, oil, and gasoline, which has increased the amount of carbon dioxide and other greenhouse gases in the atmosphere. Deforestation is another factor, because it reduces the amount of carbon dioxide that can be absorbed and stored in plants.

In its third assessment report, *Climate Change 2001*, the IPCC said it had a clearer understanding of the causes and consequences of climate change, largely because so much climate research and environmental monitoring had been undertaken. The IPCC described the effect that global warming would have on weather patterns, water resources, the seasons, ecosystems, and extreme climate events, and it

FIGURE 9.1

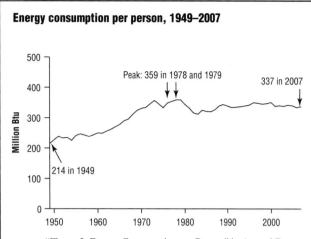

Energy consumption per person, 1949–2007

SOURCE: "Figure 2. Energy Consumption per Person," in *Annual Energy Review 2007*, U.S. Department of Energy, Energy Information Administration, Office of Energy Markets and End Use, June 2008, http://www.eia.doe.gov/aer/pdf/aer.pdf (accessed June 28, 2008)

FIGURE 9.2

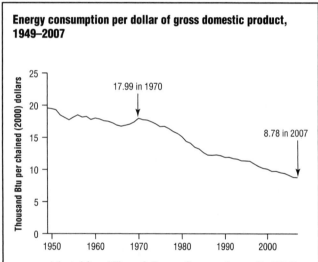

Energy consumption per dollar of gross domestic product, 1949–2007

SOURCE: Adapted from "Figure 3. Energy Consumption per Real Dollar of Gross Domestic Product," in *Annual Energy Review 2007*, U.S. Department of Energy, Energy Information Administration, Office of Energy Markets and End Use, June 2008, http://www.eia.doe.gov/aer/pdf/aer.pdf (accessed June 28, 2008)

urged governments to move quickly with policies to protect the planet.

In 2007 the IPCC won the Nobel Peace Prize, which was shared with the former vice president Albert Gore Jr. (1948–), for two decades of scientific reports on global warming and other climate change issues and their relationship to human activity. Also in 2007 the IPCC published its fourth assessment report, *Climate Change 2007*. The report noted that climate change, including global warming, was "unequivocal," meaning that it is a certainty and undeniable. The report is extensive, but a few of its key points are that many natural systems are being affected by climate

change and that some of the effects of climate change can be reduced, delayed, or avoided by taking action now, such as by reducing our emissions of greenhouse gases. The IPCC report forecasts that the earth will warm approximately 0.4° Fahrenheit (0.2° C) per decade.

The Kyoto Protocol

In December 1997 the United Nations convened a 160-nation conference on global warming in Kyoto, Japan, to develop a treaty on climate change that would place binding caps on industrial emissions. The initial draft of the treaty, called the Kyoto Protocol to the United Nations Framework Convention on Climate Change (or simply the Kyoto Protocol), bound industrialized nations to reducing their emissions of six greenhouse gases below 1990 levels. It marked the first time nations made such sweeping pledges to cut emissions.

Each country had a different target to reach by 2012: the United States was to cut emissions by 7%, most European nations by 8%, and Japan by 6%. Reductions were to begin by 2008. Developing nations were not required to make such pledges. The United States had proposed a program of voluntary pledges by developing nations, but that section was deleted, as was a tough system of enforcement. Instead, each country was to decide for itself how to achieve its goal. The draft treaty provided market-driven tools for reducing emissions. For example, nations would be allowed to sell emissions credits to other nations. The draft treaty also set up a Clean Development Fund to help poorer nations with technology to reduce their emissions.

Getting the treaty ratified proved difficult, however. President Bill Clinton (1946–) signed the protocol, but the U.S. Senate did not ratify it. To save the treaty, diplomats from 178 nations met in Bonn, Germany, in July 2001 and drafted a compromise treaty. In October 2001 two thousand delegates from 160 countries worked for twelve days in Marrakech, Morocco, to complete a final draft of the Kyoto Protocol.

President George W. Bush (1946–) (June 11, 2001, http://www.climatevision.gov/statements.html) rejected that final draft of the Kyoto Protocol, characterizing it as "fatally flawed." He said implementation of the treaty would harm the U.S. economy and unfairly require only the industrial nations to cut emissions. In particular, he noted that neither China, the world's second largest emitter of greenhouse gases, nor India, another high emitter, were bound by the protocol. He said at the time:

> Our country, the United States, is the world's largest emitter of manmade greenhouse gases. We account for almost 20 percent of the world's man-made greenhouse emissions. We also account for about one-quarter of the world's economic output. We recognize the responsibility to reduce our emissions. We also recognize the other part of the story—that the rest of the world emits

80 percent of all greenhouse gases. And many of those emissions come from developing countries....

We recognize our responsibility and will meet it—at home, in our hemisphere, and in the world. My Cabinet-level working group on climate change is recommending a number of initial steps, and will continue to work on additional ideas. The working group proposes the United States help lead the way by advancing the science on climate change, advancing the technology to monitor and reduce greenhouse gases, and creating partnerships within our hemisphere and beyond to monitor and measure and mitigate emissions.

When Russia ratified the treaty in November 2004, the Kyoto Protocol had support from countries whose emissions totaled 55% of the world's greenhouse gases, which was the minimum needed for the treaty to go into effect. At the end of that year, 130 countries had signed on, including all the European Union members, Japan, and Norway. The Kyoto Protocol took effect on February 16, 2005, without the support of the United States and Australia.

U.S. attitudes about the Kyoto Protocol varied widely. Most business leaders said the treaty went too far and was too costly for the U.S. economy, whereas environmentalists said the treaty's standards did not go far enough. Some experts doubted that any action emerging from Kyoto would be sufficient to prevent the doubling of greenhouse gases. In May 2005—in response to the Bush administration's policies—mayors from 132 cities in the United States joined a bipartisan coalition to fight global warming on the local level. The coalition pledged to have their cities meet Kyoto Protocol requirements for the United States: a reduction of heat-trapping gas emissions to 7% below 1990 levels by 2012.

Is Kyoto working? In "Time to Ditch Kyoto" (*Nature*, vol. 449, October 25, 2007), Gwyn Prins and Steve Rayner suggest that the Kyoto Protocol has failed to achieve greenhouse gas emissions reductions and slow global warming thus far. They suggest that including so many countries in the treaty was a mistake, making the initiative unwieldy. Prins and Rayner note that "fewer than 20 countries are responsible for about 80% of the world's emissions," so they suggest that only those countries be targeted. The researchers urge that those high-emissions countries should spend as much money on climate change research as they spend on their military. In addition, Prins and Rayner support a bottom-up approach to the problem, in which "countries would choose policies that suit their particular circumstances." Paul Vallely reports in "The Big Question: Is the Kyoto Treaty an Outdated Failure Based on the Wrong Premises?" (*The Independent* [London, England], October 26, 2007) that other scientists and researchers believe that huge investments are needed in climate change research but are wary of abandoning the Kyoto process, which might delay progress as new international agreements are constructed.

Levels of greenhouse gas emissions for the United States for 1990, 1995, and from 2000 through 2006 are shown in Table 9.1 in teragrams (Tg) of carbon dioxide equivalents. A teragram is a trillion grams. Each gas in the table is reported by its global-warming potential in teragrams, which allows these numbers to be compared. Higher numbers indicate greater harm done to the environment by the gas. Conversely, numbers in parentheses are for sources, such as land-use change and forestry, which reduce greenhouse gas emissions by the carbon equivalents shown. In 2006 emissions of greenhouse gases in the United States reached 7,054.2 Tg, which was 905.9 Tg (15%) higher than emissions in 1990.

ENERGY EFFICIENCY IN TRANSPORTATION

The U.S. transportation system plays a central role in the economy. Highway transportation is dependent on vehicles with internal combustion engines, which are fueled almost exclusively by petroleum. According to the Energy Information Administration (EIA), in *Annual Energy Review 2007* (June 2008, http://www.eia.doe.gov/aer/pdf/aer.pdf), the transportation sector accounted for nearly 29% of all energy consumed in the United States in 2007. Americans used 29 quadrillion Btu of energy for transportation that year, of which petroleum made up 97%. Despite the improvements in transportation efficiency in recent decades, the EIA predicts in *Annual Energy Outlook 2008* (June 2008, http://www.eia.doe.gov/oiaf/aeo/pdf/0383 (2008).pdf) that the transportation sector will consume 33 quadrillion Btu in 2030.

Automotive Efficiency

Policy makers interested in the energy used for transportation have an array of conservation options. (See Table 9.2.) However, not all options are mutually supportive. For example, efforts to promote a freer flow of automobile traffic, such as high-occupancy vehicle lanes or free parking for car pools, may sabotage efforts to shift travelers to mass transit or to reduce trip lengths and frequency.

In the United States light-duty vehicles dominate the transportation sector; cars, light trucks, and motorcycles used 60.1% of all transportation energy in 2006, as reported by the U.S. Department of Energy's Center for Transportation Analysis, in *Transportation Energy Data Book: Edition 27* (2008 http://cta.ornl.gov/data/tedb27/Edition27_Full_Doc.pdf). Furthermore, the EIA notes in *Annual Energy Review 2007* that motor gasoline, which is divided among passenger cars, motorcycles, light-and heavy-duty trucks, and miscellaneous other modes of transportation, made up 45% of the total petroleum products supplied in the United States in 2007.

The major growth in fuel use since the 1970s has been that consumed by trucks, whereas fuel consumption

TABLE 9.1

Trends in greenhouse gas emissions and sinks, 1990, 1995, and 2000–06

Gas/source	1990	1995	2000	2001	2002	2003	2004	2005	2006
CO₂	**5,068.5**	**5,394.2**	**5,939.7**	**5,846.2**	**5,908.6**	**5,952.7**	**6,038.2**	**6,074.3**	**5,983.1**
Fossil fuel combustion	4,724.1	5,032.4	5,577.1	5,507.4	5,564.8	5,617.0	5,681.4	5,731.0	5,637.9
Electricity generation	1,809.6	1,939.3	2,282.3	2,244.3	2,253.7	2,283.1	2,314.9	2,380.2	2,328.2
Transportation	1,485.1	1,599.4	1,798.2	1,775.6	1,828.9	1,807.6	1,856.4	1,869.8	1,856.0
Industrial	844.9	876.5	860.3	852.5	854.8	856.0	857.7	847.3	862.2
Residential	340.1	356.5	372.1	363.6	360.5	382.9	368.3	358.5	326.5
Commercial	216.1	225.8	228.0	222.3	222.8	236.5	230.6	221.9	210.1
US territories	28.3	35.0	36.2	49.0	44.0	51.0	53.5	53.2	54.9
Non-energy use of fuels	117.2	133.2	141.4	131.9	135.9	131.8	148.9	139.1	138.0
Iron and steel production	86.2	74.7	66.6	59.2	55.9	54.7	52.8	46.6	49.1
Cement manufacture	33.3	36.8	41.2	41.4	42.9	43.1	45.6	45.9	45.7
Natural gas systems	33.7	33.8	29.4	28.8	29.6	28.4	28.1	29.5	28.5
Municipal solid waste combustion	10.9	15.7	17.5	18.0	18.5	19.1	20.1	20.7	20.9
Lime manufacture	12.0	14.0	14.9	14.3	13.7	14.5	15.2	15.1	15.8
Ammonia manufacture and urea consumption	16.9	17.8	16.4	13.3	14.2	12.5	13.2	12.8	12.4
Limestone and dolomite use	5.5	7.4	6.0	5.7	5.9	4.8	6.7	7.4	8.6
Cropland remaining cropland	7.1	7.0	7.5	7.8	8.5	8.3	7.6	7.9	8.0
Soda ash manufacture and consumption	4.1	4.3	4.2	4.1	4.1	4.1	4.2	4.2	4.2
Aluminum production	6.8	5.7	6.1	4.4	4.5	4.5	4.2	4.2	3.9
Petrochemical production	2.2	2.8	3.0	2.8	2.9	2.8	2.9	2.8	2.6
Titanium dioxide production	1.2	1.5	1.8	1.7	1.8	1.8	2.1	1.8	1.9
Carbon dioxide consumption	1.4	1.4	1.4	0.8	1.0	1.3	1.2	1.3	1.6
Ferroalloy production	2.2	2.0	1.9	1.5	1.3	1.3	1.4	1.4	1.5
Phosphoric acid production	1.5	1.5	1.4	1.3	1.3	1.4	1.4	1.4	1.2
Zinc production	0.9	1.0	1.1	1.0	0.9	0.5	0.5	0.5	0.5
Petroleum systems	0.4	0.3	0.3	0.3	0.3	0.3	0.3	0.3	0.3
Lead production	0.3	0.3	0.3	0.3	0.3	0.3	0.3	0.3	0.3
Silicon carbide production and consumption	0.4	0.3	0.2	0.2	0.2	0.2	0.2	0.2	0.2
Land use, land-use change, and forestry (sink)[a]	*(737.7)*	*(775.3)*	*(673.6)*	*(750.2)*	*(826.8)*	*(860.9)*	*(873.7)*	*(878.6)*	*(883.7)*
Wood biomass and ethanol consumption[b]	*219.3*	*236.8*	*227.3*	*203.2*	*204.4*	*209.5*	*224.8*	*227.4*	*234.7*
International bunker fuels[b]	*113.7*	*100.6*	*101.1*	*97.6*	*89.1*	*103.6*	*119.0*	*122.6*	*127.1*
CH₄	**606.1**	**598.9**	**574.3**	**558.8**	**563.5**	**559.4**	**545.6**	**539.7**	**555.3**
Enteric fermentation	126.9	132.3	124.6	123.6	123.8	124.6	122.4	124.5	126.2
Landfills	149.6	144.0	120.8	117.6	120.1	125.6	122.6	123.7	125.7
Natural gas systems	124.7	128.1	126.5	125.3	124.9	123.3	114.0	102.5	102.4
Coal mining	84.1	67.1	60.4	60.3	56.8	56.9	59.8	57.1	58.5
Manure management	31.0	35.2	38.8	40.2	41.3	40.7	40.1	41.8	41.4
Petroleum systems	33.9	32.0	30.3	30.2	29.9	29.2	28.7	28.3	28.4
Forest land remaining forest land	4.5	4.7	19.0	9.4	16.4	8.7	6.9	12.3	24.6
Wastewater treatment	23.0	24.3	24.6	24.2	24.1	23.9	24.0	23.8	23.9
Stationary combustion	7.4	7.2	6.6	6.2	6.2	6.4	6.5	6.5	6.2
Rice cultivation	7.1	7.6	7.5	7.6	6.8	6.9	7.6	6.8	5.9
Abandoned underground coal mines	6.0	8.2	7.4	6.7	6.2	6.0	5.8	5.6	5.4
Mobile combustion	4.7	4.3	3.4	3.3	3.0	2.7	2.6	2.5	2.4
Composting	0.3	0.7	1.3	1.3	1.3	1.5	1.6	1.6	1.6
Petrochemical production	0.9	1.1	1.2	1.1	1.1	1.1	1.2	1.1	1.0
Iron and steel production	1.3	1.3	1.2	1.1	1.0	1.0	1.0	1.0	0.9
Field burning of agricultural residues	0.7	0.7	0.8	0.8	0.7	0.8	0.9	0.9	0.8
Ferroalloy production	+	+	+	+	+	+	+	+	+
Silicon carbide production and consumption	+	+	+	+	+	+	+	+	+
International bunker fuels[b]	*0.2*	*0.1*	*0.1*	*0.1*	*0.1*	*0.1*	*0.1*	*0.2*	*0.2*
N₂O	**383.4**	**395.6**	**385.9**	**392.9**	**376.1**	**356.6**	**353.5**	**370.1**	**367.9**
Agricultural soil management	269.4	264.8	262.1	277.0	262.0	247.3	246.9	265.2	265.0
Mobile combustion	43.5	53.4	52.5	49.9	45.9	42.3	39.7	36.3	33.1
Nitric acid production	17.0	18.9	18.6	15.1	16.4	15.4	15.2	15.8	15.6
Stationary combustion	12.8	13.4	14.6	14.1	14.0	14.3	14.6	14.8	14.5
Manure management	12.1	12.8	13.7	14.0	14.0	13.6	13.8	13.9	14.3
Wastewater treatment	6.3	6.9	7.6	7.8	7.6	7.7	7.8	8.0	8.1
Adipic acid production	15.3	17.3	6.2	5.1	6.1	6.3	5.9	5.9	5.9
N₂O from product uses	4.4	4.6	4.9	4.9	4.4	4.4	4.4	4.4	4.4
Forest land remaining forest land	0.5	0.6	2.2	1.3	2.0	1.2	1.1	1.6	2.8
Composting	0.4	0.8	1.4	1.4	1.4	1.6	1.7	1.7	1.8
Settlements remaining settlements	1.0	1.2	1.2	1.4	1.5	1.5	1.6	1.5	1.5
Field burning of agricultural residues	0.4	0.4	0.5	0.5	0.4	0.4	0.5	0.5	0.5

TABLE 9.1

Trends in greenhouse gas emissions and sinks, 1990, 1995, and 2000–06 [CONTINUED]

Gas/source	1990	1995	2000	2001	2002	2003	2004	2005	2006
Municipal solid waste combustion	0.5	0.5	0.4	0.4	0.4	0.4	0.4	0.4	0.4
International bunker fuels[b]	*1.0*	*0.9*	*0.9*	*0.9*	*0.8*	*0.9*	*1.1*	*1.1*	*1.1*
HFCs	**36.9**	**61.8**	**100.1**	**97.9**	**106.3**	**104.5**	**116.6**	**121.4**	**124.5**
Substitution of ozone depleting substances[c]	0.3	28.5	71.2	78.0	85.0	92.0	99.1	105.4	110.4
HCFC-22 production	36.4	33.0	28.6	19.7	21.1	12.3	17.2	15.8	13.8
Semiconductor manufacture	0.2	0.3	0.3	0.2	0.2	0.2	0.2	0.2	0.3
PFCs	**20.8**	**15.6**	**13.5**	**7.0**	**8.7**	**7.1**	**6.1**	**6.2**	**6.0**
Semiconductor manufacture	2.2	3.8	4.9	3.5	3.5	3.3	3.3	3.2	3.6
Aluminum production	18.5	11.8	8.6	3.5	5.2	3.8	2.8	3.0	2.5
SF_6	**32.7**	**28.0**	**19.1**	**18.7**	**18.0**	**18.1**	**18.0**	**18.2**	**17.3**
Electrical transmission and distribution	26.7	21.5	15.1	15.0	14.4	13.8	13.9	14.0	13.2
Magnesium production and processing	5.4	5.6	3.0	2.9	2.9	3.4	3.2	3.3	3.2
Semiconductor manufacture	0.5	0.9	1.1	0.7	0.7	0.8	0.8	1.0	1.0
Total	**6,148.3**	**6,494.0**	**7,032.6**	**6,921.3**	**6,981.2**	**6,998.2**	**7,078.0**	**7,129.9**	**7,054.2**
Net emissions (sources and sinks)	**5,410.6**	**5,718.7**	**6,359.0**	**6,171.1**	**6,154.4**	**6,137.3**	**6,204.3**	**6,251.3**	**6,170.5**

+Does not exceed 0.05 Tg CO_2 Eq.

[a]The net CO_2 flux total includes both emissions and sequestration, and constitutes a sink in the United States. Sinks are only included in net emissions total. Parentheses indicate negative values or sequestration.

[b]Emissions from international bunker fuels and wood biomass and ethanol consumption are not included in totals.

[c]Small amounts of PFC emissions also result from this source.

Note: Totals may not sum due to independent rounding.

SOURCE: "Table 2–1. Recent Trends in U.S. Greenhouse Gas Emissions and Sinks (TgCO₂Eq.)," in *Inventory of U.S. Greenhouse Gas Emissions and Sinks: 1990–2006*, U.S. Environmental Protection Agency, April 2008, http://www.epa.gov/climatechange/emissions/usinventoryreport.html (accessed July 18, 2008)

by vans, pickup trucks, and sport utility vehicles increased slightly during the 1970s, but has since slowly dropped. (See Table 9.3.) Fuel consumption by passenger cars rose slightly in the early 1970s, then dropped slightly in the mid-1970s, leveling off for a few years, dropping slightly once again in 1980, and remaining fairly constant since then. The use of automobile fuel has remained fairly constant because increases in fuel efficiency have offset the growth in car miles traveled. Boosting efficiency of all vehicles, especially trucks, will become increasingly important in controlling the demand for oil.

THE CORPORATE AVERAGE FUEL ECONOMY STANDARDS. The 1973 oil embargo by the Organization of the Petroleum Exporting Countries painfully reminded the United States how dependent it had become on foreign sources of fuel. It prompted Congress to pass the 1975 Energy Policy and Conservation Act, which set the initial Corporate Average Fuel Economy (CAFE) standards. The standards were modified in 1980 with the Automobile Fuel Efficiency Act.

The standards required domestic automakers to increase the average mileage of new cars sold to 27.5 miles per gallon (mpg; 8.6 L/100 km) by 1985. Manufacturers could still sell large, less efficient cars, but to meet the average fuel efficiency rates, they also had to sell smaller, more efficient cars. Automakers that failed to meet each year's standards were fined; those that managed to surpass the rates earned credits that they could use in years when they fell below the requirements. Even though keeping their cars relatively large and roomy, companies managed to improve mileage with inno-

vations such as electronic fuel injection, which supplied fuel to an automotive engine more efficiently than its predecessor, the carburetor.

The standards have had a significant effect. (See Table 9.3.) Fuel economy of all motor vehicles (which includes passenger cars, vans, pickup trucks, sport utility vehicles, and trucks) increased from 11.9 mpg (19.8 L/100 km) in 1973 to 17.2 mpg (13.7 L/100 km) in 2006. Greater gains have been made in the economy of passenger cars. In 1974, just after the oil embargo, cars averaged 13.6 mpg (17.3 L/100 km); in 2006 the average new-car fuel economy was 22.4 mpg (10.5 L/100 km).

The U.S. Environmental Protection Agency (EPA) computes the data in a different way by using a procedure called an adjusted real-world estimate, which takes into account factors that affect fuel economy, such as higher highway speeds, more aggressive driving, and greater use of air conditioning than in previous years. Using this estimate, the EPA indicates that the fuel economy of cars and trucks increased rapidly from 1975 to the early 1980s. (See Figure 9.3.) The increase slowed through 1987, declined gradually through 2004, and then increased slightly.

Cheap gasoline prices throughout the 1990s took away the sense of urgency surrounding fuel efficiency, which was demonstrated by the high growth of large-vehicle sales. (See Figure 9.4.) In addition, after repeal of the federal law that set the speed limit at 55 miles per hour (88.5 km/hr), many states allowed higher speed limits, which lowered fuel efficiency.

TABLE 9.2

Transportation conservation options

Improve the technical efficiency of vehicles

1. Higher fuel economy requirements—CAFE standards (R)
2. Reducing congestion: smart highways (E,I), flextime (E,R), better signaling (I), improved maintenance of roadways (I), time of day charges (E), improved air traffic controls (I,R), plus options that reduce vehicular traffic
3. Higher fuel taxes (E)
4. Gas guzzler taxes, or feebate schemes (E)
5. Support for increased R&D (E,I)
6. Inspection and maintenance programs (R)

Increase load factor

1. HOV lanes (I)
2. Forgiven tolls (E), free parking for carpools (E)
3. Higher fuel taxes (E)
4. Higher charges on other vmt trip-dependent factors (E): parking (taxes, restrictions, end of tax treatment as business cost), tolls, etc.

Change to more efficient modes

1. Improvements in transit service
   a. New technologies—maglev, high speed trains (E,I)
   b. Rehabilitation of older systems (I)
   c. Expansion of service—more routes, higher frequency (I)
   d. Other service improvements (I)—dedicated busways, better security, more bus stop shelters, more comfortable vehicles
2. Higher fuel taxes (E)
3. Reduced transit fares through higher US. transit subsidies (E)*
4. Higher charges on other vmt/trip-dependent factors for less efficient modes (E)—tolls, parking
5. Shifting urban form to higher density, more mixed use, greater concentration through zoning changes (R), encouragement of "infill" development (E,R,I), public investment in infrastructure (I), etc.

Reduce number or length of trips

1. Shifting urban form to higher density, more mixed use, greater concentration (E,R,I)
2. Promoting working at home or at decentralized facilities (E,I)
3. Higher fuel taxes (E)
4. Higher charges on other vmt/trip-dependent factors (E)

Shift to alternative fuels

1. Fleet requirements for alternative fuel-capable vehicles and actual use of alternative fuels (R)
2. Low-emission/zero emission vehicle (LEV/ZEV) requirements (R)
3. Various promotions (E): CAFE credits, emission credits, tax credits, etc.
4. Higher fuel taxes that do not apply to alternative fuels (E), or subsidies for the alternatives (E)
5. Support for increased R&D (E,I)
6. Public investment—government fleet investments (I)

Freight options

1. RD&D of technology improvements (E, I)

*U.S. transit subsidies, already among the highest in the developed world, may merely promote inefficiencies.
Notes: CAFE=corporate average fuel economy; E=economic incentive; HOV=high-occupancy vehicle; I=public investment; maglev=trains supported by magnetic levitation; R=regulatory action; R&D=research and development; RD&D=research, development, and demonstration; vmt=vehicle-miles traveled.

SOURCE: "Table 5-1. Transportation Conservation Options," in *Saving Energy in U.S. Transportation*, U.S. Congress, Office of Technology Assessment, July 1994, http://govinfo.library.unt.edu/ota/Ota_1/DATA/1994/9432.PDF (accessed July 18, 2008)

The total fuel economy of automobiles is expected to increase, however, as more fuel-efficient cars enter the market and older, less fuel-efficient autos drop out of operation. Nonetheless, new-car fuel economy has risen only slightly since 1986, and nearly all gains in automobile efficiency have been offset by increased weight and power in new vehicles since 1988. Recently, however, changes have been made to the CAFE standards.

During President Bush's administration (2001 to 2009), changes were made twice to the CAFE standards by increasing mileage requirements for light trucks. The president also addressed fuel efficiency standards for passenger vehicles in his 2007 State of the Union address, with a "Twenty in Ten" policy (January 2007, http://www.whitehouse.gov/stateoftheunion/2007/initiatives/energy.html) of reducing by 20% the amount of gasoline Americans used within the next ten years by increasing the CAFE standards and using alternative fuels. Congress responded by developing the Energy Independence and Security Act (EISA) of 2007, which mandated that fuel producers make at least 36 billion gallons (136.3 billion L) of biofuel annually by 2022. EISA also required that the CAFE standard be raised for cars and light trucks to 35 miles per gallon (6.7 L/100 km) by model year 2020.

On April 22, 2008, the U.S. secretary of transportation Mary Peters (1948–; http://www.dot.gov/affairs/peters042208.htm) announced new proposed fuel standards that would achieve a 25% improvement in fuel economy between 2010 and 2015—a 4.5% average annual increase. (The mandate from Congress had been at least a 3.3% average annual increase in fuel economy.) For automobiles, a 25% increase in fuel economy would mean raising the mpg average from 27.5 to 35.7 (8.6 L to 6.7 L/100 km). For light trucks, that would mean raising the mpg average from 23.5 to 28.6 (10 L to 8.2 L/100 km). Peters projected that these fuel economy increases would save nearly 55 billion gallons (208.2 L) of fuel and $100 billion in fuel costs over the lifetime of the affected vehicles.

Alternative Fuel Vehicles

NUMBERS AND TYPES. In 2003, 533,999 alternative fuel vehicles were on U.S. roads. (See Table 9.4.) By 2006 this total had increased to 634,562. These totals include vehicles originally manufactured to run on alternative fuels as well as gasoline or diesel vehicles that had been converted. The manufacture of new alternative fuel vehicles has increased steadily.

A number of different types of fuels are used in these vehicles (see Table 9.4):

• Compressed natural gas is natural gas that is stored in pressurized tanks. When burned, it releases one-tenth the carbon monoxide, hydrocarbon, and nitrogen of gasoline. It powered 18% of alternative fuel vehicles in 2006.

• Electricity, used by 8% of alternative fuel vehicles in 2006, can be used for battery-powered, fuel-cell, or hybrid vehicles.

• Ethanol is ethyl alcohol, a grain alcohol, mixed with gasoline and sold as gasohol. The 85% formulation of gasohol was the most common fuel for alternative fuel vehicles in 2006, powering 47% of them.

TABLE 9.3

Motor vehicle mileage, fuel consumption, and fuel rates, selected years 1949–2006

	Passenger cars[a]			Vans, pickup trucks, and sport utility vehicles[b]			Trucks[c]			All motor vehicles[d]		
	Mileage	Fuel consumption	Fuel rate	Mileage	Fuel consumption	Fuel rate	Mileage	Fuel consumption	Fuel rate	Mileage	Fuel consumption	Fuel rate
Year	Miles per vehicle	Gallons per vehicle	Miles per gallon	Miles per vehicle	Gallons per vehicle	Miles per gallon	Miles per vehicle	Gallons per vehicle	Miles per gallon	Miles per vehicle	Gallons per vehicle	Miles per gallon
1949	9,388	627	15.0	(e)	(e)	(e)	9,712	1,080	9.0	9,498	726	13.1
1950	9,060	603	15.0	(e)	(e)	(e)	10,316	1,229	8.4	9,321	725	12.8
1955	9,447	645	14.6	(e)	(e)	(e)	10,576	1,293	8.2	9,661	761	12.7
1960	9,518	668	14.3	(e)	(e)	(e)	10,693	1,333	8.0	9,732	784	12.4
1965	9,603	661	14.5	(e)	(e)	(e)	10,851	1,387	7.8	9,826	787	12.5
1970	9,989	737	13.5	8,676	866	10.0	13,565	2,467	5.5	9,976	830	12.0
1971	10,097	743	13.6	9,082	888	10.2	14,117	2,519	5.6	10,133	839	12.1
1972	10,171	754	13.5	9,534	922	10.3	14,780	2,657	5.6	10,279	857	12.0
1973	9,884	737	13.4	9,779	931	10.5	15,370	2,775	5.5	10,099	850	11.9
1974	9,221	677	13.6	9,452	862	11.0	14,995	2,708	5.5	9,493	788	12.0
1976	9,418	681	13.8	10,127	934	10.8	15,438	2,764	5.6	9,774	806	12.1
1978	9,500	665	14.3	10,968	948	11.6	18,045	3,263	5.5	10,077	816	12.4
1980	8,813	551	16.0	10,437	854	12.2	18,736	3,447	5.4	9,458	712	13.3
1982	9,050	535	16.9	10,276	762	13.5	19,931	3,647	5.5	9,644	686	14.1
1984	9,248	530	17.4	11,151	797	14.0	22,550	3,967	5.7	10,017	691	14.5
1986	9,464	543	17.4	10,764	738	14.6	22,143	3,821	5.8	10,143	692	14.7
1988	9,972	531	18.8	11,465	745	15.4	22,485	3,736	6.0	10,721	688	15.6
1990	10,504	520	20.2	11,902	738	16.1	23,603	3,953	6.0	11,107	677	16.4
1992	10,857	517	21.0	12,381	717	17.3	25,373	4,210	6.0	11,558	683	16.9
1994	10,992	531	20.7	12,156	701	17.3	25,838	4,202	6.1	11,683	698	16.7
1996	11,330	534	21.2	11,811	685	17.2	26,092	4,221	6.2	11,813	700	16.9
1998	11,754	544	21.6	12,173	707	17.2	25,397	4,135	6.1	12,211	721	16.9
2000	11,976	547	21.9	11,672	669	17.4	25,617	4,391	5.8	12,164	720	16.9
2001	11,831	534	22.1	11,204	636	17.6	26,602	4,477	5.9	11,887	695	17.1
2002	12,202	555	22.0	11,364	650	17.5	27,071	4,642	5.8	12,171	719	16.9
2003	12,325	556	22.2	11,287	697	16.2	28,093	4,215	6.7	12,208	718	17.0
2004	12,460	553	22.5	11,184	690	16.2	27,023	4,057	6.7	12,200	714	17.1
2005	R12,510	R567	R22.1	R10,920	R617	R17.7	R26,235	R4,385	R6.0	R12,082	R706	R17.1
2006P	12,427	554	22.4	10,986	612	18.0	25,290	4,300	5.9	12,016	697	17.2

[a]Through 1988, includes motorcycles.
[b]Includes a small number of trucks with 2 axles and 4 tires, such as step vans.
[c]Single-unit trucks with 2 axles and 6 or more tires, and combination trucks.
[d]Includes buses and motorcycles, which are not separately displayed.
[e]Included in "trucks."
R = Revised.
P = Preliminary.
Web pages: For all data beginning in 1949, see http://www.eia.doe.gov/aer/consump.html. For related information, see http://www.fhwa.dot.gov/policy/ohpi/hss/index.htm.

SOURCE: Adapted from "Table 2.8. Motor Vehicle Mileage, Fuel Consumption, and Fuel Rates, Selected Years, 1949–2006," in *Annual Energy Review 2007*, U.S. Department of Energy, Energy Information Administration, Office of Energy Markets and End Use, June 2008, http://www.eia.doe.gov/aer/pdf/aer.pdf (accessed June 28, 2008)

• Hydrogen is a gas, but its pure, gaseous form is not found in nature. It must be made from other energy sources, such as fossil fuels. In hydrogen fuel cells, oxygen and hydrogen react to produce water and electricity. Alternatively, hydrogen can be burned in an engine, much like gasoline. Less than 0.1% of alternative fuel vehicles were powered by hydrogen in 2006.

• Liquefied natural gas is primarily methane that has been liquefied by reducing its temperature to −260° Fahrenheit (−162.2° C). It was used by only 0.4% of all alternative fuel vehicles in 2006.

• Liquefied petroleum gas is a mixture of propane and butane. Twenty-six percent of all alternative fuel vehicles ran on liquefied petroleum gas in 2006.

• Biodiesels (not listed in Table 9.4) are liquid biofuels made from soybean, rapeseed, or sunflower oil. They can also be made from animal tallow and from agricultural by-products such as rice hulls.

In 2006 the largest numbers of alternative fuel vehicles (not including hybrid vehicles) were being used in California (105,594), Texas (92,968), Florida (29,280), New York (28,064), and Arizona (26,862). (See Table 9.5.) In 2006 manufacturers made available 1,723 alternative fuel buses (not including those already in operation). Most were transit buses (See Table 9.6.)

ALTERNATIVE FUEL VEHICLES AND THE MARKETPLACE. A fuel supply must be readily available if alternative fuel vehicles are to become a viable transportation option. Ideally, an infrastructure for supplying alternative

FIGURE 9.3

Fuel economy by model year, 1975–2007

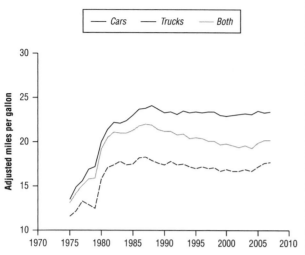

SOURCE: "Adjusted Fuel Economy by Model Year (Annual Data)," in *Light-Duty Automotive Technology and Fuel Economy Trends: 1975 through 2007 Executive Summary*, U.S. Environmental Protection Agency, Compliance and Innovative Strategies Division and Transportation and Climate Division, Office of Transportation and Air Quality, September 2007, http://www.epa.gov/OTAQ/cert/mpg/fetrends/420s07001.pdf (accessed July 19, 2008)

TABLE 9.4

Estimated number of alternative-fueled vehicles in use, by fuel, 2003–06

Fuel type	2003	2004	2005	2006
Compressed natural gas (CNG)	114,406	118,532	117,699	116,131
Electric[a]	47,485	49,536	51,398	53,526
Ethanol, 85 percent (E85)[b, c]	179,090	211,800	246,363	297,099
Hydrogen	9	43	119	159
Liquefied natural gas (LNG)	2,640	2,717	2,748	2,798
Liquefied petroleum gas (LPG)	190,369	182,864	173,795	164,846
Other fuels[d]	0	0	3	3
Total	**533,999**	**565,492**	**592,125**	**634,562**

[a]Excludes gasoline-electric and diesel-electric hybrids because the input fuel is gasoline or diesel rather than an alternative transportation fuel. The Department of Energy, which has Energy Policy Act implementation authority, ruled that gasoline-electric and diesel-electric hybrids are not "alternative fuel vehicles."
[b]The remaining portion of 85-percent ethanol is gasoline.
[c]In 1997, some vehicle manufacturers began including E85-fueling capability in certain model lines of vehicles. For 2006, the Energy Information Administration (EIA) estimates that the number of E-85 vehicles that are capable of operating on E85, gasoline, or both, is about 6 million. Many of these alternative-fueled vehicles (AFVs) are sold and used as traditional gasoline-powered vehicles. In this table, AFVs in use include only those E85 vehicles believed to be used as AFVs. These are primarily fleet-operated vehicles.
[d]May include P-series fuel or any other fuel designated by the Secretary of Energy as an alternative fuel in accordance with the Energy Policy Act of 1995.
Notes: Vehicles in use do not include concept and demonstration vehicles that are not ready for delivery to end users. Vehicles in use represent accumulated acquisitions, less retirements, as of the end of each calendar year. The estimated number of neat methanol (M100), 85-percent methanol (M85), and 95-percent ethanol (E95) vehicles in use is zero for all years included in this table. Therefore, those fuels are not shown.

SOURCE: "Table V1. Estimated Number of Alternative Fueled Vehicles in Use in the United States, by Fuel Type, 2003–2006," in *Alternatives to Traditional Transportation Fuels 2006 (Part II—User and Fuel Data)*, U.S. Department of Energy, Energy Information Administration, May 2008, http://www.eia.doe.gov/cneaf/alternate/page/atftables/afvtransfuel_II.html#in use (accessed July 19, 2008)

FIGURE 9.4

Market share of cars and light trucks, by vehicle type, 1975–2007

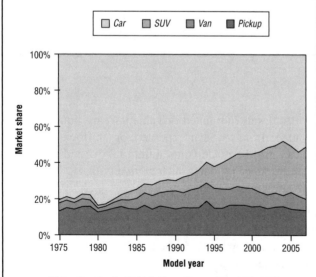

SOURCE: "Sales Fraction by Vehicle Type (Annual Data)," in *Light-Duty Automotive Technology and Fuel Economy Trends: 1975 through 2007 Executive Summary*, U.S. Environmental Protection Agency, Compliance and Innovative Strategies Division and Transportation and Climate Division, Office of Transportation and Air Quality, September 2007, http://www.epa.gov/OTAQ/cert/mpg/fetrends/420s07001.pdf (accessed July 19, 2008)

fuels would be developed simultaneously with the vehicles. Table 9.7 shows the types and numbers of alternative fuel stations available in each state. In July 2008, 5,689 alternative fueling sites were in operation in the United States.

In the early days of the automobile, electric cars outnumbered vehicles with internal combustion engines. However, with the introduction of technology for producing low-cost gasoline, electric vehicles fell out of favor. As cities became choked with air pollution, the idea of an efficient electric car reemerged. To make it acceptable to the public, several considerations have had to be addressed: How many miles could an electric car be driven before it needed to be recharged? How lightweight would the vehicle need to be? And could the electric car keep up with the speed and driving conditions of busy freeways and highways?

Electric vehicles can be battery powered, run on fuel cells, or be hybrids, which are powered by both an electric motor and a small conventional engine. EV1, a two-seater by General Motors (GM), was the first commercially available electric car. In 1999 the company introduced its second-generation electric car, the Gen II, which used a lead-acid battery pack and had a driving range of approx-

TABLE 9.5

Estimated number of alternative-fueled vehicles in use, by state and fuel type, 2006

State	Compressed natural gas (CNG)	Electric[a]	Ethanol, 85 percent (E85)[b]	Hydrogen	Liquefied natural gas (LNG)	Liquefied Petroleum gas (LPG)	Other fuels[c]	Total
Alabama	732	620	5,286	0	0	2,297	0	8,935
Alaska	456	40	1,388	0	0	109	0	1,993
Arizona	10,038	2,984	7,263	0	770	5,807	0	26,862
Arkansas	180	34	1,147	0	0	1,456	0	2,817
California	32,993	28,818	28,987	0	1,284	13,512	0	105,594
Colorado	1,326	192	8,660	0	1	3,594	0	13,773
Connecticut	2,043	48	3,064	0	0	235	0	5,390
Delaware	111	0	1,940	0	0	64	0	2,115
District of Columbia	1,196	60	4,790	0	0	400	0	6,446
Florida	3,561	896	20,661	0	0	4,162	0	29,280
Georgia	2,438	1,677	7,076	0	12	6,474	0	17,677
Hawaii	15	57	3,325	0	0	441	0	3,838
Idaho	319	0	2,207	0	85	895	0	3,506
Illinois	2,771	114	12,418	0	0	2,441	0	17,744
Indiana	2,289	68	2,584	0	0	2,999	0	7,940
Iowa	32	4	3,859	0	0	990	0	4,885
Kansas	253	0	2,889	0	0	822	0	3,964
Kentucky	307	0	4,737	0	0	1,092	0	6,136
Louisiana	536	0	3,374	0	0	1,036	0	4,946
Maine	5	0	842	0	0	426	0	1,273
Maryland	2,319	328	8,402	0	12	563	0	11,624
Massachusetts	2,081	3,170	2,370	0	0	721	0	8,342
Michigan	414	2,068	9,064	0	0	2,891	0	14,437
Minnesota	154	39	5,903	0	8	3,489	0	9,593
Mississippi	101	50	1,802	0	0	3,209	0	5,162
Missouri	231	0	6,867	0	0	3,728	0	10,826
Montana	35	34	1,498	0	0	456	0	2,023
Nebraska	332	0	2,286	0	0	298	0	2,916
Nevada	3,477	37	4,284	0	0	3,083	0	10,881
New Hampshire	58	50	558	0	0	250	0	916
New Jersey	4,853	597	6,657	0	0	2,286	0	14,393
New Mexico	1,156	67	7,177	0	0	1,956	0	10,356
New York	9,788	8,641	8,089	0	0	1,546	0	28,064
North Carolina	560	336	13,947	0	0	4,126	0	18,969
North Dakota	23	0	1,508	0	0	228	0	1,759
Ohio	1,187	304	7,713	0	0	2,818	0	12,022
Oklahoma	2,820	34	2,437	0	6	7,109	0	12,406
Oregon	1,445	890	4,623	0	7	1,049	0	8,014
Pennsylvania	2,240	0	8,366	0	9	990	0	11,605
Rhode Island	1,635	161	927	0	0	64	0	2,787
South Carolina	206	100	8,126	0	0	1,210	0	9,642
South Dakota	4	0	1,025	0	0	157	0	1,186
Tennessee	383	133	8,179	0	0	808	0	9,503
Texas	11,026	108	15,042	0	550	66,242	0	92,968
Utah	2,809	0	3,444	0	0	296	0	6,549
Vermont	15	241	437	0	0	267	0	960
Virginia	2,191	78	10,534	0	0	1,803	0	14,606
Washington	1,505	314	12,040	0	3	953	0	14,815
West Virginia	61	49	1,167	0	0	267	0	1,544
Wisconsin	955	0	4,954	0	0	2,269	0	8,178
Wyoming	435	66	1,176	0	0	368	0	2,045
State unknown	31	19	0	159	51	94	3	357
Total	**116,131**	**53,526**	**297,099**	**159**	**2,798**	**164,846**	**3**	**634,562**

[a]Excludes gasoline-electric and diesel-electric hybrids.
[b]Excludes E85 vehicles used by private individuals (non-fleet users) because most of those are believed to be in use as traditional gasoline-powered vehicles.
[c]May include P-Series fuel or any other fuel designated by the Secretary of Energy as an alternative fuel in accordance with the Energy Policy Act of 1995.
Notes: Vehicles in use do not include concept and demonstration vehicles that are not ready for delivery to end users. The estimated number of neat methanol (M100), 85-percent methanol (M85), and 95-percent ethanol (E95) vehicles in use is zero for the year included in this table. Therefore, those fuels are not shown. Totals may not equal sum of components due to independent rounding.

SOURCE: "Table V3. Estimated Number of Alternative Fueled Vehicles in Use, by State and Fuel Type, 2006," in *Alternatives to Traditional Transportation Fuels 2006 (Part II—User and Fuel Data)*, U.S. Department of Energy, Energy Information Administration, May 2008, http://www.eia.doe.gov/cneaf/alternate/page/atftables/afvtransfuel_II.html#inuse (accessed July 19, 2008)

imately 95 miles (153 km). The Gen II was also offered with an optional nickel-metal hydride battery pack, which increased its range to 130 miles (209 km). However, after the California Air Resources Board relaxed automobile-emissions requirements by phasing them in through 2017 rather than by 2003, GM found that it could no longer market the electric cars effectively. When leases on the cars ran out in 2003, GM began reclaiming them.

TABLE 9.6

Number of alternative-fuel and hybrid vehicles, by vehicle type, made available in 2006

Vehicle class/type	Vehicles
Automobiles	**514,306**
Auto-subcompact[a]	722
Auto-compact[a]	232,628
Auto-midsize[a]	28,886
Auto-fullsize	252,070
Vans	**12,470**
Minivan	11,275
Light duty van	1,170
Medium duty van	25
Pickup trucks	**382,227**
Light duty pickup	265,154
Medium duty pickup	117,073
Other trucks	**321,396**
Light duty SUV[a]	321,104
Light duty truck	0
Medium duty truck	35
Heavy duty truck	257
Buses	**1,723**
Bus-school	199
Bus-transit (<27ft 6in)	56
Bus-transit (>27ft 6in)[b]	1,276
Bus-trolley bus	192
Bus-intercity	0
Other onroad vehicles	**2,533**
Low speed vehicle (NEV)	2,433
Motorcycle	100
Total	**1,234,655**

[a]Includes gasoline-electric hybrid vehicles which are outside EPACT92's definition of alternative fuel vehicle.
[b]Includes diesel-electric hybrid vehicles which are outside EPACT92's (Energy Policy Act of 1992) definition of alternative fuel vehicle.
Notes: Light duty includes vehicles less than or equal to 8,500 gross vehicle weight rating (GVWR).
Medium Duty includes vehicles 8,501 to 26,000 GVWR.
Heavy duty includes vehicles 26,001 and over GVWR.

SOURCE: "Table S4. Number of Onroad Alternative Fuel and Hybrid Vehicles Made Available, by Detailed Vehicle Type, 2006," in *Alternatives to Traditional Transportation Fuels 2006 (Part 1—Supplier Data)*, U.S. Department of Energy, Energy Information Administration, May 2008, http://www.eia.doe.gov/cneaf/alternate/page/atftables/atf14-20_05.html (accessed July 20, 2008)

TABLE 9.7

Alternative fuel station counts, by state and fuel type, as of July 17, 2008

State	BD	CNG	E85	ELEC	HY	LNG	LPG	Totals by state
Alabama	14	3	4	0	0	0	46	67
Alaska	0	1	0	0	0	0	10	11
Arizona	10	41	16	11	1	5	50	134
Arkansas	2	3	4	0	0	0	40	49
California	39	186	9	370	25	29	199	857
Colorado	22	20	45	2	0	0	55	144
Connecticut	1	9	2	3	1	0	16	32
Delaware	3	1	1	0	0	0	3	8
Dist. of Columbia	1	1	3	0	1	0	0	6
Florida	12	15	15	3	2	0	47	94
Georgia	28	18	25	0	0	0	38	109
Hawaii	7	0	0	4	1	0	3	15
Idaho	5	7	4	0	0	1	25	42
Illinois	4	17	180	1	1	0	54	257
Indiana	6	13	107	0	0	0	28	154
Iowa	5	0	89	0	0	0	24	118
Kansas	5	2	23	0	0	0	46	76
Kentucky	1	0	9	0	0	0	13	23
Louisiana	1	6	3	0	0	0	10	20
Maine	3	1	0	0	0	0	8	12
Maryland	7	15	9	0	0	0	15	46
Massachusetts	7	11	1	18	0	0	23	60
Michigan	17	14	53	0	7	0	69	160
Minnesota	1	1	339	0	0	0	30	371
Mississippi	5	0	2	0	0	0	36	43
Missouri	8	7	76	0	1	0	75	167
Montana	4	3	2	0	0	0	31	40
Nebraska	3	2	35	0	0	0	20	60
Nevada	14	11	17	0	2	0	28	72
New Hampshire	11	3	1	8	0	0	11	34
New Jersey	0	11	0	0	0	0	10	21
New Mexico	6	9	7	0	0	0	49	71
New York	4	96	14	1	1	0	27	143
North Carolina	66	13	13	0	0	0	45	137
North Dakota	0	4	24	0	0	0	14	42
Ohio	21	9	58	0	0	0	66	154
Oklahoma	6	50	5	0	0	0	68	129
Oregon	36	12	8	9	0	0	29	94
Pennsylvania	5	26	16	0	1	0	63	111
Rhode Island	0	7	0	2	0	0	4	13
South Carolina	73	4	60	0	0	0	21	158
South Dakota	0	0	69	0	0	0	17	86
Tennessee	50	4	13	0	0	0	52	119
Texas	53	17	35	1	0	4	522	632
Utah	6	60	5	0	0	0	23	94
Vermont	2	1	0	2	1	0	5	11
Virginia	13	10	6	1	1	0	21	52
Washington	35	12	9	0	0	0	52	108
West Virginia	1	2	3	0	0	0	7	13
Wisconsin	3	19	95	0	0	0	45	162
Wyoming	14	8	5	0	0	0	31	58
Totals by fuel:	**640**	**785**	**1519**	**436**	**46**	**39**	**2,224**	**5,689**

Notes: CNG=Compressed Natural Gas, E85–85%=Ethanol, LPG=Propane, ELEC=Electric, BD=Biodiesel, HY=Hydrogen and LNG=Liquefied Natural Gas.

SOURCE: "Alternative Fueling Station Total Counts by State and Fuel Type," in *Alternative Fuels and Advanced Vehicles Data Center*, U.S. Department of Energy, Energy Efficiency and Renewable Energy, July 17, 2008, http://www.eere.energy.gov/afdc/fuels/stations_counts.html?print (accessed July 19, 2008)

Fuel-cell electric vehicles use an electrochemical process that converts a fuel's energy into usable electricity. Fuel cells produce very little sulfur and nitrogen dioxide and generate less than half the carbon dioxide of internal combustion engines. Rather than needing to be recharged, they are simply refueled. Hydrogen, natural gas, methanol, and gasoline can all be used with a fuel cell.

DaimlerChrysler's Mercedes-Benz division unveiled the first driveable fuel-cell car in 1999. Called the New Electric Car, it produced zero emissions, ran on liquid hydrogen, and traveled 280 miles on a full 11-gallon (42-L) tank. Since then, several models have been road tested. Ecostar, an alliance between Ford, DaimlerChrysler, and Ballard Power Systems, is also working on developing new fuel cells to power vehicles. In his 2003 State of the Union address, President Bush announced the Hydrogen Fuel Initiative (http://www1.eere.energy.gov/hydrogenandfuelcells/presidents_initiative.html), which appropriated funds and set a research agenda to bring hydrogen and hydrogen fuel cell vehicles to consumers by 2020. In 2006 about three hundred fuel cell cars were being tested worldwide. Harry Stoffer reports in

"Study: Hydrogen Research Worth the Cost" (*Automotive News*, March 24, 2008) that in March 2008 the National Research Council released a comprehensive study on research progress on hydrogen and hydrogen fuel cell vehicles. The council concluded that considerable progress had been made and that the research had the potential to provide enormous benefits to Americans.

In 2008 hybrid cars were the type of alternative fuel vehicle primarily available to consumers. Hybrid cars have both an electric motor and a small internal combustion engine. A sophisticated computer system automatically shifts from the electric motor to the gas engine, as needed, for optimum driving. The electric motor is recharged while the car is driving and braking. Because the gasoline engine does only part of the work, fuel economy is high. The engines are also designed to produce low emissions.

The commercialization of hybrid cars began in 2002 in the United States with the Toyota Prius, a sedan with front and back seating, and the two-passenger Honda Insight. Both cars were sold in Japan for several years before being introduced to the U.S. market. In model year 2005 Ford offered the first hybrid sport utility vehicle, the Escape, which won the 2004 North American Truck of the Year Award. The vehicle was reported to get 35 mpg (6.7 L/100 km) with city driving and traveling about 400 miles (644 km) on a 15-gallon (57-L) tank. By model year 2006, many auto manufacturers—including Honda, Ford, Toyota, Lexus, and Mercury—offered gas-electric hybrids. Table 9.6 shows the number of alternative fuel and hybrid vehicles, by vehicle type, made available in the United States in 2006. By model year 2008, Chevrolet, GMC, Mazda, Nissan, and Saturn offered hybrid car models to consumers as well.

MANDATING ALTERNATIVE FUELS. Several laws have been passed to encourage or mandate the use of vehicles powered by fuels other than gasoline. The Clean Air Act Amendments of 1990 required certain businesses and local governments with fleets of ten or more vehicles in twenty-one metropolitan areas to phase in alternative fuel vehicles over time—20% of those fleets had to be alternative fuel vehicles by 1998. Even though great strides have been made, compliance with the mandates cannot be determined because reporting and enforcement methods are inadequate.

The Energy Policy Act of 1992 was passed in the wake of the 1991 Persian Gulf War to conserve energy and increase the proportion of energy supplied domestically. It required that 75% of all vehicles purchased by the federal government in 1999 and thereafter be alternative fuel vehicles. Agency budget cuts and inadequate enforcement have slowed compliance with these regulations. Still, many municipal governments and the U.S. Postal Service have put into operation fleets of natural gas vehicles, such as garbage trucks, transit buses, and postal vans. The number of alternative fuel and hybrid

trucks and buses made available by manufacturers in 2006 is shown in Table 9.6.

Air Travel Efficiency

Flying carries an environmental price, as it is an energy-intensive form of transportation. In much of the industrialized world, air travel is replacing more energy-efficient rail or bus travel. According to the Bureau of Transportation Statistics (2008, http://www.bts.gov/publications/national_transportation_statistics/html/table_04_05.html), jet fuel consumption rose from 12.7 billion gallons (47.9 billion L) in 1995 to 13.5 billion gallons (50.9 billion L) in 2006.

Jet fuel consumption affects global warming. Airplanes spew nitrogen oxide and carbon dioxide into the air, much of it while cruising in the tropospheric zone, which is about 5 miles (8 km) above the planet, where ozone is formed. (See Figure 9.5.) The IPCC notes that emissions deposited directly into the atmosphere do greater harm than those released at ground level. In *Aviation and the Environment: Aviation's Effects on the Global Atmosphere Are Potentially Significant and Expected to Grow* (February 2000, http://www.gao.gov/new.items/rc00057.pdf), the U.S. General Accounting Office (now the U.S. Government Accountability Office) estimates that in 2000 air traffic accounted for about 3% of all global greenhouse warming. Jane Kay reports in "There's Something in the Air" (*San Francisco Chronicle*, December 5, 2007) that by 2007 the EPA reported it accounted for up to 12% of the greenhouse gases produced by all forms of transportation in the United States. For this reason, and because air traffic is expected to rise, the EPA reduced the limits on emissions of nitrogen oxides for new commercial aircraft engines beginning in 2005.

Even though each generation of airplane engines gets cleaner and more fuel efficient, there are also other engines in the airline industry—those in the trucks, cars, and carts that service airplane fleets. Electric utility companies, including the Edison Electric Institute and the Electric Power Research Institute, launched a program in 1993 to electrify airports. By converting terminal transport buses, food trucks, and baggage-handling carts to electricity, airports could reduce air pollution considerably. As of December 2005, only a few U.S. airports and airlines were operating significant numbers of electric ground support equipment.

In *Cost Benefit Analysis Modeling Tool for Electric vs. ICE Airport Ground Support Equipment—Development and Results* (February 2007, http://avt.inl.gov/pdf/airport/GSECostBenefitSmall.pdf), Kevin Morrow, Dimitri Hochard, and James Francfort evaluate the costs associated with airports operating their current baggage tractors, belt loaders, and pushback tractors versus the costs associated with changing to and operating electric versions of this equipment. Morrow, Hochard, and Francfort provided airports with the tools necessary to conduct their own cost-benefit analyses for their

FIGURE 9.5

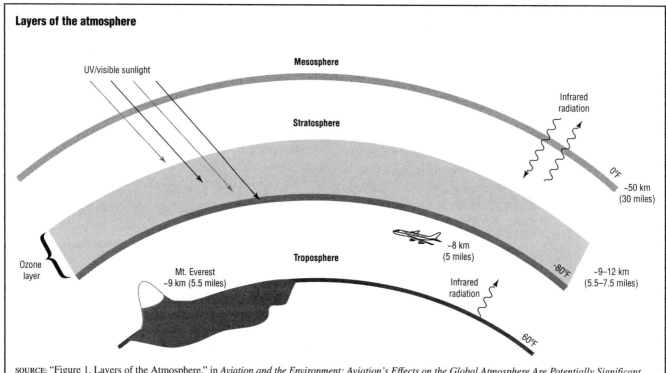

Layers of the atmosphere

SOURCE: "Figure 1. Layers of the Atmosphere," in *Aviation and the Environment: Aviation's Effects on the Global Atmosphere Are Potentially Significant and Expected to Grow*, U.S. General Accounting Office, February 2000, http://www.gao.gov/new.items/rc00057.pdf (accessed July 19, 2008)

own particular situations, and they conclude that replacing current baggage tractors and belt loaders with electric equipment would be cost-effective and that replacement of pushback tractors could be cost effective if implemented properly.

RESIDENTIAL AND COMMERCIAL CONSERVATION

Total energy use in buildings in the United States has increased because the numbers of people, households, and offices has increased. However, energy use per unit area (commercial) or per person (residential) has roughly stabilized due to a variety of efficiency measures. The sources of energy in buildings have changed dramatically. The use of fuel oil has dropped, with natural gas making up most of the difference. At the same time, other energy demands have risen. Electronic office equipment, such as computers, fax machines, printers, and copiers, has sharply increased electricity loads in commercial buildings. According to the EIA, in *Annual Energy Review 2007*, energy use in the residential and commercial sectors accounted for an increasing share of total U.S. energy consumption: 29% in 1950, 33% in 1970, and 39% in 2007.

Building Efficiency

Energy conservation in buildings in both the residential and commercial sectors has improved considerably since the early 1980s. Among the techniques for reducing energy use are advanced window designs, "daylighting" (letting light in from the outside by adding a skylight or building a large building around an atrium), solar water heating, landscaping, and planting trees.

Residential energy consumption has been reduced by building more efficient new housing and appliances, improving energy efficiency in existing housing, and building more multiple-family units. Also, many people have migrated to the South and West, where their combined use of heating and cooling has generally been lower than usage in other parts of the country.

In the residential sector the largest share of energy savings has been the result of better construction, higher quality insulation, and more energy-efficient windows and doors. According to the Department of Energy, in "Energy Savers: Tips on Saving Energy and Money at Home" (May 31, 2006, http://www1.eere.energy.gov/consumer/tips/windows.html), from 10% to 25% of the energy used to heat and cool buildings can be lost through its windows. Before the 1973 energy crisis, most new windows sold were single glazed (only a single pane of glass). By 1990, because of changes in building codes and public interest, most windows sold were double glazed, which dramatically cut energy loss. Double-glazed windows have two panes of glass sandwiched together with a small space in between. The glass may be specially treated or the space between

FIGURE 9.6

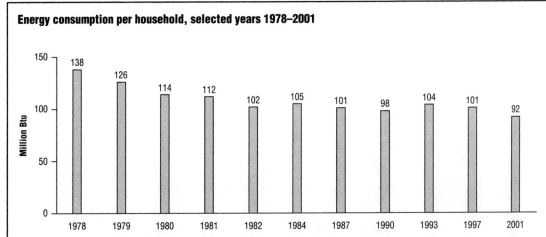

Energy consumption per household, selected years 1978–2001

Notes: Data include natural gas, electricity, distillate fuel oil, kerosene, and liquefied petroleum gases; data do not include wood. For years not shown, there are no data available. Data for 1978–1984 are for April of the year shown through March of following year; data for 1987 forward are for the calender year.

SOURCE: Adapted from "Figure 2.4. Household Energy Consumption: Consumption per Household, Selected Years, 1978–2001," in *Annual Energy Review 2007*, U.S. Department of Energy, Energy Information Administration, Office of Energy Markets and End Use, June 2008, http://www.eia.doe.gov/aer/pdf/aer.pdf (accessed June 28, 2008)

the panes may be filled with a gas, either of which increases the insulating effectiveness of the window.

Overall, however, energy consumption per household has remained fairly steady since 1982. Technology gains have been offset by an increase in the size of new homes and more demand for energy services. (See Figure 9.6.)

As in the residential sector, improved technology, materials, and construction methods have helped slow the growth of energy use in commercial buildings. Glass-walled buildings, especially, have undergone transformation: certain types of glass are now chosen for their ability to divert the heat of the sun and reduce the amount of energy needed for cooling. Like homes, many commercial structures are now designed to take advantage of breezes in the summer and to deflect cold winds in the winter.

Home Appliance Efficiency

The number of households in the United States is increasing, which is increasing the demand for energy-intensive products and services such as air conditioning. According to the EIA, in *Annual Energy Review 2007*, residential energy use accounted for 21% of total national energy consumption in 2007. In 2001 (the most recent year for which the EIA has compiled data) space heating used 47% of the total residential energy consumed, down from 51% in 1997; appliances 30%, up from 27%; water heating 17%, down from 19%; and air conditioners 6%, up from 4%.

The number of electrical appliances in U.S. households has increased steadily over the past few of decades. (See Figure 9.7.) By 2005 about 99% of American homes had color televisions, 88% had microwave ovens, 83% had clothes washers, and 68% had personal computers.

In 1987 Congress passed the National Appliance Energy Conservation Act, which gave the Department of Energy the authority to formulate minimum efficiency requirements for thirteen classes of consumer products. It could also revise and update those standards as technologies and economic conditions changed. Table 9.8 shows the products affected and the years in which appliance efficiency standards were established or revised for each.

Energy efficiency has increased for all major household appliances but most dramatically for refrigerators and freezers. In *Good Stuff? A Behind-the-Scenes Guide to the Things We Buy* (2006, http://www.worldwatch.org/system/files/GS0000.pdf), the World Watch Institute explains that since 1972 the energy efficiency of new refrigerators and freezers has more than tripled because of better insulation, motors, compressors, and accessories such as automatic defrost. These improvements have been accomplished at relatively low cost to manufacturers. In addition, efficiency labels are now required on appliances, which makes purchasing efficient models easier.

Besides concerns about efficiency, appliance makers—especially those who make refrigerators and air conditioning systems—are developing alternative cooling techniques to replace chlorofluorocarbons (CFCs), which are ozone-damaging chemicals that can no longer be legally sold in the United States. CFCs were initially substituted with somewhat less dangerous hydrochlorofluorocarbons (HCFCs), but they are now being replaced with hydroflourocarbons (HFCs), which lack chlorine. In Europe other substances, such as propane and butane, are being used as refrigerants. Known as greenfreeze technology, these materials are rapidly replacing HCFCs.

FIGURE 9.7

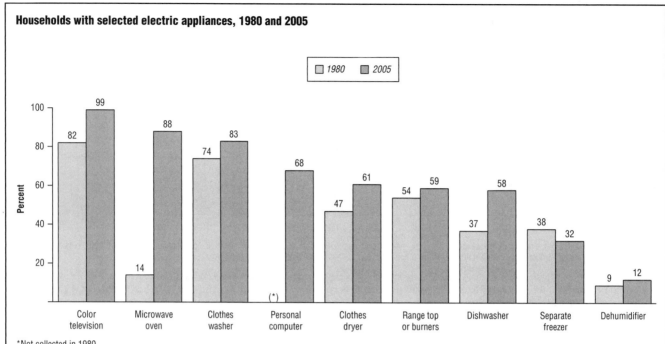

Households with selected electric appliances, 1980 and 2005

*Not collected in 1980.

SOURCE: Adapted from "Figure 2.6. Households with Selected Appliances and Types of Main Heating Fuel: Households with Selected Electric Appliances, 1980 and 2005," in *Annual Energy Review 2007*, U.S. Department of Energy, Energy Information Administration, Office of Energy Markets and End Use, June 2008, http://www.eia.doe.gov/aer/pdf/aer.pdf (accessed June 28, 2008)

TABLE 9.8

Effective dates of appliance efficiency standards, selected years 1988–2007

Product	1988	1990	1992	1993	1994	1995	2000	2001	2003	2004	2005	2006	2007
Clothes dryers	X				X								
Clothes washers	X				X					X			X
Dishwashers	X				X								
Refrigerators and freezers		X		X				X					
Kitchen ranges and ovens		X											
Room air conditioners		X					X						
Direct heating equipment		X											
Fluorescent lamp ballasts		X									X		
Water heaters		X								X			
Pool heaters		X											
Central air conditioners and heat pumps			X									X	
Furnaces													
Central (>45,000 Btu per hour)			X										
Small (>45,000 Btu per hour)			X										
Mobile home		X											
Boilers			X										
Fluorescent lamps, 8 foot					X								
Fluorescent lamps, 2 and 4 foot (U tube)						X							
Commercial water-cooled air conditioners										X			
Commercial natural gas furnaces										X			
Commercial natural gas water heaters										X			

SOURCE: "Table 2. Effective Dates of Appliance Efficiency Standards, 1988–2007," in *Annual Energy Outlook 2002*, U.S. Department of Energy, Energy Information Administration, Office of Integrated Analysis and Forecasting, December 2001, http://www.eia.doe.gov/oiaf/archive/aeo02/pdf/0383(2002).pdf (accessed July 2, 2008)

INTERNATIONAL COMPARISONS OF CONSERVATION EFFORTS

One test of a country's efficiency is the amount of energy it consumes for every dollar of goods and services it produces. According to the EIA, in *International Energy Annual 2005* (October 2007, http://www.eia.doe.gov/emeu/iea/contents.html), the United States lags behind some industrialized countries in energy efficiency and conservation efforts but is also considerably ahead of others. In 2005 the United States consumed 9,113 Btu per dollar (in 2000 U.S. dollars) of GDP, compared to 7,994 Btu per dollar for France, 7,396 Btu per dollar for Germany, and 4,519 Btu per dollar for Japan. That same year, however, Canada consumed 17,404 Btu per dollar of GDP; Belgium, 10,352 Btu per dollar; and Spain, 9,681 Btu per dollar.

The EIA also determines the carbon intensity of countries by comparing the metric tons of carbon dioxide they produce per thousand dollars of GDP. The figures for 2005 show that the carbon intensity of the United States was substantially higher than that of many other industrialized nations. For example, the carbon intensity of the United States was 0.15, which was equal to that of Belgium. Other industrialized nations' carbon intensity was lower: Germany's was 0.12, France's was 0.08, and Japan's was 0.07. Spain's carbon intensity was 0.16, slightly higher than that of the United States, whereas Canada's was much higher at 0.21.

FUTURE TRENDS IN CONSERVATION

In *Annual Energy Outlook 2008*, the EIA notes that U.S. total energy consumption is expected to increase at a fairly steady rate from nearly 100 quadrillion Btu in 2006 to about 118 quadrillion Btu in 2030, even with efficiency standards for new equipment taken into consideration. This represents a 19% increase and an average rate of 0.7% per year. Per capita energy use is expected to remain relatively stable from 2006 through 2030. (See Figure 9.8.)

According to the projections, homes will be larger in 2030, but electricity will be used more efficiently. Higher energy prices will encourage conservation. Even though annual personal highway and air travel will increase, efficiency improvements will offset much of that increase. The EIA also suggests that growth will continue in lower energy intensive industries. Thus, energy use per dollar of GDP is expected to decrease at an average annual rate of 1.7% from 2006 to 2030 as energy gains more than offset a higher demand for energy. (See Figure 9.8.)

Transportation fuel efficiency for light-duty vehicles is also projected to improve dramatically from 2006 through 2020 due to EISA, which sets a new CAFE standard of 35 miles per gallon (6.7 L/100 km) for cars and light trucks by model year 2020. After 2020, fuel efficiency in these light-duty vehicles is projected to increase minimally, but fuel efficiency will increase more in higher-priced, high-technology vehicles than in lower-priced vehicles. (See Figure 9.9.)

The EIA predicts that the market for alternative fuel vehicles will grow as a result of EISA. By 2030 about 7.7 million alternative fuel vehicles of all types are expected to be sold in that year—about 42% of total light-duty vehicle sales.

FIGURE 9.8

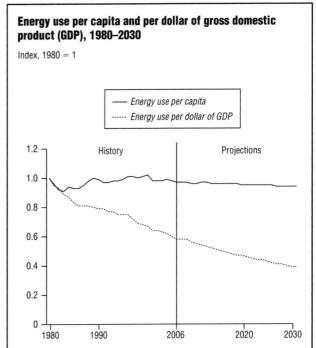

Energy use per capita and per dollar of gross domestic product (GDP), 1980–2030

SOURCE: "Figure 4. Energy Use per Capita and per Dollar of Gross Domestic Product, 1980–2030 (Index, 1980=1)," in *Annual Energy Outlook 2008*, U.S. Department of Energy, Energy Information Administration, Office of Integrated Analysis and Forecasting, June 2008, http://www.eia.doe.gov/oiaf/aeo/pdf/0383(2008).pdf (accessed July 2, 2008)

FIGURE 9.9

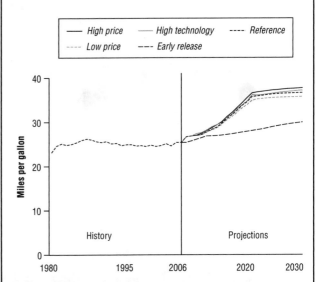

Past and projected average fuel economy of new light-duty vehicles, 1980–2030

SOURCE: "Figure 57. Average Fuel Economy of New Light-Duty Vehicles, 1980–2030 (Miles per Gallon)," in *Annual Energy Outlook 2008*, U.S. Department of Energy, Energy Information Administration, Office of Integrated Analysis and Forecasting, June 2008, http://www.eia.doe.gov/oiaf/aeo/pdf/0383(2008).pdf (accessed July 2, 2008)

IMPORTANT NAMES
AND ADDRESSES

American Gas Association
400 N. Capitol St. NW, Ste. 450
Washington, DC 20001
(202) 824-7000
URL: http://www.aga.org/

American Petroleum Institute
1220 L St. NW
Washington, DC 20005-4070
(202) 682-8000
URL: http://www.api.org/

American Wind Energy Association
1501 M St. NW, Ste. 1000
Washington, DC 20005
(202) 383-2500
FAX: (202) 383-2505
E-mail: windmail@awea.org
URL: http://www.awea.org/

Bureau of Land Management
1849 C St. NW
Washington, DC 20240
E-mail: woinfo@blm.gov
URL: http://www.blm.gov/

Edison Electric Institute
701 Pennsylvania Ave. NW
Washington, DC 20004-2696
(202) 508-5000
E-mail: electricsolutions@eei.org
URL: http://www.eei.org/

Electric Power Research Institute
3420 Hillview Ave.
Palo Alto, CA 94304
(650) 855-2121
1-800-313-3774
URL: http://www.epri.com/

Energy Information Administration
1000 Independence Ave. SW
Washington, DC 20585
(202) 586-8800
E-mail: infoctr@eia.doe.gov
URL: http://www.eia.doe.gov/

Environmental Defense
257 Park Ave. South
New York, NY 10010
(212) 505-2100
FAX: (212) 505-2375
URL: http://www.edf.org/

Friends of the Earth
1717 Massachusetts Ave., Ste. 600
Washington, DC 20036
(202) 783-7400
FAX: (202) 783-0444
URL: http://www.foe.org/

Greenpeace USA
702 H St. NW
Washington, DC 20001
(202) 462-1177
1-800-326-0959
E-mail: info@wdc.greenpeace.org
URL: http://www.greenpeace.org/usa

National Mining Association
101 Constitution Ave. NW, Ste. 500 East
Washington, DC 20001-2133
(202) 463-2600
FAX: (202) 463-2666
E-mail: craulston@nma.org
URL: http://www.nma.org/

Natural Gas Supply Association
805 Fifteenth St. NW, Ste. 510
Washington, DC 20005
(202) 326-9300
FAX: (202) 326-9330
URL: http://www.ngsa.org/

Natural Resources Defense Council
40 W. Twentieth St.
New York, NY 10011
(212) 727-2700
FAX: (212) 727-1773
E-mail: nrdcinfo@nrdc.org
URL: http://www.nrdc.org/

Nuclear Energy Institute
1776 I St. NW, Ste. 400
Washington, DC 20006-3708
(202) 739-8000
FAX: (202) 785-4019
URL: http://www.nei.org/

Public Citizen
1600 Twentieth St. NW
Washington, DC 20009
(202) 588-1000
URL: http://www.citizen.org/

Sierra Club
85 Second St., Second Fl.
San Francisco, CA 94105
(415) 977-5500
FAX: (415) 977-5799
E-mail: information@sierraclub.org
URL: http://www.sierraclub.org/

**Solid Waste Association
of North America**
1100 Wayne Ave., Ste. 700
Silver Spring, MD 20910
1-800-467-9262
FAX: (301) 589-7068
URL: http://www.swana.org/

**Union of Concerned
Scientists**
2 Brattle Sq.
Cambridge, MA 02238-9105
(617) 547-5552
FAX: (617) 864-9405
URL: http://www.ucsusa.org/

U.S. Department of Energy
1000 Independence Ave. SW
Washington, DC 20585
(202) 586-5000
1-800-342-5363
FAX: (202) 586-4403
E-mail: The.Secretary@hq.doe.gov
URL: http://www.energy.gov/

U.S. Environmental Protection Agency
Ariel Rios Bldg.
1200 Pennsylvania Ave. NW
Washington, DC 20460
(202) 272-0167
URL: http://www.epa.gov/

U.S. House of Representatives Committee on Natural Resources
1324 Longworth Bldg.
Washington, DC 20515
(202) 225-6065
FAX: (202) 225-1931
URL: http://resourcescommittee.house.gov/

U.S. Nuclear Regulatory Commission
Washington, DC 20555-0001
(301) 415-7000
1-800-368-5642
URL: http://www.nrc.gov/

U.S. Senate Committee on Energy and Natural Resources
304 Dirksen Senate Bldg.
Washington, DC 20510
(202) 224-4971
URL: http://energy.senate.gov/

Waste Isolation Pilot Plant U.S. Department of Energy
4021 National Parks Hwy.
Carlsbad, NM 88220
1-800-336-9477
E-mail: infocntr@wipp.ws
URL: http://www.wipp.energy.gov/

Worldwatch Institute
1776 Massachusetts Ave. NW
Washington, DC 20036
(202) 452-1999
FAX: (202) 296-7365
E-mail: worldwatch@worldwatch.org
URL: http://www.worldwatch.org/

RESOURCES

The U.S. Department of Energy's Energy Information Administration is the major source of energy statistics in the United States. It publishes weekly, monthly, and yearly statistical collections on most types of energy, which are available in libraries and online at http://www.eia.doe.gov/. The *Annual Energy Review* provides a complete statistical overview, and the *Annual Energy Outlook* projects future developments in the field. The *International Energy Annual* presents a statistical overview of the world energy situation, and the *International Energy Outlook* forecasts future industry developments. The Energy Information Administration also provides the *Natural Gas Annual* and the *Electric Power Annual*. The *U.S. Crude Oil, Natural Gas, and Natural Gas Liquids Reserves Annual Report* discusses reserves of coal, oil, and gas. In addition, the Department of Energy makes available information on the development of alternative vehicles and fuels, renewable energy sources, and electric industry restructuring.

The Energy Policy Act of 2005 is available at http://www.epa.gov/oust/fedlaws/publ_109-058.pdf. The 2006 Advanced Energy Initiative is available at http://www.whitehouse.gov/stateoftheunion/2006/energy/print/index.html. The Energy Independence and Security Act of 2007 is available at http://frwebgate.access.gpo.gov/cgi-bin/getdoc.cgi?dbname=110_cong_bills&docid=f:h6enr.txt.pdf.

The U.S. Department of Transportation's Bureau of Transportation Statistics provides transportation information in its *Transportation Statistics Annual Report*.

The U.S. Environmental Protection Agency maintains Web sites for the Yucca Mountain Repository (http://www.epa.gov/radiation/yucca/about.html) and for the Waste Isolation Pilot Plant (http://www.epa.gov/radiation/wipp/background.html). The agency also provides *Light-Duty Automotive Technology and Fuel Economy Trends* and *Inventory of U.S. Greenhouse Gas Emissions and Sinks*.

The U.S. Nuclear Regulatory Commission is also an important source of information. It provides the documents *NRC—Regulator of Nuclear Safety* and *Information Digest*.

INDEX